The Corporate Insider's Guide to U.S. Patent Practice

The Corporate Insider's Guide to U.S. Patent Practice

Charles R. Macedo
Partner
Amster, Rothstein & Ebenstein LLP

Oxford University Press, Inc., publishes works that further Oxford University's objective of excellence in research, scholarship, and education.

Oxford New York
Auckland Cape Town Dar es Salaam Hong Kong Karachi Kuala Lumpur Madrid Melbourne Mexico City Nairobi New Delhi Shanghai Taipei Toronto

With offices in
Argentina Austria Brazil Chile Czech Republic France Greece Guatemala Hungary Italy Japan Poland Portugal Singapore South Korea Switzerland Thailand Turkey Ukraine Vietnam

Published by Oxford University Press, Inc.
198 Madison Avenue, New York, New York 10016

Library of Congress Cataloging-in-Publication Data

Macedo, Charles R.
The corporate insider's guide to U.S. patent practice / Charles R. Macedo.
p. cm.
Includes bibliographical references and index.
ISBN 978-0-19-538117-7 ((pbk.) : alk. paper)
1. Patent laws and legislation—United States. 2. Patent practice—United States. 3. Patent infringement—United States. I. Title.
KF3114.85.M33 2010
346.7304'86—dc22 2009011947

---

1 2 3 4 5 6 7 8 9

Printed in the United States of America on acid-free paper

Note to Readers
This publication is designed to provide accurate and authoritative information in regard to the subject matter covered. It is based upon sources believed to be accurate and reliable and is intended to be current as of the time it was written. It is sold with the understanding that the publisher is not engaged in rendering legal, accounting, or other professional services. If legal advice or other expert assistance is required, the services of a competent professional person should be sought. Also, to confirm that the information has not been affected or changed by recent developments, traditional legal research techniques should be used, including checking primary sources where appropriate.

(Based on the Declaration of Principles jointly adopted by a Committee of the American Bar Association and a Committee of Publishers and Associations.)

Contents

About the Author

Charles R. Macedo is a Partner at ***Amster, Rothstein & Ebenstein, LLP.*** His practice specializes in intellectual property issues including litigating patent, trademark and other intellectual property disputes, prosecuting patents before the U.S. Patent and Trademark Office and other patent offices throughout the world, registering trademarks and service marks with U.S. Patent and Trademark Office and other trademark offices throughout the world, and drafting and negotiating intellectual property agreements.

Mr. Macedo has a BS and MS in Physics from the Catholic University of America, 1986, and a JD from Columbia Law School, 1989. He graduated from the Catholic University of America, *summa cum laude*, Phi Beta Kappa, and Phi Eta Sigma. He was also the recipient of the prestigious Clyde Cowan Award in Physics. Mr. Macedo graduated from Columbia Law School as a Harlan Fiske Stone Scholar and was the Managing Editor of COLUMBIA BUSINESS LAW REVIEW. He was also the recipient of the prestigious Robert C. Watson Award from the American Intellectual Property Law Association in 1989.

Mr. Macedo has written extensively on intellectual property topics in law reviews, business journals, and bar association publications. His writings have been reprinted in numerous text books and cited to the U.S. Supreme Court as authority. He lectures on intellectual property topics and has been a frequent guest columnist for IP LAW 360 and JOURNAL OF INTELLECTUAL PROPERTY LAW AND PRACTICE. He has also been often quoted in the media on intellectual property law topics.

He can be reached at cmacedo@arelaw.com.

Acknowledgments

The author wishes to acknowledge and thank his partners, senior counsel, and associates, both past and present, who assisted him in developing the thoughts, concepts, and material used in this Guide. In particular, the author wishes to thank Anthony Lo Cicero, Daniel Ebenstein, Joseph Casino, Abraham Kasdan, Kenneth Bernstein, Michael Kasdan, Marion Metelski, Matthew Fox, Norajean McCaffrey, David Boag, Robert Burak, Reiko Kaji, Liel Hollander, David Mitnick, Howard Wizenfeld, Serge Krimnus, Parashos Kalaitzis, Ellen Leviss, David Goldberg, Daniel Almont, Jennifer Doran, and Gerri Renna for their helpful comments, guidance, and support throughout this project.

He also acknowledges and thanks his family for their support during the preparation of this Guide and for tolerating the many weekends and evenings that were devoted to writing it.

The author thanks his many clients over the years for teaching him what type of information they need in order to intelligently navigate the process and procedures associated with obtaining patent protection and litigating patent disputes.

Finally, the author thanks Matt Gallaway and Oxford University Press for taking on this project and bringing it to fruition.

Charles R. Macedo, 2009

Foreword

The Corporate Insider's Guide to U.S. Patent Practice (this "Guide") is intended to assist potential inventors, business people, general counsel, corporate officers, and other decision-makers involved in the patent process to better understand the patent process and to quickly spot issues that can affect the decisions being made. This Guide is *not* intended to be a "How To" guide for the non-patent practitioner that replaces the need to seek out and obtain competent outside counsel. As is often said, "a man who represents himself has a fool for a client." This is further amplified when he has no experience.

Further, it is important to understand that the statements made herein are general statements that may not apply in every instance. This Guide is not intended to be legal advice or a substitute for seeking the advice of competent legal counsel. Particular factual scenarios may raise issues or concerns not addressed in this Guide, and should be presented to legal counsel to address.

Finally, the views expressed herein are not necessarily those of Amster, Rothstein & Ebenstein LLP and/or its clients.

CHAPTER 1

What Is a Patent?

A patent is a form of "intellectual property." Phrased another way, it is property of the mind. A patent turns an intangible idea from the mind of the inventor(s) into an asset that is tangible and identifiable.[1] When an inventor is awarded a patent, the government issues a document (the "issued patent") which states what rights are being granted. It is like a property deed, which sets out the boundaries (called "metes and bounds") of the rights being granted. Thus, a patent turns the invention that was in the mind of the inventor(s) into a written, clearly defined deed that is intended to set forth the boundaries which separate the patent holder's protected invention from that which the public is free to use.

Practice Note:
A patent turns an intangible idea into an asset that is tangible.

A U.S. Patent is a time-limited right (twenty years from filing)[2] granted by the U.S. government[3] to the first and true inventors[4] of a new,[5] not obvious[6] and useful[7] invention to exclude others from practicing that invention.[8] This right to exclude is granted in exchange for the public disclosure of how to practice the invention.[9] (Each of these concepts will be discussed in greater detail throughout this Guide.)

Practice Note:
A U.S. Patent is a time-limited right to exclude others from practicing an invention in exchange for a public disclosure of how to practice the invention.

Everyone has no doubt heard of great ideas which have been the subject of one or more patents:

- the Wright brothers' airplane;[10]
- Samuel Morse's telegraph;[11]
- Alexander Graham Bell's telephone;[12] and
- Thomas Edison's light bulb.[13]

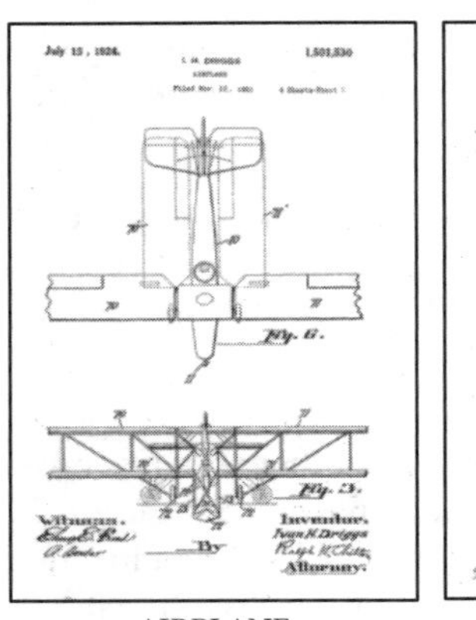

AIRPLANE

MORSE CODE/
TELEGRAPH

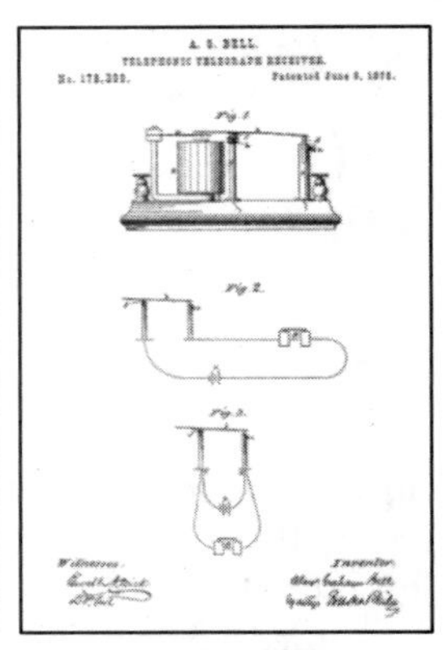

TELEPHONE

FIGURE 1.1 Historical Examples of Patents on Well-Known Devices.

More modern examples include

- A video tape recorder;[14]
- A cellular phone;[15]
- A digital music player;[16]
- An e-mail pager;[17]
- A plasma display device;[18] and
- A touch screen telephone.[19]

Some of these patents cover the basic idea, while others are directed to smaller improvements.

Most people have also heard the news media reports[20] about some ideas that seem a little silly (or too simple) and yet have been issued a patent:

- A method of swinging on a swing;[21] and
- A method of making a crustless peanut butter and jelly sandwich.[22]

Further, most people have also heard of some ideas that have been patented for which the public questions whether a patent should have been granted:

- Amazon.com's "one click" ordering process;[23] and
- the Y2K "fix" patent.[24]

While these silly and other dubious quality patents exist,[25] the focus of this Guide is more serious patents which disclose and claim legitimate inventions.

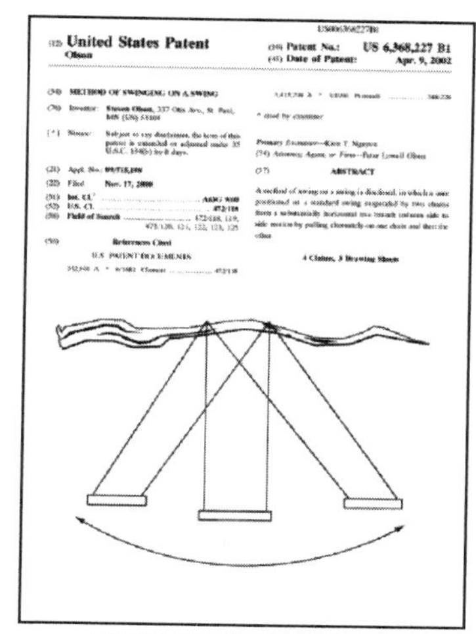
United States Patent
Olson
Patent No.: US 6,368,227 B1
Date of Patent: Apr. 9, 2002

METHOD OF SWINGING ON A SWING

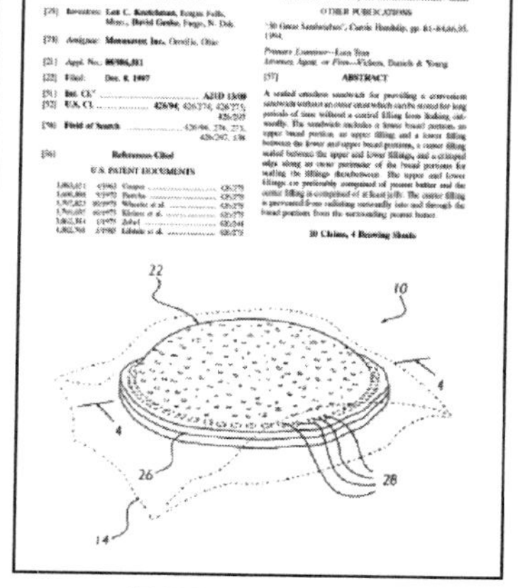
United States Patent
Kretchman et al.
Patent Number: 6,004,596
Date of Patent: Dec. 21, 1999

SEALED CRUSTLESS SANDWICH

FIGURE 1.2 Examples of Silly Patents.

Practice Note:

Generally, patents cover serious subject matter. However, some silly patents and other dubious quality patents have also been granted.

One recent case that brought patents to the public's attention was *NTP v. RIM*, where a patent-holding company was on the verge of obtaining an injunction against the maker of the BlackBerry® handheld pager.[26] No one liked the prospect that they might not be able to e-mail their colleagues and friends from anywhere in the United States. This prospect both scared and inspired many. It let the public understand that obtaining a patent could be very useful and that infringing a patent could be very risky.

Practice Note:

High profile patent litigation has scared and inspired many to understand that obtaining a patent can be useful and that infringing a patent can be risky.

One goal of the U.S. Patent System is to promote innovation by protecting new inventions in exchange for public disclosure of the inventions. It is a bargain between the government and the inventor. The concept is that in order to promote the "useful arts" (or innovation), the government will grant a limited right to exclude others from practicing a new invention: if the inventor can show that his innovation was not already within the public's knowledge and if the inventor teaches the public how it can practice the invention. Once a patent expires, the patentee then dedicates his invention to the public.

Practice Note:
A patent protects new ideas in exchange for a public disclosure of how to practice the invention.

The U.S. Patent System seeks to promote innovation by various means. One way is by awarding inventors an exclusive monopoly to their invention (for a limited time period) in exchange for teaching the world how to practice the invention. This motivates individual inventors and organizations (large and small) to innovate by allowing them to recoup their investment in research and development, without the risk of an unauthorized third party entering the marketplace and copying the invention. In many industries, such as pharmaceuticals, for example, without such protection, it simply is not economical to invest in research and development.

This point was made by Abraham Lincoln, a famous patent holder,[27] who happened also to be the sixteenth president of the United States, when he explained that "the patent system . . . added the fuel of interest to the fire of genius."[28]

Another way that innovation can be promoted is by the full and complete disclosure of inventions. For example, consider the area of software development. Prior to 1998, many software developers did not appreciate the availability of patent protection for inventions related to software. While new software was obviously developed during this period, the software inventions were not readily available to the public. Rather, those inventions were often buried in software code, which may or may not have been publicly available and, even if available, would have been difficult for most people to decipher and appreciate.

After the 1998 decision by the U.S. Court of Appeals for the Federal Circuit ("the Federal Circuit")[29] in *State Street Bank & Trust Co. v. Signature Financial Group, Inc.*,[30] when the possibility of patent protection for software (when properly claimed) became widespread, public knowledge, a flood of patent disclosures were submitted to the U.S. Patent and Trademark Office ("USPTO"). This flood of disclosures led to the widespread dissemination of previously withheld "secrets" on how to program a computer to reach a useful, concrete, and tangible result.[31] Even if many of these applications were not deserving of patent protection because their claims were obvious or due to some other reason (*see* Chapter 3), the dialogue created by these submissions and their subsequent publication as published applications or issued patents, has resulted in the promotion of innovation and the dissemination of information.

Depending upon an organization's line of business, appropriate patent protection can be the difference between the organization being in business or a competitor being in business. In recent years, since *State Street* confirmed that even so-called "business methods" could be patented,[32] patents have become more important in a more diversified range of business activities. Today, not only do traditional consumer manufacturing and pharmaceutical industries grapple with patent issues, but other industries, like financial services and Internet-based businesses, also have to deal with similar issues.[33]

Practice Note:

Patents are important because of the broad range of products and processes that can be patented.

This Guide provides a basic explanation of how patents can pertain to a business, why patents should be sought, how patents are obtained, how patents are used, and how to avoid using another's patents. The discussions herein are generally related to patent law and practice in the United States. It is important to remember that this Guide is not intended to teach anyone to be a patent attorney or agent, or to replace a patent attorney or agent. Rather, this Guide is intended to give patent users a foundational understanding about patents so that discussions with a licensed patent practitioner are more efficient, useful and productive.

CHAPTER 2

Why Seek Patent Protection?

Before determining whether to seek patent protection and what kind of patent protection should be sought, it is important to understand not only what a patent is, as discussed in Chapter 1, but why an organization should seek patent protection. Patents can be valuable assets and can serve a wide variety of purposes. But patents can also be a waste of money if not sought for the right reasons and in a manner that does not achieve the ultimate goals.

Practice Note:

It is important to first understand why patent protection is being sought to focus efforts properly.

There are many reasons seeking patent protection can be useful to an organization.

- Patents can turn an intangible asset into something tangible and well defined;

- Patents are evidence of the organization's level of innovation and thus can be used as a marketing tool;
- Patents can protect a product or product line and potentially keep out competitors;
- Patents can be used as a source of revenue;
- Patents can be used as something to trade when others start asserting patents;
- Patents can create prior art to others;
- Patents can help establish an effective "design around"; and/or
- Patents can be an impressive decorative item on the wall.

Understanding why patent protection is being sought for a particular invention before beginning the patenting process can prevent an organization from wasting a lot of time and money on misplaced emphasis. Of course, more than one motivation may drive an organization's desire to seek patent protection for any given invention. Similarly, different motivations may drive an organization's desire to seek patent protection for different inventions. This chapter explains each of these potential motivations.

2.1 Patents Can Turn an Intangible Asset into Something Tangible and Well Defined

In general, business plans start with an idea and seek to implement that idea. The idea may be developing a new and innovative product or service that customers will desire. Figuring out how to turn the intangible idea that is the center of a business plan into something tangible and well defined brings value to an organization. This value can be important regardless of whether the organization is a start-up or an established business which has been operating for a long time.

A patent can be a crucial element in crystallizing an intangible invention and turning it into something tangible. As discussed in Chapter 1, patents are concrete, written documents that define an invention in the form of claims that are intended to define what the patentee owns and what the public is free to use. Despite the complexity that is often involved in interpreting patents (*see* Chapter 11), patents are definable assets. Patents can be valued (*see* Chapter 15) and identified as "intangible assets" on an organization's books.[1] As such, patents can enhance the value of an organization beyond the value of the invention itself.

Practice Note:

Patents turn intangible inventions into tangible things that add value to the organization.

Consider the following illustration. An organization is working on a new invention, for example developing a new commercial product, as JVC did in the late 1970s and early 1980s with the VHS recorder. Obtaining patent protection, even on small but crucial elements of that invention, can provide the organization with exclusive access to the market for up to twenty years.[2] Moreover, seeking and obtaining improvement patents for the technology as a product line evolves—for example, the VHS recorder evolved into Super VHS and other forms of VHS—can allow the organization to continue its exclusive or leading role in the industry even longer.

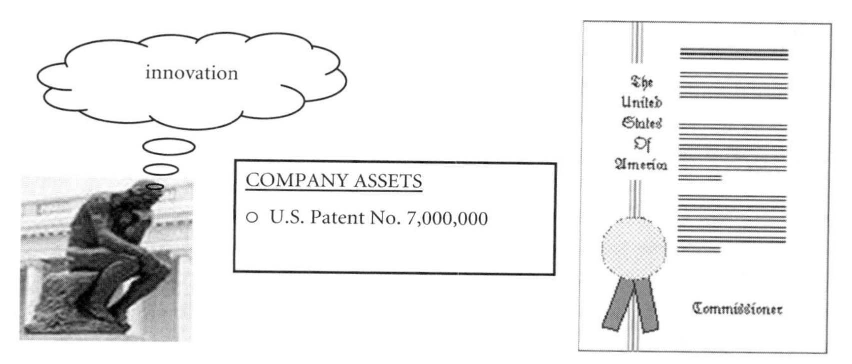

FIGURE 2.1 Patents Can Turn an Intangible Asset into Something Tangible and Well Defined.

2.2 Patents Can Evidence That an Organization Is an Innovator and Thus Can Be Used as an Effective Marketing Tool

Patents can be, and often are, used as marketing tools. Many products or services, when marketed to consumers, make reference to the fact that the product is "patented" or has a "patent pending." Why do marketing folks like to make reference to an issued patent or pending patent application with respect to a product being offered for sale?

First, the fact that patent protection is being sought or has been obtained suggests to the consuming public that the product is innovative and special. Consider a cleaning solution that is so powerful it uses a "special patented formula." Likewise, consider a method of manufacturing bicycles that is so effective and efficient that it uses a "patented process." A prerequisite to the marketing plan of many infomercials is that the product or service being offered be "patented" or at least have a "patent pending." In each instance, the ability to state that the product is patented is used to convey to the consumer the impression that there is something special and innovative about the product.

Practice Note:

Making reference to patents in marketing suggests that the product or service is innovative.

Further, identifying a product or service as being subject to patent protection also suggests exclusivity. In other words, the quality of the product or service that makes it patentable is only available from a limited number of sources.

In the cleaning solution example above, the reference to a special patented formula creates the impression that this is the *only* cleaning solution available that uses that special patented formula. Thus, if the consumer wants to have *access* to the cleaning power that the special patented formula provides, he or she will have to purchase the patented product.

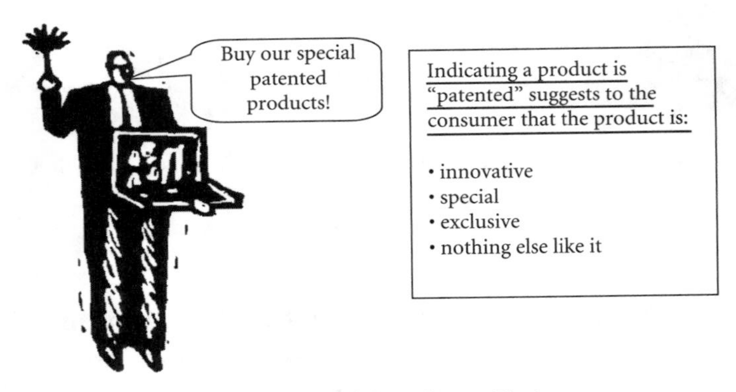

FIGURE 2.2 Patents Can Be Used as a Useful Marketing Tool.

Practice Note:

Making reference to patents in marketing suggests that the product or service is exclusive.

However, it is important to remember that it is *not* appropriate to mark a product or service as "patented" or "patent pending" when such a statement is not true. False patent marking is a violation of U.S. patent law[3] and can lead to a host of other causes of actions.[4]

Practice Note:

Products or services should not be marked as "patented" or "patent pending" if such a statement is not true.

For a more detailed discussion of patent marking, *see* Chapter 15, Section 15.5.1.

2.3 Patents Can Protect a Product or Product Line and Potentially Keep Out Competitors

One of the most important remedies available to a patent owner is an injunction. In other words, a court may issue an order to *exclude* others from practicing the claimed invention. Thus, a patent owner can prevent others in the industry from offering a competing product or service.[5] This remedy is an important and powerful aspect of having a patent and is often a major reason patent protection is sought.

Practice Note:

Patents can potentially exclude competitors from practicing your invention.

Over the past few years, this right to exclude others has been substantially limited as a result of the negative publicity surrounding the BlackBerry® case between *NTP and RIM*[6] and the subsequent decision by the U.S. Supreme Court in *eBay v. Mercantile Exchange.*[7] As discussed in more detail in Chapter 17, these cases have limited a patent owner's right to obtain an injunction when the patent owner itself does not sell a product that competes with the infringer's product.

Historically, patentees would write to competitors or potential licensees to put them on "notice" of their patent portfolio. By carefully crafting such letters, patentees could start the period in which damages against the letter recipient would begin for patent infringements. At the same time, such notification would not make the patentee susceptible to a declaratory judgment lawsuit by the letter recipient at a time and place chosen by the recipient which might not be desirable to the patentee. (*See also* Chapter 14.

In a declaratory judgment lawsuit, an accused infringer seeks a declaration (or statement) by a court that a patent is invalid, not infringed, and/or unenforceable.)

In 2007, the U.S. Supreme Court's decision in *MedImmune*[8] and subsequent decisions by the Federal Circuit,[9] changed this paradigm. These cases redefined when a court has the authority to hear a patent dispute in the form of a declaratory judgment action, raised by an accused infringer, and further discouraged patentees from writing to their competitors or potential licensees to assert their patents prior to bringing a lawsuit. As a result of *MedImmune* and its progeny, if a patentee writes a pre-lawsuit notice letter, even a carefully crafted one, then the patentee risks being sued for a declaratory judgment that its patent is invalid, not infringed, and/or unenforceable at a time and in a place of the accused infringer's choice. This change in U.S. patent law has made patentees more likely to sue first and discuss settlement later.[10]

Practice Note:
Since 2007, the fear of declaratory judgment actions has made patentees more likely to sue first and write letters later.

Even without a lawsuit or a notice letter, the mere existence of a published application or issued patent can deter a would-be competitor from entering a market. As part of best business practices, many organizations perform what are called "right-to-use" or "clearance" searches before launching a new product and, periodically, when implementing new improvements. As a result of such patent searches, these competitors become aware of other organizations' patents and may choose to change the design of their products or perhaps to not even enter a market. Thus, the mere fact that a patent application is on file, or that a patent has issued, may deter future competitors from entering the marketplace without the organization that owns the published patent application or the patent ever realizing it.

Practice Note:
The act of merely seeking and publishing a patent application or obtaining an issued patent can be a deterrent to would-be competitors.

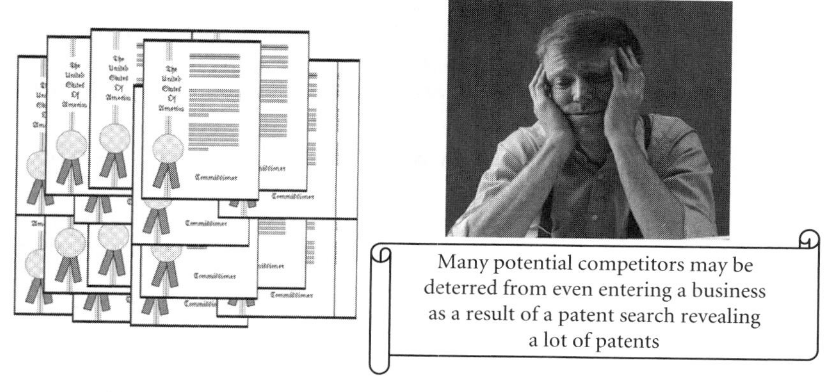

FIGURE 2.3 Patents Act as a Deferent to Competitors.

2.4 Patents Can Be Used as a Source of Revenue

Many organizations use patents as a source of revenue. IBM, Texas Instruments, Honeywell, Xerox, Alcatel-Lucent, Kodak, and others have all turned their vast patent portfolios into a source of revenue.[11] Licensing out non-core patents (or even in some cases core patents) has been a strategy invoked by many technology leaders. (A "core" patent is a patent directed to the organization's main business, while a "non-core" patent is a patent directed to a device or process that is not a part of the organization's main business.) While generating licensing revenue was not the original reason these organizations sought to develop patent portfolios, it has certainly become a practical reality in many instances.

Other organizations have been founded solely on the concept of obtaining patents for the purpose of licensing such patents to third parties. These organizations are often referred to as "patent-holding companies" or "non-practicing entities." Some of these organizations have also been referred to as "trolls," invoking images of the mythical creatures standing in front of bridges extracting tolls from those innocents seeking passage. Regardless of what they are called, these organizations seek (often successfully) to monetize their patent portfolios.

Practice Note:
Patents can be a source of revenue, by either directly licensing or litigating them.

To avoid a claim for patent infringement, it is common for an organization to pay for the right to use a claimed invention. Even when an organization does not voluntarily agree to pay for the right to use an invention, as a result of litigation, an organization may nonetheless be compelled to pay for its use of a patented technology.[12] Organizations may license or cross-license their patents to competitors or others in exchange for patent rights, some other desired asset, or even cash.

Even organizations that traditionally did not seek to use their patent portfolio in an affirmative manner seek revenue from their competitors using their patent portfolio.[13] Of course, many patents are not licensed and do not generate any licensing stream of income. If the goal in obtaining a patent is to seek licensing income, careful consideration is required when determining whether a potential patent application covers a useful or desirable technology, the lifetime of the product that will be covered, and whether the organization would be willing to let others have access to the technology.

2.5 Patents Can Be Used as Something to Trade When Others Start Asserting Patents

One reason many organizations seek patents is for defensive purposes. For example, consider the situation where an organization decides to use its patent portfolio to raise revenue. When the organization is deciding which organizations to target in its patent enforcement program, it is likely to consider as an undesirable target any organization that has its own relevant patent portfolio. Such a target organization could respond with its own counter-patent assertion and perhaps demand that a balancing payment be made in its favor. At a minimum, the existence of a relevant patent portfolio can allow the target organization to request a cross-license, thereby reducing the balancing payment that might otherwise be due.

Practice Note:
Having a strong patent portfolio can reduce or shift a balancing payment that is due when a competitor seeks a cross-license.

Even if a non-competitor starts asserting patents against the organization, having a non-core patent that can be traded for a license may be an inexpensive way to resolve a patent dispute. Some organizations use non-core patents as assets to trade with patent-holding companies.

Practice Note:

Some organizations use non-core patents as assets that can be used in negotiating with patent-holding companies.

2.6 Patents Can Create Prior Art to Others

By promptly seeking and disclosing its inventions in patent applications which get published or become issued patents, an organization can create an easily verifiable source of prior art. (Prior art, as discussed in Chapter 8, is what is used to determine if a patented invention is new and not obvious.) It is much simpler and cheaper in a patent litigation to develop the evidence necessary to establish that a published application or an issued patent is prior art (*see* Chapter 8), than it is to establish that a commercial product is prior art that had the patented features and was "on sale" in the United States during the relevant time period. Also, when a patent application is prepared and filed, it can disclose more alternatives than might otherwise be present in the organization's commercial embodiment of the invention. By including a wider range of descriptions, or alternatives, a patent application can potentially invalidate others' patents more effectively than the actual product which was intended to be covered by the patent application.

Practice Note:

By seeking patent protection, an organization can create prior art to be used to defend against future patent assertions.

2.7 Patents Can Help Establish an Effective "Design Around"

When faced with another's patent, an organization may choose to develop a design that avoids the claims of that patent. This process is often referred to as "designing around" the patent. In this case, seeking a patent on the new design may also be a good idea.

However, even when a potential "design around" literally removes one or more elements of a patent claim from a potentially accused product or service, a patentee may, nonetheless, assert that the equivalent of the missing element is present. (*See* Chapter 12, Section 12.1.) If the organization gets its own patent on the new design, which is granted over the design of the earlier patent, this "separate patentability" of the "design around" may be evidence to support that the change is significant and not merely the equivalent of the patent element. Thus, when an organization chooses to design around a patent instead of paying a royalty for a license, seeking and obtaining a separate patent on the new design, if available, can be beneficial.

Practice Note:

Obtaining patent protection on new designs which seek to avoid other patents can be beneficial.

However, it is important to understand that a later patent may be valid, but a product incorporating that invention may still infringe an earlier patent. The patent right is a right to exclude; it does not necessarily grant a right to practice the invention. In other words, just because a patent can be used to stop someone else from practicing the claimed invention, it does not mean that the patent owner can actually practice the invention disclosed and claimed in the patent. The patent owner may be precluded from practicing the claimed invention because someone else owns another earlier patent which covers that product too.

2.8 Patents Can Be an Impressive Decorative Item on the Wall

Finally, some organizations (and individuals) obtain patents just to say they have them. Some people like patents as vanity plaques. Minimal effort and expense should be incurred for these types of patents.

CHAPTER 3

What Is Patentable?

In order to be entitled to a patent, a claimed invention must be

- New (or "novel");
- Not obvious;
- Useful; and
- Patent-eligible subject matter.

Each of these criteria for patentability must be met for a claim to be entitled to be patented. However, it is important to keep in mind that in order to determine whether an invention meets these criteria, the inquiry begins with the claim being analyzed.

3.1 "New" (or "Novel")

First, the invention for which a U.S. Patent is being sought must be "new" or "novel."[1] Phrased another way, no one else has come up with the same invention before. The test that U.S. patent law applies to determine whether an invention meets the "novelty" requirement is whether no single reference has all of the elements of the claim either directly or inherently.[2] In other words, if every element recited in a claim is identically disclosed in a single prior art reference, then that claim is anticipated and patentability is precluded.[3]

Practice Note:
Patentable ideas must be "new" (or "novel"), i.e., no single reference has all the elements of the claim.

A reference is considered to explicitly "anticipate" a claimed invention when each of the elements of an invention sought to be patented is expressly discussed in the prior art reference.

To illustrate this point, consider the situation where the invention is a new type of chair as shown here.

The organization's new chair

What is claimed is:

1. A chair, comprising:
   a. a rectangular seat;
   b. a rectangular back;
   c. two arms; and
   d. four legs.

FIGURE 3.1 The Invention.

In this example, a claim is drafted that seeks to encompass the inventive aspects of this new chair as follows:

What is claimed is:

1. A chair, comprising:
   a. a rectangular seat;
   b. a rectangular back;
   c. two arms; and
   d. four legs.

In order to meet the "novelty" requirement, there must be no single prior art reference that discloses a chair having each of these elements.

Now, assume a piece of prior art (*see* Chapter 8)—like a sales brochure or flyer offering for sale an older design of a different chair—discloses a chair with each of these elements (or parts). In U.S. patent law, that prior art reference is said to "anticipate" the invention since there is nothing new about the alleged invention.

Taking the example "Claim 1" a little further, consider the above claim as analyzed against the prior art flyer for a chair being sold in the United States.

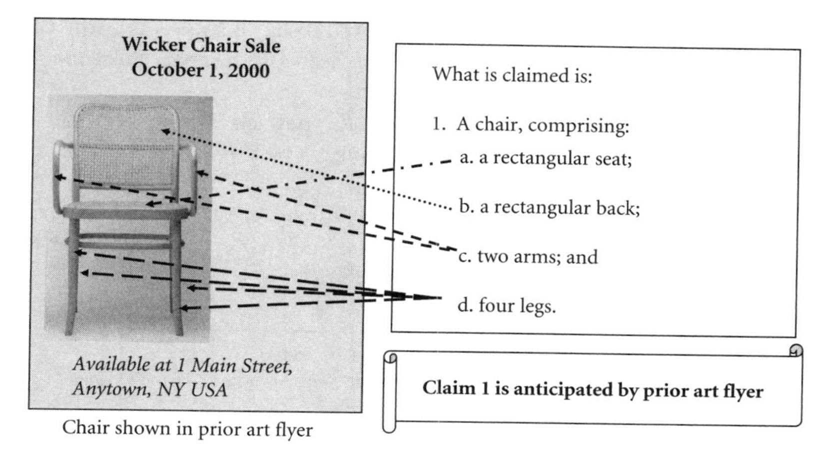

FIGURE 3.2 Claim to a Chair Anticipated by a Prior Art Flyer.

As this analysis shows, even though the earlier chair in the flyer looks very different from the new chair, because the claim is drafted so broadly, each element in the claim is met by the chair shown in the flyer.

Practice Note:

Even prior art that looks different from the original invention can still anticipate a patent claim.

Of course, this claim can be rewritten to describe the new chair in a different way, where the chair in the earlier flyer does not show each of the elements of the claim. For example, the claim could be redrafted as follows:

> What is claimed is:
> 1. A chair, comprising:
>   a. a *flexible* rectangular seat;
>   b. a *flexible* rectangular back;
>   c. two arms; and
>   d. *two pairs of* legs, wherein each pair of legs is crossed.

(The italicized text shows additional concepts added to the claim.)[4]

In the revised claim, the following changes have been made to the claim to distinguish the prior art flyer:

- Both the seat and back are now required to be "flexible," as is the case with the new chair design, but not the case with the chair shown in the earlier flyer.
- While both claims require four legs, the new claim requires that the four legs be "two pairs of legs, wherein each pair of legs is crossed."

As shown below, the new chair design will meet this claim, but the prior chair disclosed in the flyer will not. Thus, this new claim will still cover the new chair, but will not be anticipated by the prior art.

The organization's new chair:

Chair shown in prior art flyer:

(Revised Claim)

What is claimed is:

1. A chair, comprising:

a. a flexible rectangular seat;

b. a flexible rectangular back;

c. two arms; and

d. two pairs of legs, wherein each pair of legs is crossed.

FIGURE 3.3 Revised Cliam to Capture Invention and Distinguish Prior Art Flyer.

U.S. patent law recognizes that even when an aspect of an alleged invention is not expressly disclosed in a prior art reference, the fact that the prior art reference includes a disclosure which "inherently" (or necessarily) discloses that aspect of the invention, it is still said to anticipate.[5]

Practice Note:

If a prior art reference "inherently" (or necessarily) discloses all aspects of the alleged invention, the invention is not "new."

In order to illustrate this concept, consider the same chair invention, except that instead of merely requiring "two arms" in the proposed claim, the claim requires "two arms *made of a stiff material.*" Even though the flyer does not state expressly that the arms are made of a stiff material, a person of ordinary skill in the art of making chairs, looking at the flyer, would understand that the "Wicker Chair" in the flyer has wood arms, as shown in the picture, and that the wood arms are necessarily made of a "stiff material." Thus, the flyer would still "inherently" disclose that claim limitation, even though the claim limitation is not expressly stated in the prior art flyer.

It is important to appreciate, however, that inherency requires that the element or limitation not explicitly disclosed must "necessarily" be as provided in the claim. The fact that the undisclosed aspect is more probable, or likely than not, to be as stated in the claim, is not enough to anticipate a claim.[6]

3.2 Not "Obvious"

Next, under U.S. patent law, the claimed invention for which the patent is being sought must also not be "obvious."[7] (Outside the United States, this concept is referred to as "inventive step.") In other words, even if a single reference does not identically disclose all the elements of a claim, U.S. patent law does not allow a claim in a patent to be issued if the claimed invention as a whole would be obvious in light of the reference or its combination with other references at the time the patent application was filed.[8] In the vernacular, obviousness is determined by combining references: 1+1 = 2.

Practice Note:
Patentable ideas must be "not obvious," e.g., 1+1 = 3.

Nearly a half century ago, the U.S. Supreme Court[9] set forth the following steps to be followed when making a determination of obviousness:

- The scope and content of the prior art are to be determined;
- The differences between the prior art and claimed invention as a whole must be determined;
- The level of ordinary skill in the art when the application was filed must be established; and
- Certain "secondary considerations" are evaluated including
  - The invention's commercial success,
  - Long-felt but unsolved needs,

- The failure of others,
- Skepticism by experts,
- Praise by others,
- Teaching away by others,
- Recognition of a problem,
- Copying of the invention by competitors, and
- Other relevant factors.

(These "secondary considerations" are also known as the "*Graham*" factors).[10]

These determinations are then used to decide whether or not the claimed invention would have been obvious to a person of ordinary skill in the art at the time the invention was made.

Until 2007, when courts applied this test, it was, in practice, very difficult to establish that a claim which was not anticipated was in fact obvious. It was especially difficult in the context of litigation over an already issued patent, since an issued patent is presumed valid.[11] In particular, according to U.S. patent law developed since the early 1980s by the Federal Circuit, the challenger of a patent claim was required to show that some teaching, suggestion, or motivation to combine the prior art references to demonstrate a claim was obvious.[12] This test has been referred to as the "TSM" test.

However, after the U.S. Supreme Court's 2007 landmark decision in *KSR v. Teleflex*,[13] it is now easier to demonstrate that a claimed invention is obvious.[14] In particular, the U.S. Supreme Court rejected rigid tests like the TSM test used by the Federal Circuit prior to that time to determine obviousness in favor of a more flexible approach.[15] This lower threshold of demonstrating obviousness has restricted the scope of patent protection ultimately found to be available.

The U.S. Supreme Court in *KSR* identified the following guidelines for this more flexible obviousness analysis:

- Merely substituting one element for another known in the field would be considered obvious unless it yields a result that is not predictable;[16]
- When the prior art teaches away from combining certain known elements, discovery of a successful means of combining them is more likely to be non-obvious;[17]
- A combination of items would be obvious if a person of ordinary skill in the art would recognize the combination to improve similar devices in the same way, unless the application of the technique is beyond his or her skill;[18] and

- "In determining whether the subject matter of a patent claim is obvious, neither the particular motivation nor the avowed purpose of the patentee controls. What matters is the objective reach of the claim. If the claim extends to what is obvious, it is invalid under § 103."[19]

U.S. patent law, applying these principles, looks to the following types of evidence to determine whether there is an apparent reason to combine the known elements in the fashion claimed by the patent at issue:

- Interrelated teachings of multiple patents;
- The effects of demands known to the design community or present in the marketplace; and
- The background knowledge possessed by a person having ordinary skill in the art.[20]

Consider, for example, U.S. Patent No. 5,026,109, entitled "Segmented Cover System." The claimed invention was directed to a "retractable segmented cover system used with a truck trailer." The scope and content of the prior art included two references, U.S. Patent Nos. 4,189,178 (Cramaro) and 3,415,260 (Hall).

- Cramaro discloses a retractable tarpaulin cover system for use in trucks. It included all the elements of the asserted claim, except it did not include "segmented tarps."
- Hall discloses a cover system divided into a number of "flexible screen members" and that its system "may be used as a truck cover."

Applying the above principles, the Federal Circuit found it would be obvious to combine the teachings of Cramaro and Hall to form the claimed segmented cover.

> In combination with each other, the cover system of Cramaro performs exactly the function that it performs independent of Hall, and the removable cover sections of Hall perform exactly the function that they perform independent of Cramaro. The elements of the cover system of Cramaro perform several functions, including protection of the cargo, containment of the cargo, and retraction of the cover. None of these functions changes upon the simple act of replacing the one-piece cover of Cramaro with the segmented cover of Hall. The segmented cover of Hall performs the function of allowing individual replacement of the cover sections. This function does not change upon incorporation into the Cramaro cover system. The combination simply mechanizes Hall's segmented cover or segments Cramaro's mechanized cover.[21]

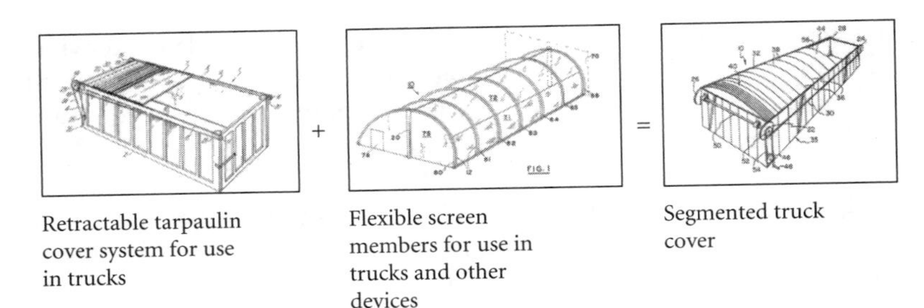

Retractable tarpaulin cover system for use in trucks

Flexible screen members for use in trucks and other devices

Segmented truck cover

FIGURE 3.4 It is Obvious to Use the Flexible Screen Members as Part of a Retractable Tarpaulin Cover.

3.3 Useful

Further, the invention must also be useful.[22]

Generally, unless the invention is a perpetual motion machine, obscene, or concerned with discovering previously unknown uses for some newly isolated biochemical or genetic compound, usefulness (or "utility") usually is not an issue.

However, when a patent claim includes a limitation that does not make sense or will not work, utility can become an issue.[23]

Practice Note:
Patentable ideas must be "useful." Generally, this criterion is not hard to meet as long as the claim makes sense.

3.4 Patent-Eligible Subject Matter

In addition to these criteria, the claimed subject matter of a U.S. Patent Application must also be so-called "patent-eligible" subject matter. U.S. patent law defines patent-eligible subject matter to include

> *any* new and useful process, machine, manufacture, or composition of matter, or any new and useful improvement thereof. . . .[24]

Congress (in adopting U.S. patent law), and U.S. courts (in interpreting U.S. patent law), recognize that the area of patent-eligible subject matter is intended to be very broad. It is considered to include "anything under the sun made by man."[25]

Thus, there are four categories of patent-eligible subject matter defined by U.S. patent law statutes:

- Processes;
- Machines;
- Manufactures; and
- Compositions of matter.[26]

Practice Note:
Processes, machines, manufactures, and compositions of matter are eligible for patent protection.

U.S. patent law has also recognized that, in addition to falling within at least one of these four statutory categories of patent-eligible subject matter, a claim must not fall in one of three judicially created exceptions:

- Laws of nature;
- Natural phenomena; and
- Abstract ideas.[27]

These exceptions have been collectively referred to as so-called "fundamental principles."[28] U.S. patent law tries to avoid the granting of patent claims that pre-empt (or remove from the public's access) such fundamental principles, which are "part of the storehouse of knowledge of all men. . . . free to all men and reserved exclusively to none."[29]

This section will first explain the concept of "fundamental principles" and then explain each of these four categories of patent-eligible subject matter.

3.4.1 Claims That Cover Merely "Fundamental Principles" Are Excluded from Patent-Eligible Subject Matter

So-called "fundamental principles," including laws of nature, natural phenomena, and abstract ideas, are the basic tools of scientific work. Thus, patent claims that preempt others from using such fundamental principles have been judicially carved out from the scope of patent-eligible subject matter. The purpose of this judicial carve-out is to prevent patents that exclude these fundamental building blocks from the public's access (even for a limited period of time). The rationale for this judicial carve-out is that it seems unfair to block others from using these fundamental building blocks.

Practice Note:

"Fundamental principles," including laws of nature, natural phenomena, and abstract ideas, are *not* eligible for patent protection.

A classic example of this concern is illustrated in the context of a patent granted to Samuel Morse, the inventor of the telegraph and Morse code. Mr. Morse's patent had eight claims including

- Claims directed to the telegraph device he developed;
- Claims directed to his system of using dots and dashes to communicate over such a device; and
- A claim to the use of electro-magnetism in general for transmitting characters, letters, or signs at any distance.[30]

Although the U.S. Supreme Court recognized that Mr. Morse developed a significant invention and was deserving of at least some patent protection, the Court also recognized that there was something troubling about Mr. Morse claiming ***any*** use of electro-magnetism, even when confined to the particular purpose of transmitting characters, letters, or signs at a distance.[31] The Court found that the scope of patent protection to which Mr. Morse was entitled should be limited to the use of the particular machine he invented, and not the law of nature (electro-magnetism) which his machine employed.[32]

The concepts of excluding claims directed merely to "fundamental principles" (like Morse's claim seeking to patent electro-magnetism)—but not excluding claims to inventions applying such principles (like Morse's claims directed to using particular structures in his device which rely upon electro-magnetism to operate)—have been applied by U.S. courts innumerable times over the past few centuries and form a foundation for what the U.S. patent system considers to be patent-eligible subject matter.

U.S. courts have also recognized that merely limiting a claim to a "fundamental principle" to a particular field of use—as Morse did for the sending of information over a distance—is not sufficient to make a potential claim patent-eligible subject matter.

Thus, U.S. courts have recognized that it would be inappropriate to grant patent protection for other fundamental principles, like

- Einstein's discovery of $E=mc^2$;
- Newton's discovery of the law of gravity; or
- Other known or yet undiscovered laws of nature.[33]

Patent-ineligible fundamental principles include not merely laws of nature and abstract ideas, but also natural phenomena like a new mineral discovered in the earth or a new plant found in the wild.[34]

However, it is important to remember that just because a patent claim relates to a fundamental principle, or even includes a fundamental principle as an element of the claim, like an equation or algorithm, does not, in itself, make the claim patent-ineligible subject matter.[35] Every invention in some way depends upon a fundamental principle to make it work. A pulley relies on basic physics to operate; a semiconductor microprocessor depends upon quantum physics; and even a method of baking a cake depends upon fundamental principles, such as when the cake mix changes from the liquid state of batter into the solid state of cake. Nonetheless, each of these inventions can be patent-eligible subject matter.

3.4.2 Statutory Classes of Patent-Eligible Subject Matter

3.4.2.1 Processes

U.S. patent law statutorily defines a "process" to mean "process, art or method, and includes a new use of a known process, machine, manufacture, composition of matter, or material."[36]

Although the statutory definition of "process" is very broad, and the ordinary meaning of the term "process" would include any process which is a series of steps or acts, U.S. courts have recognized that not every process is a patent-eligible process. Instead, U.S. courts have found that processes that preempt (or merely cover) fundamental principles (as discussed in Section 3.4.1) are not patent-eligible processes.

While various tests have been developed by lower courts and the USPTO over the years to try to distinguish between claims that cover patent-eligible processes and claims that cover processes that are not patent-eligible,[37] the current state of U.S. patent law is that there is only one "governing" test available: the so-called "machine-or-transformation test."

Under the "machine-or-transformation test," an applicant may show that a process claim is patent-eligible subject matter by either

- Showing that his claim is tied to a particular machine; or
- Showing that his claim transforms an article.[38]

Practice Note:
A process must be tied to a machine or transform an article in order to be patent-eligible.

U.S. courts have further recognized that in addition to meeting one and/or the other of these two tests, the analysis should consider that

- The use of a specific machine or transformation of an article must impose meaningful limits on the claim's scope to impart patent-eligibility; and

- The involvement of the machine or transformation in the claimed process must not merely be insignificant, extra-solution activity.[39]

Practice Note:

The machine or transformation must impose meaningful limits and not be merely insignificant, extra-solution activity.

However, an analysis of whether a claimed process is patent-eligible does not include an evaluation of

- Whether the invention is new or not obvious; those considerations are addressed separately as discussed above;[40] or
- Whether one or more of the steps may be directed to a fundamental principle or other patent-ineligible subject matter, as long as the claim "as a whole" meets the machine-or-transformation test.[41]

Practice Note:

The machine or transformation test does not consider novelty or obviousness and must be based on the claim "as a whole."

In applying this test, U.S. patent law recognizes that patent-eligible processes include *methods of making or using something*, like the chair discussed above, at least when the process transforms or reduces the article to a different state or thing, or is performed by, for example, some other device or article.

Thus, taking the chair example above, a patent-eligible process would include the method of manufacturing the chair, such as illustrated by the following claim:

What is claimed is:

1. A method of manufacturing a chair, comprising:
    a. providing a flexible rectangular seat;
    b. providing two arms;
    c. attaching the two arms to the flexible rectangular seat;
    d. attaching a flexible rectangular back to the flexible rectangular seat;
    e. providing two pairs of legs; and
    f. attaching the two pairs of legs to the flexible rectangular seat so that each pair of legs is crossed.

In this case, the method of manufacturing the chair claimed is transforming several articles (the various parts of the chair) into a different state or thing (an assembled chair). U.S. patent law would recognize this process to be patent-eligible. Of course, this does not mean a U.S. Patent would necessarily be granted for this process, since the other requirements of patentability discussed above—e.g., new, not obvious, useful, etc.—must also be met.

What is claimed is:

1. A method of manufacturing a chair, comprising:
   a. providing a flexible rectangular seat;
   b. providing two arms;
   c. attaching the two arms to the flexible rectangular seat;
   d. attaching a flexible rectangular back to the flexible rectangular seat;
   e. providing two pairs of legs; and
   f. attaching the two pairs of legs to the flexible rectangular seat so that each pair of legs is crossed.

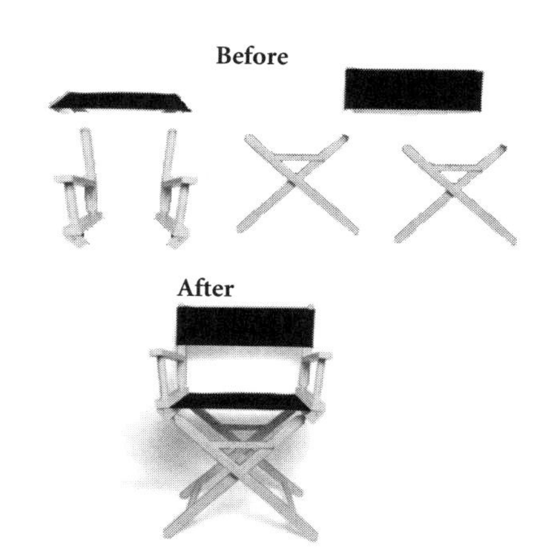

FIGURE 3.5 Example Method of Manufacturing Claim.

Another type of patent-eligible process includes *a method of using something*. For example, consider the following claim directed to a method of taking a picture which uses a camera and a roll of film:

What is claimed is:

1. A method of taking a picture, comprising:
   a. providing a camera having a lens;
   b. inserting a roll of film in the camera;
   c. pointing the lens at a desired object or scene to be photographed;
   d. activating a picture-taking switch of the camera;
   e. advancing the roll of film in the camera;
   f. developing the film; and
   g. using the developed film to form an image.

In this example, the film is transformed when the picture is taken with the camera, and the film is developed. Thus, while this claim may not be new (and thus would not be entitled to patent protection), it nonetheless claims a patent-eligible method.

What is claimed is:

1. A method of taking a picture, comprising:
   a. providing a camera having a lens;
   b. inserting a roll of film in the camera;
   c. pointing the lens at a desired object or scene to be photographed;
   d. activating a picture-taking switch of the camera;
   e. advancing the roll of film in the camera;
   f. developing the film; and
   g. using the developed film to form an image.

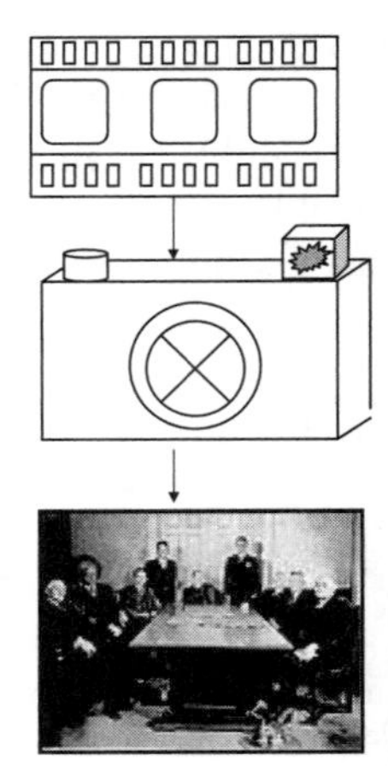

FIGURE 3.6 Example Method of Using Claim.

Another example of a patent-eligible process tied to a machine is *a computer-implemented method*. Consider, for example, a new inventory control system which involves the method of providing a database, receiving an order, identifying in the database whether the order is available, processing the order, and confirming the order. This type of computer-implemented process could be claimed in the following fashion:

What is claimed is:

1. A computer-implemented method for processing orders, comprising the steps of:
   a. providing a database stored on a computer-readable medium comprising inventory information;
   b. receiving at a processor operatively connected to a communication device from a computer associated with a customer comprising order information data regarding an order by the customer;
   c. comparing, at the processor, the order information data with the inventory information data to identify which portion, if any, of the order is available to fill;
   d. generating, at the processor, available-to-fill data based on the portion of the order identified as available to fill; and
   e. sending, from the processor to the computer associated with the customer, the available-to-fill data.

Patent-eligible processes also include *methods that transform matter from one state to another*. Historical examples of where chemical processes or physical acts transform a raw material into a finished product include processes like

- Tanning;
- Dyeing;
- Waterproofing cloth;
- Vulcanizing Indian rubber; and
- Smelting ores.[42]

Thus, a method of vulcanizing rubber (e.g., converting molten rubber into a rubber tire) could be a patent-eligible process. In this example, the molten rubber is transformed into a new and different state of matter, i.e., vulcanized rubber.

Another example of such a patent-eligible process would be a claim directed to the *process of manufacturing a compound,* such as table salt, like the following claim:

> What is claimed is:
> 1. A method of manufacturing table salt, comprising the steps of:
>   a. providing sodium hydroxide;
>   b. providing potassium chloride; and
>   c. mixing the sodium hydroxide with the potassium chloride to form sodium chloride and potassium hydroxide.

While this process may not be novel, for example, and thus it would be too late to obtain patent protection for it, it would nonetheless be a patent-eligible process, because it transforms the two initial chemicals (sodium hydroxide (NaOH) and potassium chloride (KCl)) into two new compositions (sodium chloride (NaCl) and potassium hydroxide (KOH)).

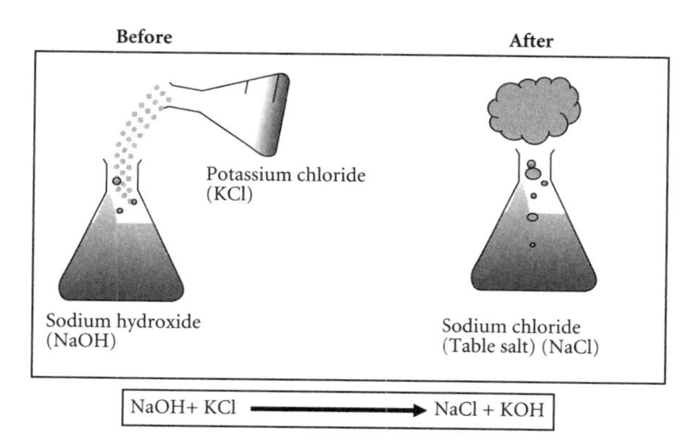

FIGURE 3.7 Example Process of Manufacturing a Compound.

3.4.2.2 Machines

U.S. patent law defines a "machine" for purposes of determining patent-eligibility as "a concrete thing, consisting of parts, or of certain devices and combination of devices."[43] This "includes every mechanical device or combination of mechanical powers and devices to perform some function and produce a certain effect or result."[44]

Practice Note:

A patent-eligible "machine" is a concrete thing, consisting of parts, or of certain devices and combination of devices.

Historical examples of patent-eligible machines include

- A rasterizer for creating a waveform;[45] and
- A sewing machine.[46]

Today, patent-eligible machines would include

- Personal display devices;
- Cellular phones;
- Plasma display projectors;
- Digital video recorders;
- Automobiles; and
- Windmill generators.

One recent example of such a type of machine which could be patent-eligible subject matter is ***a computer system*** with a processor, memory, and software programmed on the memory to cause the processor to perform certain specified steps. In a recent case, the Federal Circuit found that a computer readable medium that has stored on it a new form of watermark signal was considered a patent-eligible machine.[47] ("Computer readable medium" is how U.S. patent law describes a data storage device like a hard disk drive, ROM, RAM, flash memory, or the like.)

Taking the inventory control example discussed earlier, the same subject matter could be rewritten to be a patent-eligible machine as follows:

What is claimed is:

1. A computer system for processing orders, comprising:
   a. a processor;
   b. a communication device operatively connected to the processor; and

c. a computer readable medium operatively connected to the processor comprising a database comprising inventory information data and software programmed to perform the following steps:
   (i) receiving, at a processor operatively connected to a communication device from a computer associated with a customer, comprising order information data regarding an order by the customer;
   (ii) comparing, at the processor, the order information data with the inventory information data to identify which portion, if any, of the order is available to fill;
   (iii) generating, at the processor, available-to-fill data based on the portion of the order identified as available-to-fill; and
   (iv) sending, from the processor to the computer associated with the customer, the available-to-fill data.

3.4.2.3 Manufactures

U.S. courts have defined "a manufacture" as something man-made or a "tangible article or commodity," like an article of merchandise, an article of clothing, etc.[48] As the U.S. Supreme Court has explained, the term "manufacture" means "the production of articles for use from raw or prepared materials by giving to these materials new forms, qualities, properties, or combinations, whether by hand-labor or by machinery."[49]

Practice Note:

A patent-eligible "manufacture" is something man-made or a tangible article or commodity.

Examples of "manufactures" include articles resulting from a process of manufacture,[50] like the chair example. In this regard, the chair may be manufactured either by hand or by a machine, and is thus a "manufacture."

3.4.2.4 Compositions of Matter

U.S. patent law defines a "composition of matter" as a "composite" or combination of "two or more substances."[51] It has been interpreted to mean "all compositions of two or more substances and . . . all composite articles, whether they be the results of chemical union, or of mechanical mixture, or whether they be gases, fluids, powders or solids."[52]

Practice Note:

A patent-eligible composition of matter is a combination of two or more substances.

A composition of matter is a substance which is made by mixing two or more chemicals to form a new compound. For example, in the ordinary table salt example discussed earlier, table salt is formed by mixing sodium hydroxide (NaOH) and potassium chloride (KCl) to form sodium chloride (NaCl). The resulting substance, sodium chloride (NaCl), is a composition of matter and is thus patent-eligible subject matter.

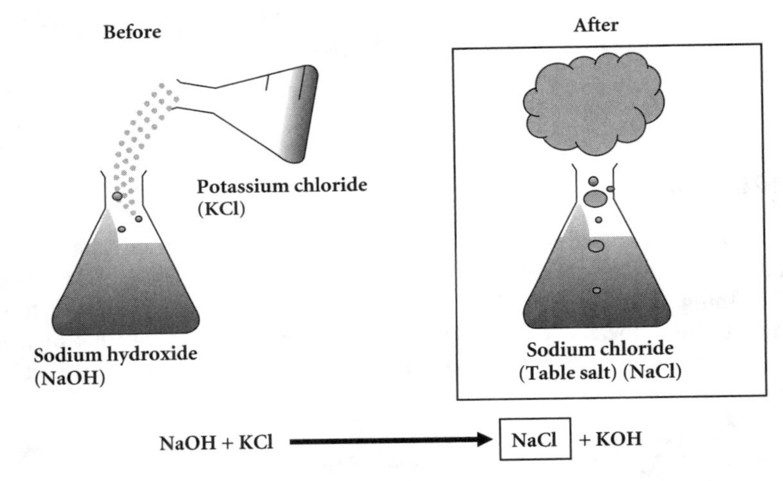

FIGURE 3.8 Patent-eligible Composition of Matter.

CHAPTER

4

What to Patent

At some point in the process, an organization that decides to seek patent protection needs to decide which inventions it will seek to patent. Since patent protection involves a significant investment of funds, time, and effort, this decision should be carefully arrived at in the first instance.

This chapter provides guidelines on best practices to identify what types of inventions to seek patent protection for and procedures to establish an effective patent program including the following recommended steps:

- Understand the business;
- Define the business and the business road map;
- Understand the details of the product lines;
- Understand where the business operations occur;
- Identify supporting systems and services (non-core business);
- Understand what is necessary to make the business work;
- Get management buy-in;
- Establish a budget;
- Set up patent policies and procedures to encourage participation of key employees; and
- Determine which inventions to pursue.

4.1 Understand the Business

In order to identify inventions an organization should patent, it is important to understand *the business of the organization*, including understanding

- The products or services offered by the organization;
- The structures and operations of the organization; and
- The decision-making processes of the organization.

Practice Note:
Understand the business of the organization in order to develop priorities.

Because it is easier to understand this process in the context of an example, the discussion in this chapter will focus on a hypothetical organization, High Tech Co., which has three basic product lines:

- **Core Processors** (special kind of microprocessor used as the brains of many products);
- **LCD Displays** (displays which are often used with computer terminals or in other devices); and
- **PDA/Pager Devices** (personal hand-held organizer, e-mail device, and entertainment center).

FIGURE 4.1 High Tech Co. Product Lines.

In addition to understanding the organization's products and services, it is important to understand *the structure and operation of the organization*, including

- The decision-making process for the organization as a whole, as well as the relevant business units in particular;
- The priorities of the organization as a whole, as well as the relevant business units in particular;
- The budget priorities for the organization as a whole, as well as for the relevant business units in particular; and

- The location of relevant information within the organization and its relevant business units in particular.

As is often the case in many organizations, in this example, High Tech Co.'s three business lines are inter-related.

Physically, the High Tech PDA/Pager devices use High Tech Core Processors. High Tech Core Processors are also used in competitors' PDA/Pager devices and other types of devices. The High Tech LCD Displays, however, do not use any Core Processors.

The areas within the organization that make these products are also related. For example, they all use the same High Tech brand on their products and are subject to oversight by High Tech's central management, which provides legal services, including guidance on intellectual property issues like patents, trademarks, copyrights, etc.

However, there are three separate business units, with separate personnel running each business unit, and separate research, development, manufacturing, sales, and distribution facilities. Although the same High Tech Co. brand is used on all three products, decisions concerning budget, management, and strategy are often independently arrived at for each business unit, with some oversight by the organization's central management structure. This means that each business unit can have its own sources of innovation and decision-makers who may need to be educated and mined for information. It also means that management may need to be included in the decision-making process.

It is important to understand this kind of information about the organization.

Practice Note:
Understand the organizational structure to understand priorities.

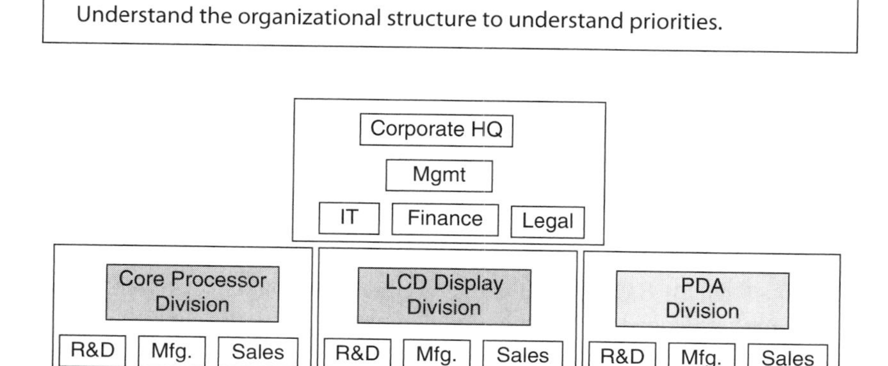

FIGURE 4.2 High Tech Co. Organization Chart.

Once the organizational structure is understood, it is important to *understand key components within the organizational structure*, including where are

- The innovation centers;
- Allies for investing in innovation; and
- Sources of funding for the projects.

Innovation centers should be identified since this is where the source of possible patentable inventions is likely to be located. In the High Tech Co. example, the innovation centers may be the R&D departments within each business unit.

Allies for investing in innovation and source of funding for projects are also important to identify. While sometimes these may be the same, in some organizations they may be different. Without funding, it is impossible to develop a patent portfolio. In the High Tech Co., the source of funding may only be from the budget established by central management or by each business unit; but the allies for innovation may be key personnel from the R&D, Sales, or Accounting departments of each of the business units, and Legal and Finance departments within central management.

Practice Note:
Target innovation centers, allies for investing in innovation, and sources of funding for projects.

In addition to understanding the products that are sold by the organization and its organizational structure, it is also important to *understand the relative importance of each of these product lines to the business*. The importance of the product lines can be measured in a variety of ways, such as in terms of

- Percentage of overall sales of the organization;
- Percentage of profits of the organization; and/or
- Other intangible factors, like the significance of the product line to the organization's history and identity.

In the High Tech Co. example, the revenue and profit of the organization as a whole are divided among the product business units as follows:

- **Core Processors** (60 percent of revenue and 55 percent of profit);
- **LCD Displays** (30 percent of revenue and 25 percent of profit); and
- **PDA/Pager devices** (10 percent of revenue and 20 percent of profit).

Alternatively, the relative importance of the revenue and profit stream from each of these business units can be summarized as follows:

- The Core Processors generate the largest part of the organization's overall revenue and profit but are less profitable than the PDA/Pager devices;
- The PDA/Pager devices are the most profitable product lines but represent only a small share overall of the organization's total revenue and profit; and
- The LCD Displays represent a significant share of the overall revenue and profit for the organization but are not as profitable as the PDA/Pager devices or Core Processors.

Understanding this kind of information helps to identify where patent protection may be more important to the organization's bottom line.

Practice Note:

Understand the relative importance of each product line to the organization to help establish priorities.

4.2 Define the Business and the Business Road Map

It is also important to understand and consider *the organization's business plans for the future*. Without understanding what products the organization expects to be important in the future, it is difficult to set priorities as to

- Which inventions are worth investing in to maximize the return on investment; and
- Which inventions require the development of a strategy of intellectual property protection.

In the High Tech Co. example, the Core Processor business unit has developed a product "road map," where it plans on selling

- A 90 nm Core Processor during the period of 2007–2010;
- A 45 nm Core Processor during the period of 2009–2013; and
- A 14 nm Core Processor during the period of 2011–2015.

Under this product road map, inventions covering the 90 nm Core Processor products are potentially less valuable to the organization than inventions which would apply to all three Core Processors that will be sold through 2015 (i.e., the 90 nm Core Processor, the 45 nm Core Processor, and the 14 nm Core Processor). An invention which covers all three types of Core Processors will cover the organization's future products though 2015, rather than merely through 2010. Thus, such an invention would potentially be more valuable to the organization since it would protect product lines for five more years into the future. Of course, this does not mean that an invention which merely applies to the current 90 nm Core Processor has no value to the organization. For example, it may be used to keep others from trailing the road map and selling cheaper competitive products using High Tech Co.'s older technology.

Practice Note:
Understand the business road map to help set priorities concerning which inventions should be sought to be patented into the future.

4.3 Understand the Details of the Product Lines

In order to be able to identify potentially patentable inventions in the organization's products, it is important *to understand the details of the product lines.* Without an intimate knowledge of the details of the product lines, it is difficult to

- Decide where an invention may lie;
- Define that invention; and
- Determine the significance of that invention.

This point can be easily demonstrated in the context of the High Tech Co. example. By examining the details of the Core Processor device, it may be that an invention lies, by way of example, in

- Some special physical structure of the product, such as the pins used to connect the core processor to the motherboard;
- A particular semiconductor layer being used to create a portion of the structure (like a gate or transistor);
- A particular material that is used in one layer or a combination of layers (like tungsten, molybdenum silicon (MoSi), etc.);
- A unique circuit design embodied in the core processor; or
- A particular software routine embedded in the core processor.

Without a thorough understanding of the various relevant component parts of the Core Processor, it is difficult to be able to identify, and define, the inventive elements of a product.

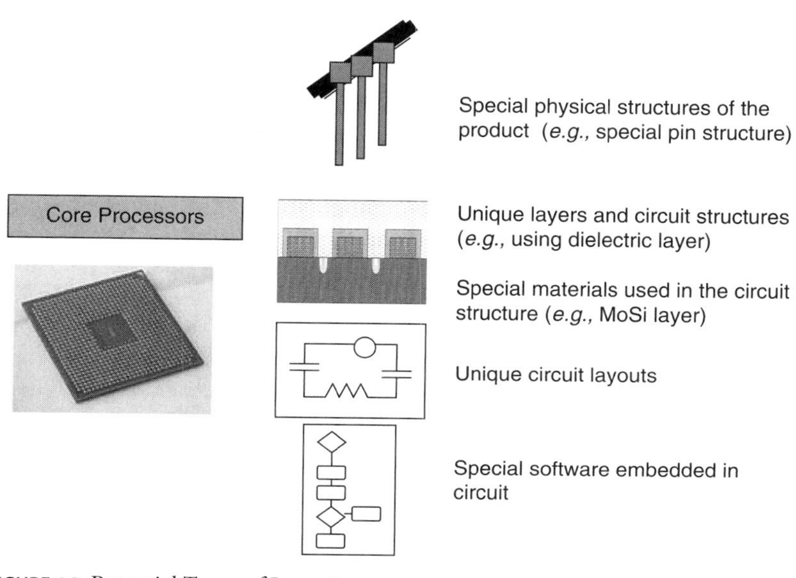

FIGURE 4.3 Potential Types of Inventions.

Practice Note:

Understand product details to help identify where inventions may be located and if such inventions are significant.

It is important to understand not only the physical structures of the organization's products, as just discussed, but also *the interrelationship of the products* with respect to

- Other products of the organization; and
- The organization's overall horizontal and vertical distribution system.

Practice Note:

Understand the product structures, as well as how the different parts function and interrelate with each other to help identify inventions.

This point can again be illustrated using the Core Processor devices in the High Tech Co. example. In this example, the Core Processor device may be used in a variety of products including

- Computers;
- Cell phones; and
- PDA/Pager devices.

Further, while High Tech Co. does not make computers or cell phones, it does make PDA/Pager devices. Thus, being able to sell the Core Processor devices for use in computers and cell phones will be significant potential markets for generating revenue outside the organization, but protecting the use of the Core Processors for PDA/Pager devices may become very important if the only entity that uses the Core Processors in PDA/Pager devices is High Tech Co.

These types of real-world factors can affect the type of patent protection that should be sought for the invention in the Core Processor. For example, it may be desirable or undesirable to claim a PDA, Computer, or Cell Phone device comprising a Core Processor with the new invention depending upon these real-world factors. (*See* Chapter 15, Section 15.3.1.4.)

Practice Note:
Understand the interrelationship of the organization's products with respect to other products of the organization and the organization's overall vertical and horizontal distribution system.

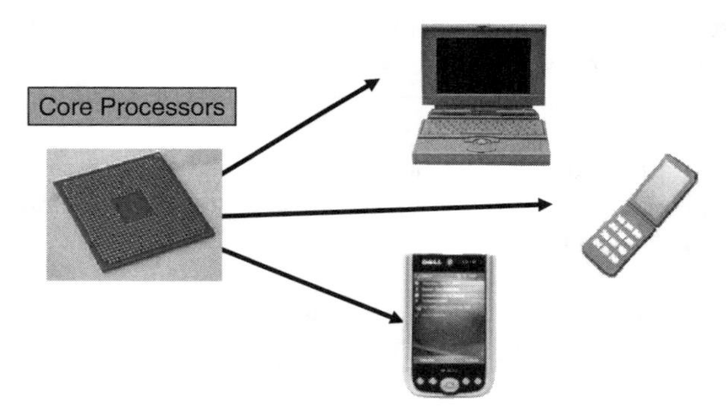

FIGURE 4.4 Uses of Core Processors.

Finally, it is also important to consider *the features the organization relies upon to market and sell its products.* Features that drive the organization's sales are the best prospects for potential patent protection, since those inventions would most likely protect the organization's profitability.

In the High Tech Co. example, the selling features of the Core Processor devices are that the processor

- Is faster;
- Is cheaper; and
- Has special functions.

Patent protection should be sought on the inventions that allow the Core Processor devices to achieve these characteristics, if possible. Obtaining exclusivity over these features can be useful in enhancing the sales of the product. Also, as discussed in Chapter 2, Section 2.2, having such patent protection may also be a useful marketing tool. Further, damages for infringing such patents could likely be higher, as discussed in Chapter 15.

Practice Note:

Patent protection should be sought to cover features that contribute to a product line's commercial success.

4.4 Understand Where the Business Operations Occur

In order to obtain effective patent protection, it is also important to know *geographically where patent protection is necessary to protect a business.* Patents are geographically limited to the country which issues the patent. For example, a U.S. Patent only applies to acts that take place in the United States and its territories or possessions. A Japanese Patent only applies to acts that take place in Japan. While there are certain collective organizations that encompass more than one country, such as the European Patent Office, a patent which issues from such organizations only applies in the countries that are specifically designated by the applicant, such as France or Germany for example, when the patent issues.

Thus, it is important to *understand geographically and functionally the life cycle of the organization's products* so that patent protection can be sought in those countries of interest and concern, and in a prioritized manner.

Practice Note:

Understand the geographic footprint of the organization to assist in identifying and prioritizing *where* to seek patent protection.

In the High Tech Co. example, the organization manufacturers its products in the following locations:

- Display products are manufactured in China;
- Core Processor devices are manufactured in Thailand; and
- PDA/Pager devices are manufactured in Singapore.

In such a case, it can be important to obtain patent protection covering manufacturing processes for these various products in these respective regions to protect High Tech Co.'s manufacturing processes.

Further, each of these products is sold by High Tech Co. for end use in Europe and the United States. In this case, it may be important to obtain patent protection that covers the use of the relevant products in the countries where the products are sold and used.

Thus, it is important not only to obtain patent protection in the right places, but also to make certain that the right type of patent protection is sought in each of those places. Patent protection that is sought in each relevant geographic location should be directed to covering the type of activities that occur in that location. For example, claims covering manufacturing processes should be sought and obtained in manufacturing countries, and use-based claims should be sought and maintained in end-use countries. Product claims should also be sought in both locations.

Practice Note:
Patent protection in each relevant geographic location should be directed to covering the type of activities that occur in that location.

FIGURE 4.5 Understanding How Products Relate to Different Countries.

It is also important to *understand the geographic and functional life cycle of competitors' products*. It may be as important (if not more so) to obtain relevant patent protection where competitors manufacture and sell products as it is where the organization itself manufactures and sells products. For example, it may be possible to gain a strategic advantage over a competitor on the competitor's home turf by obtaining relevant patent protection on the manufacturing processes where the competitor manufactures products.

Practice Note:

Competitors' geographic landscapes should be considered in determining where and what type of patent protection to seek.

4.5 Identify Supporting Systems and Services (Non-Core Business)

In addition to obtaining patents that directly relate to the main products (often called "core" products) that an organization sells (like the Core Processor devices, LCD Displays, and PDA/Pager devices in the High Tech Co. example), patent protection on "non-core" businesses may also be useful. For example, manufacturing organizations like the High Tech Co. often have their own proprietary inventory control and ordering systems. While the organization may not be in the business of developing software or hardware systems for others, there may be substantial commercial investment in such systems, and such systems may provide a significant competitive advantage.

Patent protection on such systems may be useful since

- It may restrict competitors' ability to effectively control inventory or manage orders; and
- A non-core patent may be a patent which could be licensed, sold, or traded in a future dispute, should the need arise.

The value of a non-core patent may, at times, exceed the value of a core patent, depending upon the line of business, the level of innovation in the core and non-core aspects of the business, the interest of competitors, and other market factors. These non-core patents may also be useful sources of income or avoiding income diversion. (*See* Chapter 2, Sections 2.4 and 2.5.)

Practice Note:

Patent protection for non-core businesses can be valuable.

4.6 Understand What Is Necessary to Make the Business Work

It is also important to understand *which factors are necessary to make the business work*. A good patent strategy seeks to complement and enhance such factors. Focusing on the wrong factors could result in a waste of organizational resources.

Practice Note:

Understanding what factors are necessary to make a business work can inform and direct an organization's patent strategy.

4.7 Get Management "Buy-In"

The projects that are most likely to succeed within an organization are those projects that have *management's support* and for which management demonstrates its support. Thus, it is important for management to "buy into" the concept of developing and maintaining a patent portfolio in order for such projects to succeed. Without such support, it is difficult to effectively implement a patent program.

Practice Note:

Management support is necessary to the success of a patent program.

Depending upon the level of existing support within management, there are various steps that can be taken to obtain management "buy-in."

First, it may be necessary to *dispel illusions about the effectiveness and desirability of relying solely upon other forms of intellectual property* protection as a substitute for patent protection.

- Many industries rely on *trade secret protection* until they try to enforce such rights. It is expensive to enforce trade secret rights since it requires bringing a lawsuit to establish that the rights exist. Further, in industries with a large turnover of creative employees, it may be difficult to maintain such protection.
- The use of *defensive publications* to create prior art to others may be useful at times, but it essentially donates the organization's inventions to competitors for free.

- While *copyright* protection can be useful, it only protects the expression of an idea, not the underlying idea.
- While a *first-mover advantage* may be useful, patent protection can extend that advantage for up to twenty years.

Thus, new and original ideas are best covered by patent protection.

Practice Note:
Dispel management's illusions about the effectiveness and desirability of relying solely upon other forms of intellectual property protection as a substitute for patent protection.

Next, it may be necessary to *review with management and key executives why having a patent portfolio is a good idea.* To do this, it is best to look at the different motivations discussed in Chapter 2 and explain the ones that are appropriate to the organization.

- Patents can turn an intangible asset into something tangible and well defined;
- Patents can be evidence that an organization is an innovator and thus can be used as effective marketing tools;
- Patents can protect a product or product line and potentially keep out competitors;
- Patents can be used as a source of revenue;
- Patents can be used as something to trade when others start asserting patents;
- Patents can create prior art to others;
- Patents can help establish an effective design around; and
- Patents can be an impressive decorative item on the wall.

Practice Note:
Review the benefits of patent protection with management.

Also point out to management *the patents that competitors are seeking and obtaining.* The fact that competitors seek and obtain patents within the industry can often have a dramatic impact on management's decision to support a patent program when its organization does not.

Practice Note:
Review competitors' patents with management.

In sum, without the support of management, any effort to implement an effective patent program is doomed to failure.

4.8 Establish an Appropriate Budget

As with all investment programs, a patent program needs an *adequate and appropriate budget* to support it.

It is easier to support a patent program if the legal department has its own budget to obtain patent protection, independent from the operating business units' budgets. Some may think that wiser resource management choices will be made if the operating business unit is required to fund patent protection efforts, but in many organizations, this can lead to less desirable results for the organization overall.

For example, the interests of a particular business unit may not always be completely aligned with the interests of the overall organization. Similarly, in some industries or organizations, the turnover rate of employees in one or more business units may be high, which could result in the individuals in those units being more reluctant to seek patent protection which could inhibit their ability to use their inventions in their next job. Further, in having a short-term vision for the organization, such employees may not be willing to sacrifice short-term profits, which could impact bonuses or compensation directly, by paying for patent protection which could help the organization over the long term.

Careful and thoughtful consideration should be used when establishing how the organization will fund its system for obtaining patents.

Practice Note:
Establish an appropriate and adequate patent budget that is funded in a sensible way.

4.9 Set Up Patent Policies and Procedures to Encourage Participation of Key Employees

In order to develop a patent portfolio effectively, it is beneficial to set up a patent policy that includes procedures to encourage key employees to contribute to the development of the portfolio, while still making sense to the organization as a whole.

The organization can take steps to achieve this goal including

- Establishing a clearly delineated patent policy and publicizing it widely within the relevant business units of the organization;
- Establishing a funding mechanism that encourages relevant business units to participate and seek patent protection;
- Following up within the organization to encourage patent generation;
- Educating business units on the value of patents and the process to obtain patents;
- Building in a reward system for patent filings and issuances, which includes appropriate monetary compensation for important milestones (submission of disclosure, approval of disclosure, filing of patent application, issuance of patent, etc.);
- Providing recognition of inventors within the organization, with public internal announcements, and giving symbols that reward efforts and successes (e.g., patent plaques, trophies, etc.); and
- Discussing success or failure of patent efforts as part of annual employee and business unit reviews.

Patent Policy

Educate Personnel

Funding

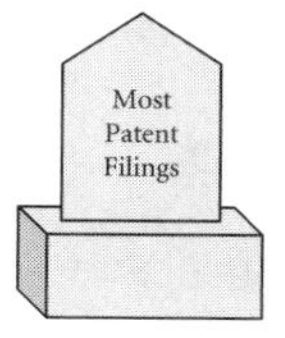

Reward Participation and Success

Cooperation of Divisions

Annual Reviews Discussing Patents

Publicize Success

FIGURE 4.6 Keys To a Successful Patent Program.

Practice Note:
Establishing appropriate patent policies can encourage key employees to participate in developing a patent portfolio in a sensible and economical way.

4.10 Determine Which Inventions to Pursue

Finally, the organization should establish priorities in determining which inventions to protect with a patent. Some organizations have a policy of seeking as many patents as possible and spending as little as possible to obtain each patent. This type of patent policy values quantity over quality.

Another approach which other organizations have taken in developing patent portfolios is to focus on fewer patents that are directed to more significant improvements. Under this approach, in order to obtain higher quality patent protection, more time and money are spent on a fewer number of patents.

CHAPTER 5

How to Protect an Invention

In order to protect a new invention, best practices would be to follow the following procedure:

- Define the invention;
- Document the development;
- Retain evidence of commercial success;
- Maintain secrecy of development and inventions;
- Search prior art;
- Act quickly and diligently;
- Understand the nature and importance of the invention; and
- Mark products and notify competitors of published patent applications and issued patents in a prudent manner.

This chapter explains each of these steps in further detail.

5.1 Define the Invention

The first step to take in protecting an invention is figuring out what it is. (*See* Chapter 6, Section 6.1.) The process of *defining the invention* involves not only writing up a description of the invention, but also understanding and explaining why the invention is different from what came before it (i.e., the prior art; *see* Chapter 8). This process includes drafting a claim and identifying what elements of the claim are different from the prior art. If you cannot define the elements of the invention, such as in the form of a claim, then an invention probably does not really exist.

Practice Note:
Define the invention in writing and understand why it is new and different.

One method used for defining an invention is the "problem-solution" approach. Although this methodology is not how U.S. patent law determines patentability, it can nonetheless be a useful way to identify and define an invention. The problem-solution approach involves the following steps:

- The "problem" the inventors are seeking to solve is identified;
- The solution the inventors came up with is described; and
- An explanation as to why this solution is new and different is provided.

This procedure is used in Europe, for example, to determine if an invention includes an "inventive step" (the European equivalent of non-obviousness).

Practice Note:
Identify the problem, the solution that was developed, and why the solution is new and different is one way to define the invention.

5.2 Document the Development

Typically, inventions that become the subject of patent applications are first developed in the context of new projects. Thus, it is important to *document the development* of any new project from the beginning including

- Contemporaneous information on the identification of new ideas to explore and the dates on which such ideas were first conceived;
- Improvements on the new ideas (even rejected concepts) and when such improvements were conceived;

- Efforts to implement the new ideas and test the hypotheses;
- Pictures of samples, experiments, or other efforts to test and/or implement the invention; and
- Source materials used in investigating the new ideas.

Historically, development records for a project would be maintained in well-documented notebooks or other business records. Many organizations issue notebooks to all employees to keep track of their developments. If the invention being developed by a project is important, it is best if the supporting documentation is dated and witnessed contemporaneously by individuals who will be available to authenticate the documentation many years later. Ideally, the witnesses should be able to verify that they "read and understood" the disclosure. This kind of documentation is among the kinds of information that is typically requested by patent counsel when drafting a patent application.

Today, many organizations maintain their records in the form of electronic files. Thus, traditional written and bound laboratory notebooks may no longer be a practical option. To the extent that electronic records are likely to be relied upon, the organization should set up a system of maintaining, storing, and accessing such records so that they can be retrieved in a reliable and verifiable manner for many years into the future. (A patent can be in effect for two decades!)

Practice Note:
Document the development of the invention in a reliable manner that can be accessed and verified in the future.

Such documentation can be used down the line if the organization needs to demonstrate when specifically it first conceived and/or developed the invention.[1] Such documentation is useful even if the organization does not seek patent protection itself.

For example, the organization may decide to keep as a trade secret a certain business method practice, which someone else independently developed and patented. Under U.S. patent law, if the organization maintains appropriate documentation, it may be entitled to keep practicing certain kinds of inventions (like methods of doing business), even after another's patent application is filed and issued under a so-called "prior user right."[2]

Further, documenting the sources used in developing a product can also be used to show that the product did not copy the intellectual property of others. This type of evidence can be useful not only in patent disputes, but in other kinds of intellectual property disputes like copyright disputes.[3]

5.3 Retain Evidence of Commercial Success

In addition to documentation regarding the development of the project itself, it is also useful to keep *documentation regarding the "commercial success" or "praise in the industry"* for the invention after it has been implemented. As discussed in Chapter 3, Section 3.2, evidence of commercial success or praise in the industry can be used to demonstrate that an invention is not obvious, and thus can support the patentability of the invention.[4]

Thus, the following types of evidence should be maintained with respect to the introduction of an invention:

- Increase in the organization's sales or profits related to the introduction of the invention;
- Articles or commentary in trade publications or other literature about the invention;
- Awards for the invention; and
- Compliments by customers, competitors, or objective third parties.

Practice Note:
Keep a file of press clippings and praise by others.

5.4 Development and Inventions Should Be Maintained in Secrecy

Until a patent application has been filed, the organization should *maintain the invention in secrecy.*

To the extent that the organization may need to work with its customers or business partners to fully develop the invention, the organization should first document the inventions it plans to contribute before contacting customers or business partners, and then should disclose the inventions only in the context of *a non-disclosure agreement.*[5]

The organization may also want to consider entering into *a joint development agreement* with the customer before it commences the project. Some issues that should be intelligently considered before entering into a joint development agreement include:

- Ownership rights of patents and other intellectual property developed under the agreements;
- Rights to use such patents and other rights under the agreements;
- Responsibility for payment of fees associated with obtaining and maintaining such rights; and

- Rights, responsibilities, and limits with respect to enforcing and licensing such rights.

In addition, joint development agreements should

- Be written and not merely oral;
- Be effective as of a date which predates the first tasks performed under the agreement;
- State that they are for purposes of "performance of experimental, developmental or research work in" the intended field of endeavor, and be promptly amended to expand the field of endeavor when the scope of work expands;
- Require all patent applications filed based on work performed within the scope of the agreement to designate that such work was performed under the scope of the agreement; and
- Specify that the parties will give up a right to separately enforce any patents obtained based on work developed under the agreement.[6]

Practice Note:

Non-disclosure agreements and joint development agreements which specify each parties' rights and responsibilities regarding intellectual property should generally be entered into before a project begins.

It is always easier to establish guidelines for how to resolve these kinds of issues at the beginning of a relationship. Often, when parties wait until a dispute arises to address such issues, resolving the disputes can be difficult and contentious. Of course, at the beginning of a relationship, it may be difficult to appreciate whether rights should be sought and/or obtained, and whether it is even worth arguing over such an issue. It may also be disadvantageous for an organization to take on the costs of seeking and maintaining patent protection to own patent rights that may add insignificant value to the organization.

5.5 Prior Art Should Be Searched

Before embarking on a new commercial project or implementing an improvement to an existing project, the organization should *search out and study the prior art*. By way of example, searching can be performed by various methods:

- In public and commercial databases;
- In public and private libraries; and
- At the USPTO and/or other patent offices.

Practice Note:

Prior art should be searched in appropriate places and ways.

There are two different kinds of searches that may be relevant:

- A "*patentability search*," which determines if an invention is new and different from the prior art (*see* Chapter 6, Section 6.2); and
- A "*clearance*" or "*right-to-use search*," which determines if a product will infringe patents owned by others.

Practice Note:

A "patentability search" determines whether patent protection should be sought.

A "clearance search" determines whether a product or service may intrude upon someone else's invention and rights.

The scope and purpose of a patentability search is not the same as a clearance search. A patentability search helps the organization understand whether an invention is worth the effort and expense of seeking patent protection. A clearance search helps the organization determine whether a product or service may infringe the rights of others.

It is important to understand that even if a patentability search is conducted and indicates that patent protection should be sought, this does not necessarily mean that the organization is free to offer the product or service which is the subject of the patentability search without infringing someone else's patent rights. An organization may be entitled to seek and obtain patent rights for a new invention, which, when implemented in a product or service, nonetheless infringe the patent rights of others. Thus, best practices would dictate in many circumstances performing one or both kinds of searches.

Practice Note:

A "patentability search" and a "clearance search" are different. A product can infringe another's patent, even though the product embodies a patentable invention which has received separate patent protection.

By identifying the rights of others early on, an organization can make intelligent decisions about whether it can design around such rights or will need to obtain an appropriate license to such rights before entering a particular market.

5.6 File Quickly and Act Diligently

File quickly and act diligently. Other than the United States (and the Philippines), all countries have a "first-to-file" system.

In a "*first-to-file*" system, if two different entities file for and claim the same invention, the first applicant to file the application will prevail in a priority battle. To meet the priority requirements of other patent systems, it is obviously important to promptly file a patent application.

Practice Note:
File quickly and act diligently to maximize potentially available rights.

FIGURE 5.1 Race to Patent Office in a First-to-File System.

Patent law in the United States is different. It is a "*first-to-invent*" system. In order to establish that an inventor is the "first-to-invent," the inventor needs to show that

- He or she was the first to "conceive" the invention; and
- He or she was the first to "reduce to practice" the invention (i.e., made the invention or filed for a patent application).[7]

In the case where one party is the first to conceive the invention, and the other party first reduced to practice the invention, then the party that is first to conceive can still be awarded priority if the prior inventor exercised "reasonable diligence toward reduction to practice from a date just prior to the other party's conception to its reduction to practice."[8] Thus, it is again important to demonstrate *diligent effort* from the time of conception to the time of reducing the invention to practice or filing the patent application (whichever is first).[9] This task requires not only diligent efforts, but also keeping records that evidence those efforts.

S	M	T	W	R	F	S
1	2 Conceive Invention	3	4 Working on making invention	5	6	7
8	9	10 Working on making invention	11	12	13 Make Invention	14
15	16	17	18	19	20 File Patent Application	21
22	23	24	25	26	27	28

FIGURE 5.2 Conception, Reduction to Practice and Diligence.

Priority of invention is a very complex issue which can be greatly simplified by acting quickly and decisively to seek patent protection.

5.7 Understand the Nature and Importance of the Invention

There are various types of inventions. One type is a *minor* improvement. A purpose for seeking patent protection on this type of invention might be more to increase the size of a patent portfolio than for any other purpose. Another type of invention is a *significant* improvement, which may be used by the organization to fend off competitors or to raise funds through licensing. The time, effort, and expenditure that should be devoted to developing patent protection for an invention should be commensurate with the importance of the invention to the business or the overall business strategy. Thus, it is important to *understand the nature and importance of the invention* to the business and the business strategy.

Practice Note:
It is important to understand the nature and importance of an invention in order to properly allocate resources.

For example, with respect to an invention that is a significant improvement over the prior art, it is useful to consider keeping alive the application in the USPTO through filing continuation applications (*see* Chapter 6, Section 6.5) so as to be able to refine the claims to insure that subtle differences advanced by potential infringers can be covered with revised claims.[10]

Likewise, for a core product line, it is useful to file improvement patent applications that cover new features (*see* Chapter 6, Section 6.5).

The value of a patent portfolio is not just based on the value of an individual patent; it is also based on how the patent claims fit together to cover the relevant product and commercial landscapes. A good patent portfolio is like a jigsaw puzzle and, when analyzed in its entirety, fully covers the product area. Thus, even minor improvement patents, when combined with other patents in a portfolio, can add significantly more value than a single patent standing alone might otherwise provide. The synergy of a patent thicket can create an effective deterrent to competitors. When all of pieces in the patent jigsaw puzzle are pieced together, a formidable wall of patent protection can be formed.

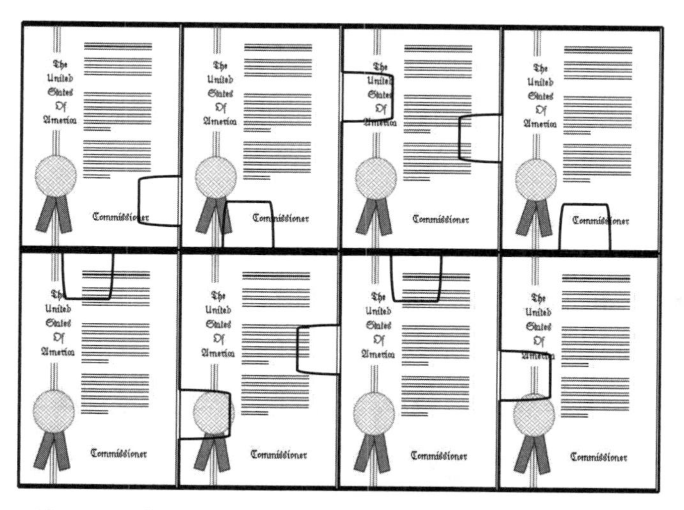

FIGURE 5.3 The Patent "Jigsaw" Puzzle: It is How the Patents Fit Together.

5.8 Mark Products and Notify Competitors of Published Patent Applications and Issued Patents in a Prudent Manner

When patent applications are published, in order to obtain the most value, the organization should *mark its products and notify competitors in a prudent manner.*

One of the benefits of the publication of patent applications is that after the application has been published, if a patentee provides an infringer with notice of the publication, and the infringer is infringing a published claim that is commensurate in scope with a claim as ultimately issued, the infringer will have to pay a reasonable royalty for its infringement beginning from the date of the notice until the patent issues.[11]

Practice Note:
Providing written notice of published patent applications may in certain circumstances provide pre-issuance damages if a patent ultimately issues.

When a patent issues, products that practice the claims of the invention should be "marked" with the patent number to the extent feasible. When a patentee or its licensee sells products covered by an apparatus claim, if they do not mark the products with the patent number, the patentee can be precluded from collecting damages for the period before it provided an infringer with actual notice of its claim for damages.[12] In order to limit the need to write notice letters, it is a best practice to mark the organization's products (or packaging materials) with issued patent numbers, to the extent it is feasible. Similarly, patentees should require their licensees to mark relevant products (or packaging materials) with patent numbers.

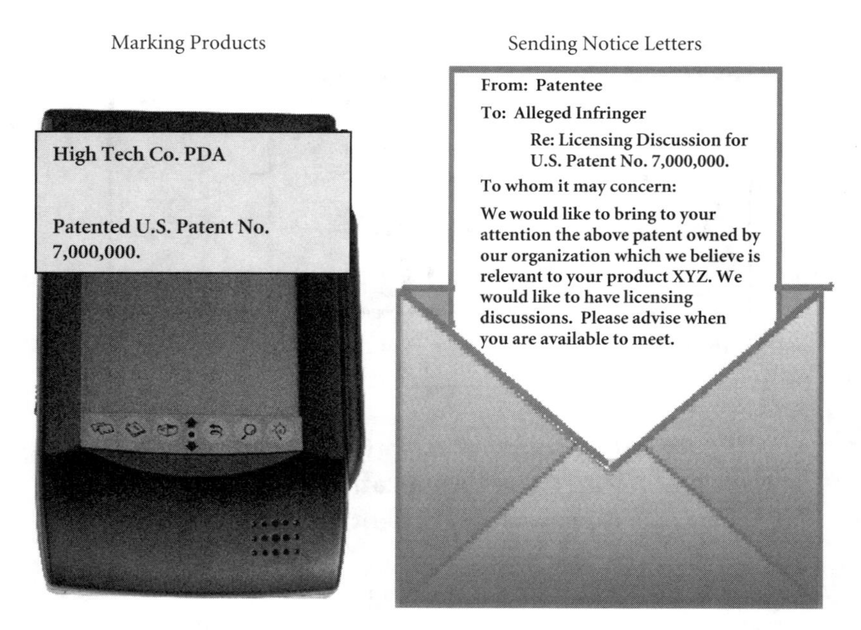

FIGURE 5.4 Marking Products vs. Sending Notice Letters.

Practice Note:

Promptly and continuously marking products with the patent numbers of patents that are practiced can avoid the need to send notice letters.

As discussed in Chapter 2, Section 2.3, one risk associated with writing notice letters, at least since the U.S. Supreme Court's decision in *MedImmune*,[13] is that writing such a letter can potentially expose the letter-writer to a lawsuit seeking a declaration that its patents are invalid, not infringed, and/or unenforceable by the recipient of the letter. Thus, the organization needs to carefully consider the benefits and detriments of writing such a letter, after consulting its patent counsel.[14]

Practice Note:

Sending a patent infringement notice letter can start the damages period for patent infringement but risks exposure to undesired lawsuits.

CHAPTER

6

How to Get a Patent

The steps involved in obtaining patent protection are relatively straightforward but require experience, strategic thought, and careful planning to be implemented most effectively. After an invention is developed and identified as potentially being the subject of patent protection, the following procedures are typically used to obtain patent protection:

- Define the invention;
- Conduct a prior art search (optional but recommended);
- Prepare and file a U.S. Patent Application (mandatory);
- Prosecute a U.S. Patent Application (mandatory);
- Prepare and file continuing U.S. Patent Application(s) (optional);
- Issuance of a U.S. Patent;
- Post-issuance activities for a U.S. Patent (mandatory to keep patent in force); and
- Seeking protection outside the U.S. with PCT and non-U.S. Patent Applications (optional).

6.1 Defining the Invention

The first step in the process of seeking a patent is to *define and crystallize the invention*. Typically, this is done in the first instance by the inventors describing to the patent practitioner their invention in the form of an "invention disclosure form."

Practice Note:

The patent process begins by defining and crystallizing the invention.

Many organizations have their own standard form for use in documenting potentially patentable inventions. Similarly, patent practitioners often provide their own type of invention disclosure forms for inventors to fill out, describing their inventions and providing other information that will be needed to prepare and prosecute a patent application.

The form used by an organization and the form used by a patent practitioner may be used for different (albeit similar and overlapping) purposes.

An organization may need a form that is directed to determining not only if a patentable invention exists, but also whether there is any commercial value to the organization in obtaining patent protection. Thus, it will include questions regarding the potential economic value of the invention to the organization such as

- Will any of the organization's products use the invention;
- What is the market size associated with the invention;
- How much will it cost to bring the invention to market; and
- What resources have already been spent in research and development.

This information enables the organization to determine whether it is worth investing the time, effort, and resources to seek patent protection.

On the other hand, the patent practitioner will need a form that is directed to soliciting sufficient information to determine whether a patentable invention exists, and, if so, to prepare a patent application. Thus, a patent practitioner's form tends to be concerned with the details of the invention and include questions such as:

- How the invention works;
- How the invention could be modified;

- What materials the inventor uses to make the invention; and
- What alternative materials can be used to make the invention.

The patent practitioner's purpose for asking such questions is to elicit sufficient details to write a patent application. When drafting an invention disclosure form, careful thought should be given to the purpose of the form and to insure that the right information is being sought and obtained.

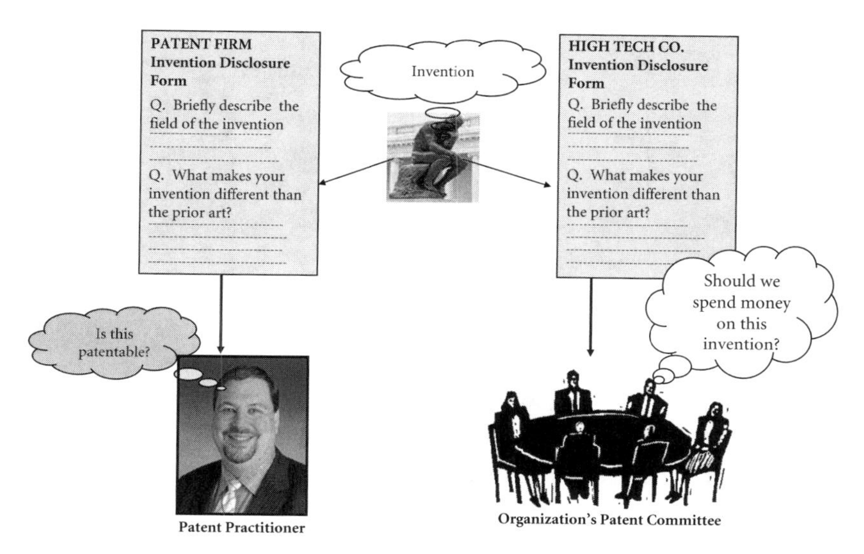

FIGURE 6.1 Different Purposes of Invention Disclosure Forms.

Practice Note:
Invention disclosure forms should be drafted to elicit the information that will be needed by the people who will be using the form.

It can be difficult at times to get inventors to complete formal invention disclosure forms. Thus, alternative forms of description may be used to provide the necessary information. For example, some inventors find it is easier to prepare a PowerPoint® presentation of the invention than to write a narrative explanation. PowerPoint® presentations can often be very useful in describing the invention.

Practice Note:

Invention disclosure forms are one way of conveying the invention to the patent practitioner, but other ways may be used too.

FIGURE 6.2 Alternative Ways to Disclose Invention.

Key information to be conveyed to the patent practitioner includes:

- What the inventor thinks the invention is;
- Why the inventor thinks that the invention is different from the prior art (i.e., that which came before);
- Different ways of implementing the invention;
- What prior art the inventor is aware of; and
- What efforts have been made by the inventor/organization to market the invention or to disclose it to others.

This information is generally the type of information that a patent practitioner uses to analyze the patentability of the invention and draft a patent application. Often, a patent practitioner will also ask questions seeking to flush out details related to these general areas of inquiry.

Practice Note:

Patent practitioners often ask questions to flush out details about the invention.

Using this information, the patent practitioner and the inventors should work together to formulate a set of claims that define what the inventor thinks is the invention.

If the invention cannot be defined in the form of one or more claims, then it makes no sense to go further. Some inventors and patent practitioners try to write a description of the invention based on product literature, without understanding and defining the invention in the first instance. While meaningful patent protection can be obtained when applications are drafted in this manner, it is often more costly, less efficient, and more likely to include extraneous details that could, in the end, limit the scope of patent protection actually obtained. Depending upon the purpose of the patent application being filed, this approach may not be the best approach to drafting a patent application.

Practice Note:
The first step in preparing a patent application is defining the invention in the form of one or more claims.

6.2 Conducting a Prior Art Search (Optional but Recommended)

Before preparing a patent application, the information provided in the invention disclosure form should be used to *formulate* and *commission a search* of the USPTO records to determine whether there is any prior art which would preclude the organization from obtaining patent claims of meaningful scope for a new invention disclosure. While conducting a patentability search is not generally a legal prerequisite to obtaining a patent, it is a prudent course of action to help maximize the best possible patent protection that may be available.

Practice Note:
Generally, a patentability search of the prior art should be conducted before drafting a patent application.

The proposed set of claims prepared to define the invention should be used to draft a patent search request. The claims should be drafted to include the limitations of the invention that the inventor thinks are most likely going to be patentable over the known prior art. Dependent claims should be included to further refine the invention and to ensure that all relevant prior art is identified. (Dependent claims are claims that incorporate limitations from other claims but add one or more additional limitations.)[1]

The costs associated with conducting a patentability search of prior art may vary, depending upon how extensive a search is to be performed. For some inventions, a search may be limited to the records of the USPTO. For others, it may be desirable to conduct other types of prior art searches, such as searches of

- Relevant technical literature in a library or applicable technical database;
- An Internet search; and/or
- A product catalog search.

In some instances it may be a good idea to also search non-U.S. Patents, e.g., European and Japanese patents.

FIGURE 6.3 Different Sources of Prior Art that Can Be Searched.

Often prior to commissioning a formal search, the inventor(s) or patent practitioner may perform preliminary searches to identify generally the scope of prior art, which can include, for example, an Internet search of

- Articles;
- Web sites;
- Product descriptions;
- Published patent applications; and/or
- Issued patents in the United States or elsewhere.

Inventors who are "in the business" often have an understanding of the relevant prior art and the actual products being offered by their organization and its competitors. A review of competitors' product catalogs, Web sites, or other product information is a useful preliminary step that the organization should undertake before conducting a formal patent search.

All information identified should be provided to the patent practitioner as part of the invention disclosure so that it can be considered prior to incurring the added expense of commissioning a formal USPTO patent search. Failure to provide such information could result in any patent to issue becoming unenforceable or invalid. (This duty is also a continuing duty, which means any prior art discovered while the patent application is pending should also be provided to the patent practitioner.)[2]

Practice Note:

Prior art searches should potentially include sources other than just patents and published patent applications.

Once the patent practitioner receives the search results, he should evaluate the prior art uncovered in the search and then typically provide an opinion as to whether the invention should be patentable.

In many cases, before the decision to proceed with filing a patent application is finally made, the inventors, as well as others from the organization who may be involved with prosecution of patent applications and who understand the technology involved in the invention and the prior art, should also review the identified prior art and provide the patent practitioner with comments and guidance on the potential scope of patent protection, as well as any differences that can help define the invention.

The proposed set of claims should be reevaluated and modified as appropriate in light of the prior art identified by the patentability search.

Practice Note:

Claims should be reevaluated and modified as appropriate in light of prior art identified by the patentability searches.

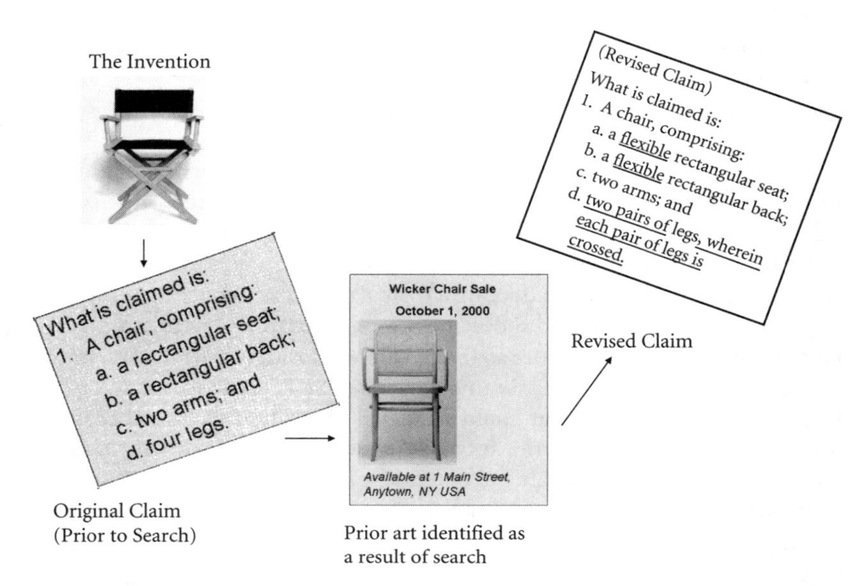

FIGURE 6.4 Refining Claim Language in View of Prior Art.

In some instances, it may be determined that the patenting process should end here because no meaningful patent protection is likely to be obtained.

6.3 Preparing a Patent Application (Mandatory)

Assuming that the invention appears to be patentable in view of the prior art identified, *a patent application can be drafted.*

It is important to remember that any patent application must be filed with the USPTO *within one year* after the first sale, offer for sale, or public use or disclosure of the patented article. (*See* Chapter 8). Moreover, to the extent any patent rights are being sought outside the United States, the patent application must first be filed *prior to* any first sale, offer for sale, or public disclosure of the patented article.

Failure of the organization to provide prompt and detailed disclosure to the patent practitioner can significantly adversely affect the costs, reliability, and effectiveness of preparing an application.

Practice Note:

Patent applications in the United States must be filed within one year of the first sale, offer for sale, or public disclosure of the invention.

Typically, the process of drafting a patent application should begin by refining the proposed set of claims used to conduct the patent search in light of the results returned by the patent search as illustrated in Figure 6.4. Since the claims define the scope of patent protection, it is important to begin drafting the patent application by focusing on the desired scope of patent protection to be sought. It is helpful to consider that if an invention cannot be defined by one or more of the claims, it is probably not an invention.

Practice Note:

Drafting of patent applications should begin with drafting claims defining the invention and an understanding of how the invention differs from the prior art.

Thereafter, drawings that help to explain the invention should be prepared (to the extent appropriate), and a detailed description should be written describing details about the invention embodied in the claims and shown in the drawings. This may be an iterative process where, for example, after the drawings are prepared, and the detail description is partially drafted, the drawings may need to be further revised or supplemented based on the detailed description.

Practice Note:

A detailed description of the invention, and, in many instances, drawings illustrating the invention, will need to be prepared.

As part of the drafting process, patent practitioners typically ask a lot of questions and seek more information and details about the invention and its preferred embodiments. Patent practitioners want to know not only how the organization plans on practicing the invention, but how competitors might modify the invention in an attempt to use the invention without infringing the claim. A patent will not keep a competitor out of the market if it does not cover the way the competitor manufactures or sells its competing product.

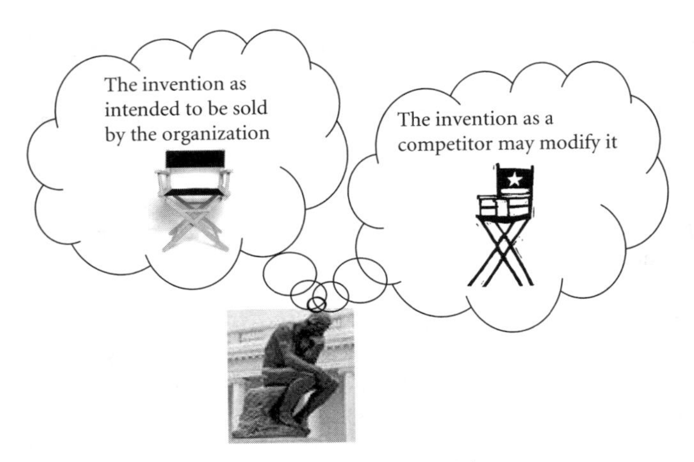

FIGURE 6.5 Consider Alternatives a Competitor May Adopt.

Sometimes the drafting process may take longer than desired, or there may not be time to fully draft a patent application. In such circumstances, patent priority can be preserved by filing a provisional patent application with the USPTO. A U.S. provisional patent application will not be substantively examined by the USPTO. A U.S. provisional patent application remains in force and effect for up to one year, at which time it will expire. However, in order to be useful, a provisional patent application must contain an enabling disclosure of the invention which is ultimately claimed. One or more non-provisional patent applications may be filed within a year claiming priority to one or more provisional patent applications.

Practice Note:
Sometimes it may be appropriate to file a provisional patent application with the USPTO.

Upon filing the patent application (or shortly thereafter), various documents must be filed with the USPTO, including, for example

- Inventor's Declaration;
- Assignment;
- Power of Attorney;
- Fee Transmittal Forms;
- Patent Application Transmittal Sheets; and
- Information Disclosure Statement(s).

These forms are typically prepared and filed either at the time of filing the patent application or soon thereafter.

Practice Note:

Paperwork associated with a patent application must be prepared and submitted to the USPTO around the time the application is filed.

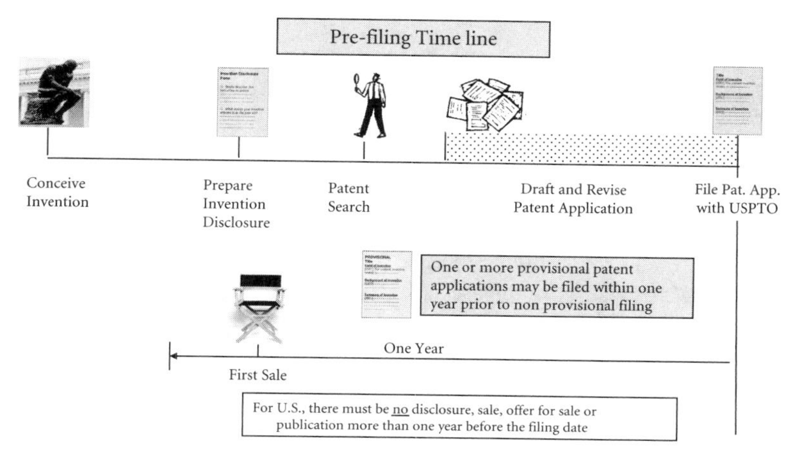

FIGURE 6.6 Pre-Filing Time Line in the U.S.

6.4 Prosecuting a U.S. Patent Application (Mandatory)

Substantive examination of U.S. Patent Applications typically commences sometime after one year from the filing date of the application. Thus, the work load of the USPTO differs greatly depending upon the Art Unit. The time it takes an examiner to first consider an application also depends upon the work load of the particular examiner in the Art Unit assigned to the application. The time it takes an examiner to first start to substantively consider a patent application depends heavily upon which part of the USPTO is assigned to examine the application (the "Art Unit") and the number of patent applications that need to be examined by the Art Unit and/or the particular examiner assigned to the patent application prior to the present application.

Practice Note:

The time it takes an examiner to first consider a patent application may vary widely, depending on which Art Unit is assigned to examine the application.

In some Art Units, the time it takes for an examiner to first consider a patent application can vary widely from around 18 months to years. Special proceedings have been developed by the USPTO to expedite the examination of certain patent applications. These procedures have certain benefits and detriments which need to be considered on a case-by-case basis to determine whether it makes sense for a particular patent application.

Practice Note:

Special expedited procedures may be appropriate for some patent applications while not appropriate (or available) for others.

More often than not, the first Office Action issued by the USPTO rejects at least some of the claims or at least raises some objections to at least some of the claims. Accordingly, it is often necessary to prepare a response to such Office Actions—typically in the form of Remarks and often in the form of an Amendment. Remarks are the explanation of why the applicant believes the examiner's objections and rejections are not justified. An Amendment includes revisions to the claims of the patent application and usually address in a "Remarks" section the objections and/or rejections raised by the USPTO. When an Amendment is filed, the Remarks will also explain the Amendments.

Once, and if, the claims are allowed, it is usually necessary to prepare various issuance forms, correct informalities (e.g., prepare formal drawings), and pay issuance and publication fees.

6.5 Continuing Patent Application(s) (Optional)

Additionally, it may be desirable under U.S. patent practice to file "continuing" patent applications based on certain "parent" patent applications which have been allowed or are otherwise pending. A continuing patent application is an application which claims "priority" in whole or in part to an earlier filed patent application (e.g., a "parent" or "grandparent" patent application).

When a patent application is identical (except for the claims) to an earlier filed application, it is called a "continuation" patent application and can claim priority in its entirety to an earlier filed patent application.

Practice Note:

A continuation patent application contains the same disclosure as an earlier filed patent application to which it claims priority.

When a patent application includes additional information not included in the previously filed patent application (called "new subject matter"), it can only claim priority "in part" to an earlier filed patent application. Such an application is called a "continuation-in-part" patent application.

Practice Note:

A continuation-in-part patent application contains at least some new and different disclosure from an earlier filed patent application to which it claims priority in part.

In this regard, it is often the case that an examiner may allow some claims while rejecting others. In such instances, allowance of claims which were not allowed or considered in the first instance may be sought in a continuation application.

Additionally, when a lot of claims have been submitted, an examiner may "restrict" certain claims from the pending application. In other words, the examiner may preclude some claims from being considered in the pending patent application on the ground that such claims are "patentably distinct" from other claims being considered. When the continuing patent application presents claims which were "restricted out" of an earlier-filed patent application, this type of patent application is called a "divisional" patent application.

Practice Note:

A divisional patent application contains the same disclosure as an earlier-filed patent application to which it claims priority, and claims that were previously presented for consideration in the earlier-filed application, but were withdrawn and/or cancelled in response to a restriction requirement.

In order to claim "priority" to an earlier filed patent application, there must be at least some overlap in the pendency of the two applications. In other words, the later-filed patent application must be filed before the issuance of the earlier-filed patent application to which priority is being claimed. If there are a series of patent applications in the chain of priority, there must be an overlap in pendency for every application in that chain with at least one other patent application in the chain, and there must be no gaps in time when no patent application is pending.

In some instances, the applicant may determine that there are certain improvements to the invention as presented in a patent application that has been made, and patent protection should be sought for those improvements.

With respect to such improvements, it may be desirable to file a continuation-in-part application, which has basically some or all of the same disclosure as the initially filed application, but adds additional or different disclosure to reflect the improvement. Depending upon how much new material is being added, it may be desirable to file a separate and independent patent application, which does not claim the benefit of the filing date of the earlier-filed patent application.

Practice Note:

Sometimes it is better to file a new and separate patent application for an improvement rather than to file a continuation-in-part patent application.

6.6 Issuance of a U.S. Patent

After the USPTO issues a Notice of Allowance and the applicant pays the issue fee, a U.S. Patent typically will issue within several months.

Once a U.S. Patent issues, it is enforceable, and the patentee can bring legal actions to enforce the patent. Prior to the time the patent issues, a legal action to enforce the patent would not be appropriate. However, in some circumstances, after a patent issues, a patentee may obtain, retroactively, pre-issuance damages as discussed in Chapter 15, Section 15.2. (*See also* Chapter 5, Section 5.8.)

Practice Note:

A U.S. Patent becomes enforceable only after it issues, although some rights to pre-issuance damages may become available retroactively, after the U.S. Patent issues.

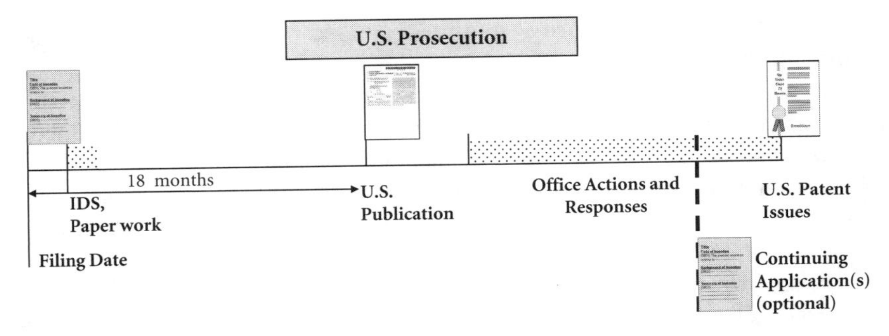

FIGURE 6.7 U.S. Patent Prosecution Time Line.

6.7 Post-Issuance of a U.S. Patent (Mandatory to Keep Patent in Force)

Once a U.S. Patent issues, to keep the patent in force and effect, the organization is required to pay maintenance fees to the USPTO at three and a half, seven and a half, and eleven and a half years after the date of issuance. The USPTO allows a small grace period in which to pay these fees, for an additional fee. Nonetheless, it is important to timely pay the maintenance fees due for an issued patent (at least within the grace period), or else the patent will lapse. Organizations often reconsider the value of a particular patent to the organization when it comes time to pay these maintenance fees.

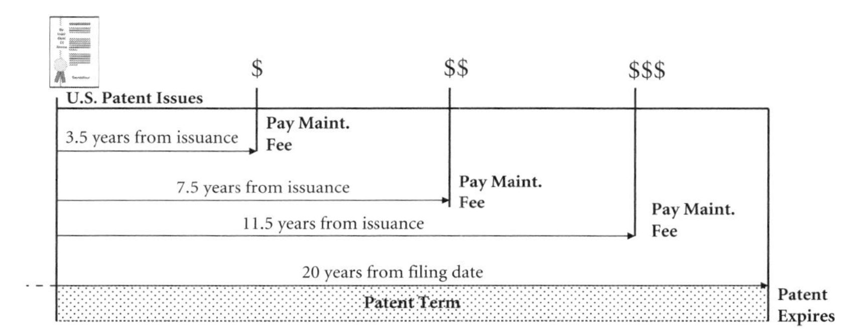

FIGURE 6.8 Post-issuance Time Line.

Practice Note:
It is important to timely pay the maintenance fees for an issued patent, or else the patent will lapse.

Often, the patent practitioner is responsible for advising a patentee that a maintenance fee is due. However, it is increasingly becoming the case that a maintenance fee service may be employed to notify the patentee of the maintenance fee due dates and to arrange for the payment of the fees. Either way, it is important to set up an appropriate docketing system to ensure that the organization does not unintentionally miss these deadlines.

Practice Note:
The organization should set up an appropriate docketing system to timely and accurately pay maintenance fees for issued patents.

Even if all the maintenance fees are paid, a patent will ultimately expire twenty years from the earliest effective filing date for the patent application.[3] If the patent does not claim priority to any earlier-filed U.S. or PCT Patent Applications, the expiration date would be twenty years from the patent application filing date. If the patent does claim priority to one or more earlier-filed U.S. or PCT Patent Applications, the expiration date would be twenty years from the earliest-filed U.S. or PCT Patent Application to which the patent properly claims priority.[4]

The patent term may be extended either due to delay by the USPTO in examining the patent application[5] or for some other special reason.[6]

Practice Note:
U.S. Patents expire no later than twenty years (plus any extensions) from the filing date of the earliest U.S. or PCT priority application.

6.8 Non-U.S. Patent Applications (Optional)

6.8.1 PCT Applications and International Search Reports

Most countries outside the United States require that a patent application be filed within one year of filing a U.S. Patent Application in order to claim the benefit of the filing date of the U.S Patent Application. Most countries of concern are members of the Patent Cooperation Treaty ("PCT"), and thus, a single "PCT Application" can be filed in which the organization can specify which PCT member countries it would like to seek patent protection. Within the first 18 months of pendency (i.e., up until the date of publication), it may be necessary to file various procedural documents.

Practice Note:
A PCT Patent Application, which claims priority to a U.S. Patent Application filed within a year of the PCT filing date, preserves the applicant's rights to seek patents in most countries of the world.

6.8.2 Non-PCT Countries

Some countries (such as Taiwan) are not members of the PCT. In non-PCT member countries, it is necessary to file a separate "national" patent application within one year of filing the U.S. Patent Application in order to claim and obtain priority to that application. Typically, national patent applications in non-PCT member countries are filed at the same time a PCT Application would be filed. A current list of PCT members should be consulted when making decisions regarding non-U.S. filings.[7]

Practice Note:

In non-PCT member countries, like Taiwan, a separate national patent application must be filed within one year of the U.S. filing date.

6.8.3 Non-U.S. National Filings for PCT Countries

For most countries of interest, within thirty months from the priority date, the organization must elect the countries within the PCT in which it seeks patent protection (called entering the "National Phase"). A separate patent application must be filed in each selected country.

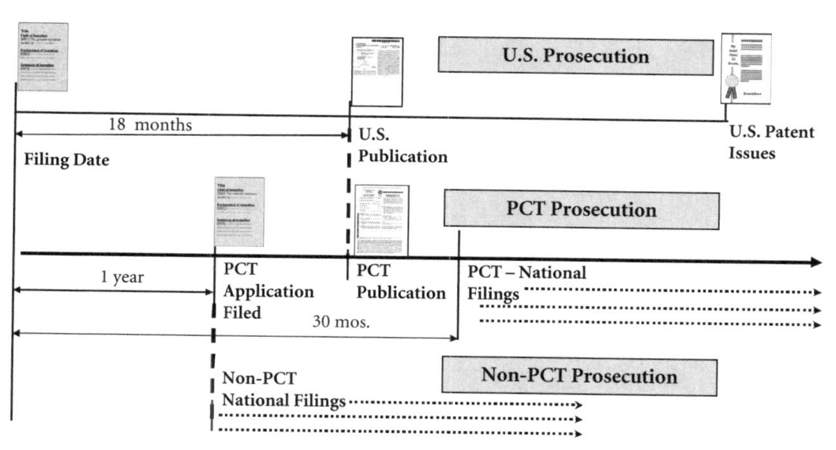

FIGURE 6.9 Non-U.S. Filings Time Line.

Filings in most European countries can be accomplished by filing a single application with the European Patent Office ("EPO") within 31 months from the priority date. This process is called "entering the European Regional Phase."

Once the National/Regional Phase is entered, each patent application must be separately prosecuted before each individual or regional patent office. Moreover, different jurisdictions have different laws and rules governing patentability. Under the European patent system, after the EPO issues a patent, it is then necessary to comply with the national requirements of each of the EPO member countries in order to obtain a patent in those countries (referred to as "entering the national phase of the EPO").

Once a patent application is filed and/or a patent issues, various maintenance fees, taxes, and annuities will be due in each country, the requirements of which vary from country to country.

Practice Note:

For most PCT countries, individual filings in each country must be separately made within 30 (or 31) months from the priority date. This process can be expensive if many countries are selected.

CHAPTER 7

How to Read a Patent

It is very difficult to discuss the value and significance of patents without first understanding how to read a patent. In order to facilitate this discussion, an example patent has been selected in which each of the parts can be discussed. In this case, the example selected is U.S. Patent No. 7,045,065 B1, which relates to a method of removing antimony from radioactive waste streams. In particular, this chapter discusses each of the different parts of the patent and the significance of each part in understanding the patent as a whole.

7.1 Identifying Information

The cover page of each U.S. Patent has identifying information about the patent including

- The title of the patent;
- The patent number;

- The issue date;
- The filing date;
- The patent application serial number;
- The prior publications (if any);
- The named inventor(s);
- The assignee(s) at the time of issuance (if any); and
- The prior art considered of record.

Each of these types of identifying information is discussed in this section.

7.1.1 Title

Every patent is required to have a "title," which is intended to indicate the general field of the disclosure and the particular improvements the patent purports to add to this field. In the example, the title reads

> "METHOD OF REMOVING RADIOACTIVE ANTIMONY FROM WASTE STREAMS."

Practice Note:
The "title" identifies the general field of the disclosure and the particular improvement added by the invention.

The title in present-day U.S. patents, like the example, appears on the cover page of the patent, next to the code "(54)." This same code is used to indicate a title in patents and patent publications throughout the world. Thus, when determining what portion of a non-U.S. Patent or Publication should be translated, the portion next to the code "(54)" is the title.

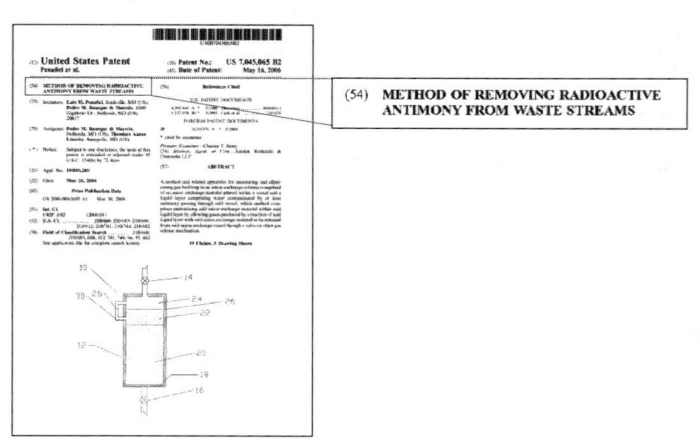

FIGURE 7.1 Title.

7.1.2 Patent Number and Issue Date

Each issued patent has a unique number assigned to it called the "patent number." A system has been developed whereby the number assigned to the document (e.g., the patent number for patents) follows the code "(10)." These numbers usually appear, at least in modern day U.S. Patent in the upper right-hand corner of the cover page of the patent document as shown in the example in Figure 7.2.

Practice Note:

Each issued U.S. Patent has a unique "patent number" assigned to it.

Likewise, each published U.S. Patent Application has a unique number assigned to it called the "publication number." In a U.S. published patent application, the publication number likewise follows the code "(10)" as show in Figure 7.2. In an issued U.S. Patent, the publication number follows the code "(65)" as shown in Figure 7.4 (*See* Section 7.1.4.)

Practice Note:

Each published U.S. Patent Application has a unique "publication number" assigned to it.

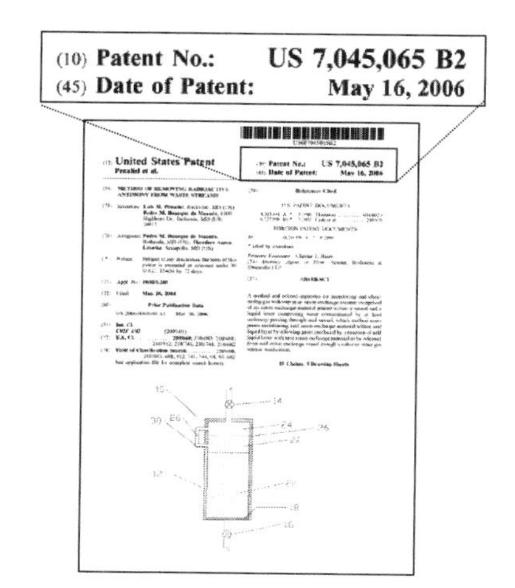

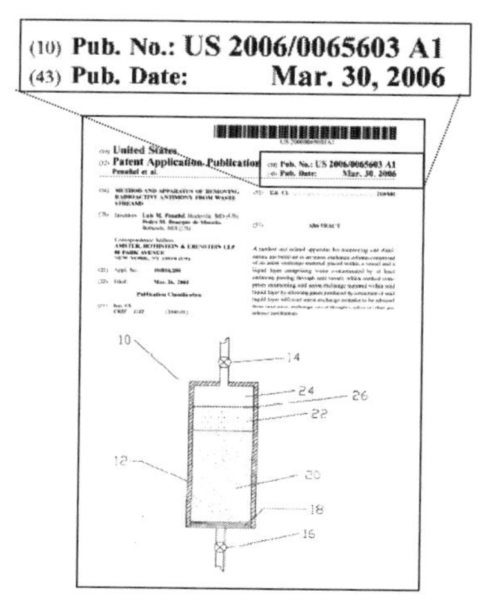

FIGURE 7.2 Patent No. and Publication Date.

While different national and regional patent systems have different number systems for assigning patent numbers and publication numbers, an international standard has been established to add a suffix at the end of the number to indicate the kind of document a particular patent document is.

Practice Note:

The suffix at the end of a patent number or a publication number identifies the type of patent document it is.

For example, in the document number, such as "2006/0065603 *A1*" in the example, a suffix starting with the letter "A," like "*A*1" or "*A*2," is used to indicate (at least in the United States) that the document is a pre-grant patent publication. Usually the "1" in "A*1*," indicates that it is the first publication of the patent application, and the "2" in "A*2*" that it is a re-publication of the patent application.[1] Thus, patent documents that have numbers ending in a suffix starting with the letter "A" are published patent applications, not final, issued patents.

In some patent systems, like the PCT or the European Patent Convention, search results are published with an application, when available. These searches typically are published with the "A1" document if completed by the time the application is original published, or they may be published as an "A2" document if prepared after the initial application is published.

Next to the document number is the date on which the document is issued. In the case of a U.S. Patent Publication, the publication date is the date next to the publication number. In the case of a U.S. Patent, the issue date appears next to the patent number. (*See* Figure 7.2.)

In the United States, after March 2001,[2] a patent document which has a number with a suffix starting with the letter "B," such as "*B*2," like US 7,045,065 *B*2 in the example, is an issued patent. In the United States, an issued patent that has not been the subject of pre-grant publication has the number "B1." Similarly, in the United States, an issued patent that as been the subject of a pre-grant publication has the number "B2."[3] In the example, since there was a pre-grant publication, the suffix is "B2."

A U.S. Patent document with a "B" number, if relevant to the organization, should be treated seriously, since it is an issued U.S. Patent. In the case of an issued patent, the date next to the patent number is the issue date of the patent. This date indicates the date on which the patent becomes effective. It is also used to determine the date on which maintenance fees will be due. (*See* Chapter 6, Section 6.7.)

Sometimes, U.S. Patents may be the subject of a reexamination proceeding. A U.S. Patent document which has a number with a suffix that starts with the letter "C," like "*C*1," is a document published as a result of such a proceeding.

(Before the United States published pre-grant patent applications, a "B" suffix was used.)[4] In Chapter 1, two examples of "Silly Patents" from the early 2000s were discussed. (*See* Figure 7.2.) In both examples, the claims in the U.S. Patents were subsequently found to be unpatentable. Reexamination certificates with the "C1" suffix were issued as shown in Figure 7.3.

Documents which result from a reissue proceeding in the USPTO have the suffix "E."[5]

> **Practice Note:**
>
> A suffix at the end of a patent document number identifies the type of patent document it is, e.g., a published patent application ("A"), an issued patent ("B"), a reexamination patent ("C"), a reissue patent ("E"), etc.

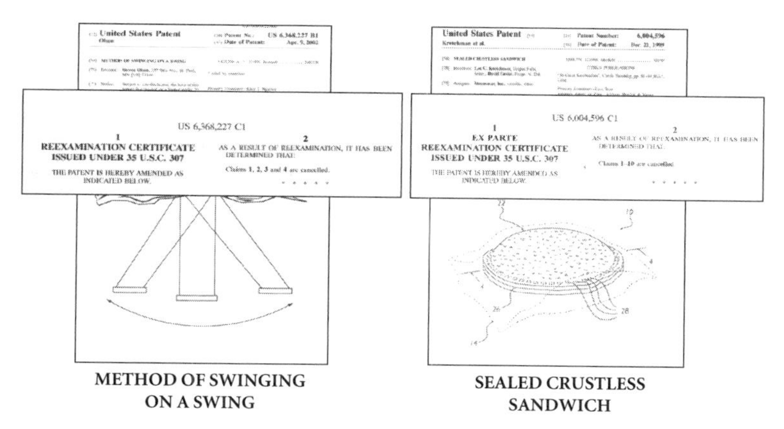

FIGURE 7.3 Reexamination Certificates.

7.1.3 Application Number and Filing Date

Each patent application is also assigned a unique identification number at the time of filing, which is called the "application number." This application number appears next to the code "(21)." The filing date of the application is listed next to the code "(22)." (*See* Figure 7.4.)

> **Practice Note:**
>
> Each U.S. Patent Application is assigned a unique "Application Serial Number" at the time it is filed with the USPTO.

An application number can be used to look up information about a published U.S. Patent Application or issued U.S. Patent on the USPTO's Web site. Thus, it is useful to know how to identify the application number.

In the example patent as shown in Figure 7.4, the application number listed is "10/810,280." The "10" in the number "10/810,280" reflects the "series" of the patent application. The USPTO assigns application numbers sequentially based on "series." All U.S. Patent Application numbers have a "series" number. Older patent applications did not always list the series number. The series number is necessary to find information from the USPTO or its public databases about the patent application based on the application number.

The filing date is also important for determining the term of the patent (i.e., how long it will remain in effect), as well as the prior art status of the patent application. (*See* Chapter 8.)

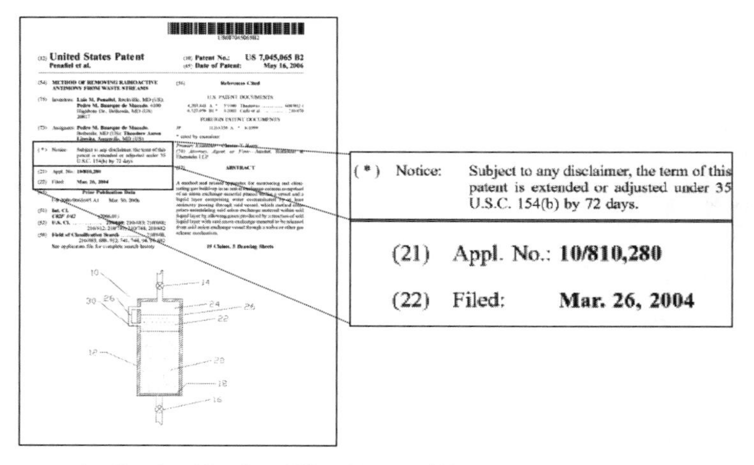

FIGURE 7.4 Application Number, Filing Date and Term Notice.

The length of time that a patent remains in effect is calculated not only by using the earliest effective filing date of the U.S. Patent Application (*see* Chapter 15, Section 15.1), but also by taking into account any "term notice." In the case of the above example patent, the term has been extended by an additional 72 days due to delay attributed to the USPTO during prosecution. This information is indicated next to an asterisk (*) and the word "Notice" on the cover of the patent. (*See* Figure 7.4.)

Patents may also include "Related Application Data," which indicates any earlier-filed patent applications to which the issued patent claims priority. These earlier-filed patent applications are important to consider in order to determine the earliest effective filing date of the patent. The earliest effective filing date of a patent claim also affects the status of which material will be considered prior art. The earliest claimed priority date also affects the length of the patent term, whether the claim is entitled to that priority date or not.

Practice Note:

"Related Application Data" identifies other patent applications and patents that are related to the instant patent application.

7.1.4 Prior Publications

Starting in March 2001, the USPTO began publishing most pending U.S. Patent Applications.[6] To the extent a U.S. Patent has been previously published, that information is provided on the cover page of modern patents next to the code "(65)," under the heading "Prior Publication Data." In the example patent shown in Figure 7.5, the publication number "2006/0065603 A1" and the publication date "March 30, 2006" are shown at this location.

Practice Note:

"Prior Publication Data" identifies the publication number and date of publication for earlier published versions of the patent application.

This information is important for identifying the prior art status of the patent as a printed publication (*see* Chapter 8, Section 8.1), as well as potential pre-issuance rights (*see* Chapter 15, Section 15.2). However, it is important to keep in mind that until a patent issues, while it may grant a patent owner some rights retroactively, a published application is not enforceable; only an issued U.S. Patent is enforceable.

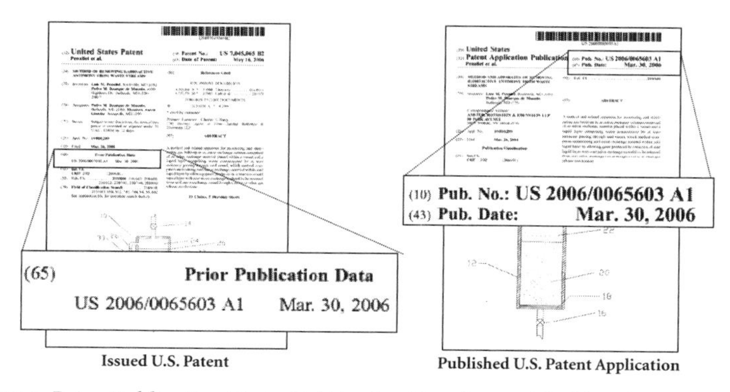

FIGURE 7.5 Prior Publication Data, Publication Number and Publication Date.

7.1.5 Inventors and Assignees

The cover page of a patent also identifies the named inventors and the owner (called the "assignee") of the patent application at the time the patent issues, if different than the named inventors. The named inventors are identified next to the code "(75)." The assignee is identified next to the code "(73)." Each patent may list one or more inventors. Similarly, each patent may list no assignee or one or more assignees. In the example in Figure 7.6, there are two inventors listed and two assignees.

Practice Note:

The cover page of a patent lists the name(s) of the inventor(s) and the owner(s) (called "assignee(s)") at the time the patent issues.

This information is useful when investigating a patent and for understanding whom to contact to learn more about a patent, either as prior art (*see* Chapter 8) or perhaps to obtain license rights (*see* Chapter 18).

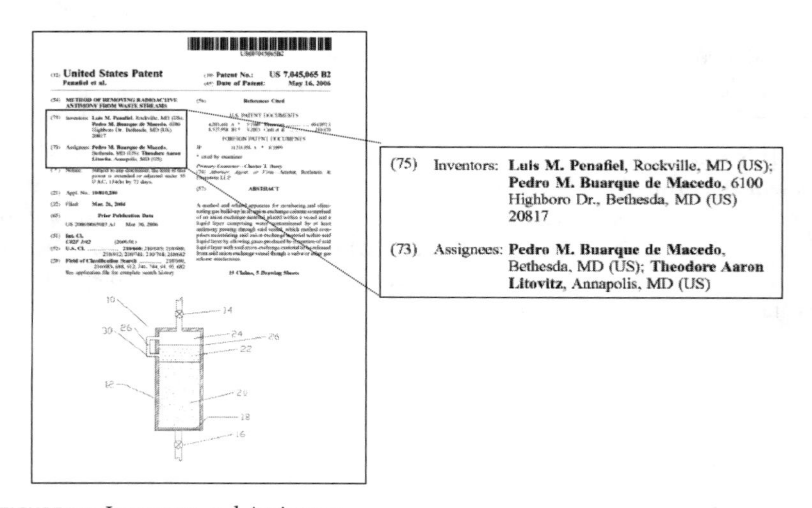

FIGURE 7.6 Inventors and Assignees.

However, while U.S. patent law provides for the recordation of assignments with the USPTO, if an existing assignment is not recorded, or not recorded until after a patent issues, the assignee on the face of the patent may not be the actual assignee. Also, post-issuance assignments, even if recorded with the USPTO, do not appear on the face of the patent. For a more thorough search of the ownership history, public assignment records for a U.S. Patent or U.S. published application are available at the USPTO, either through an in-person search, which allows access to copies of recorded assignments, or though the USPTO's Web site (*see* assignments.uspto.gov), which provides abstracts of the recorded assignments.

Practice Note:

Additional information on ownership claims to a patent may be available from the USPTO office or its Web site.

Also, all relevant information about who has rights to a U.S. Patent may not necessarily be filed with the USPTO. For example, licenses, even exclusive licenses, need not be recorded with the USPTO.

7.1.6 Prior Art of Record/"References Cited"

The patent cover page of a U.S. Patent also identifies the prior art (*see* Chapter 8) that was considered by the USPTO when deciding whether to issue the patent. In recently issued patents, the prior art that is cited (or identified) by the examiner has an asterisk (*) next to it. When prior art is cited by the examiner, it is generally (but not necessarily) considered the most relevant prior art. This information is shown in the "Reference Cited" section as shown in Figure 7.7.

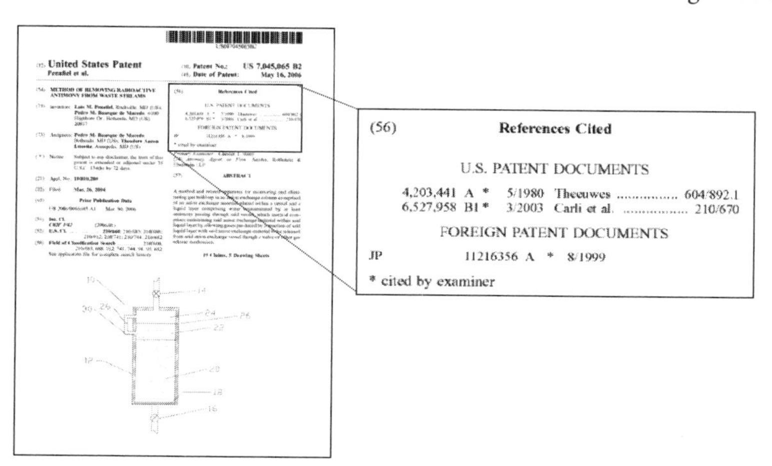

FIGURE 7.7 References Cited.

Practice Note:

The "References Cited" portion of a U.S. Patent identifies the prior art that is considered by the examiner when granting the issued patent.

References Cited can include various types of documents, such as

- Issued U.S. Patents; or
- U.S. Published Patent Applications.

These types of references are listed under the caption "U.S. Patent Documents." (*See* Figure 7.7.)

Reference Cited may also be an issued or registered patent or published patent application by a different patent office, including, for example, the Japanese Patent Office, the European Patent Office, or some other patent office outside the United States. These references are listed under the caption "Foreign Patent Documents." In the example patent shown in Figure 7.7, a reference issued by the Japanese Patent Office is listed (JP 11216356A).

Non-patent publications may also be cited as prior art and are listed under the caption "Other Publications," such as

- Journal articles;
- Newspapers articles;
- Government reports and filings;
- Product brochures;
- Manuals; and
- Schematics.

The actual back and forth between the applicant and the USPTO is called the "prosecution history." In some instances, an examiner may decide not to consider prior art or other references that were identified by the patent applicant, in which case, such art does not appear on the cover of the patent. Thus, it is always a good idea to review the prosecution history of a U.S. Patent to identify with certainty all of the potentially relevant prior art or references available.

7.2 Abstract

The cover page of a U.S. Patent also includes an "Abstract" of the patent. (*See* Figure 7.8.) The Abstract provides the reader with a summary understanding of the basic nature of the invention in two or three sentences, without including all of the details required to practice the invention. Patent practitioners often draft the abstract by turning into sentence form the broadest independent claim as originally filed.

Practice Note:
The "Abstract" of a patent briefly identifies the general subject matter of the claimed invention.

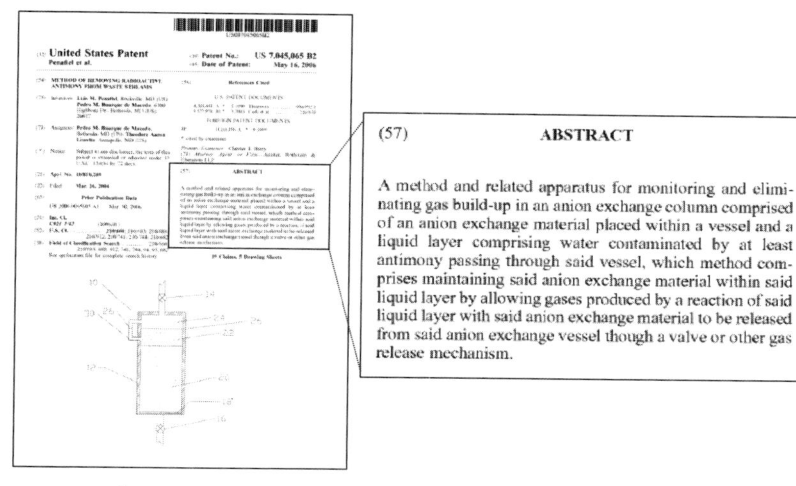
United States Patent
Peñafiel et al.
Patent No.: US 7,045,065 B2
Date of Patent: May 16, 2006

(57) ABSTRACT

A method and related apparatus for monitoring and eliminating gas build-up in an anion exchange column comprised of an anion exchange material placed within a vessel and a liquid layer comprising water contaminated by at least antimony passing through said vessel, which method comprises maintaining said anion exchange material within said liquid layer by allowing gases produced by a reaction of said liquid layer with said anion exchange material to be released from said anion exchange vessel though a valve or other gas release mechanism.

FIGURE 7.8 Abstract.

7.3 Field of Invention

At the beginning of a U.S. Patent is a "Field of Invention" section which identifies generally the types of products or processes to which the invention relates. (*See* Figure 7.9.)

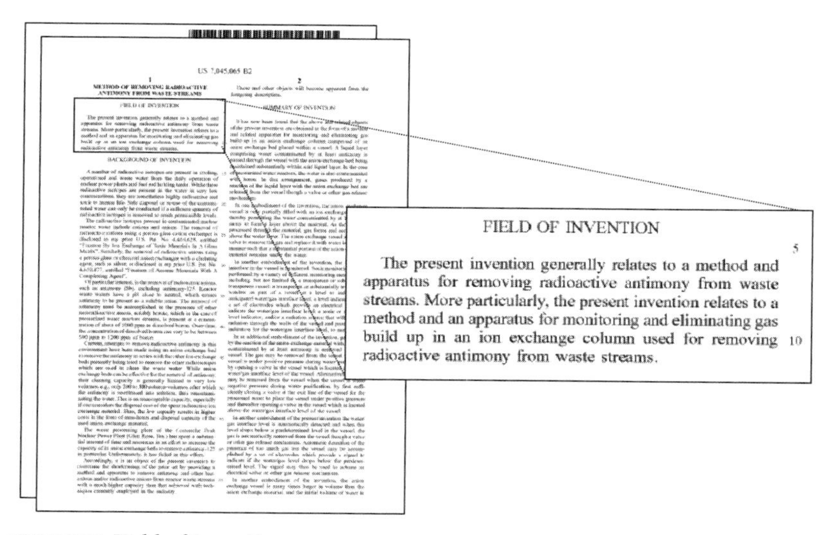
US 7,045,065 B2

FIELD OF INVENTION

The present invention generally relates to a method and apparatus for removing radioactive antimony from waste streams. More particularly, the present invention relates to a method and an apparatus for monitoring and eliminating gas build up in an ion exchange column used for removing radioactive antimony from waste streams.

FIGURE 7.9 Field of Invention.

Practice Note:

The "Field of Invention" section of a U.S. Patent identifies generally the types of products or processes to which the invention relates.

7.4 Background of Invention

A "Background of Invention" section may be included in a U.S. Patent. (*See* Figure 7.10.) This section is intended to provide a context in which the invention was developed. It may include a description of prior art which the invention is meant to improve upon. Often it contains discussions as to the problems with the prior art and/or how the prior art requires improvements. Sometimes the prior art discussed in the Background of Invention section may not be listed as a "Reference Cited." If it is not listed, the examiner did not necessarily consider this material when granting the patent. Thus, it is important in analyzing a patent to review not only the References Cited that are listed on the cover page, and references that have otherwise been submitted during the prosecution history (as discussed in Section 7.1.6), but also each of the references discussed in the body of the patent, including, for example, within the Background of Invention section. Each of these references may have a significant impact on the validity or construction of the patented claims.

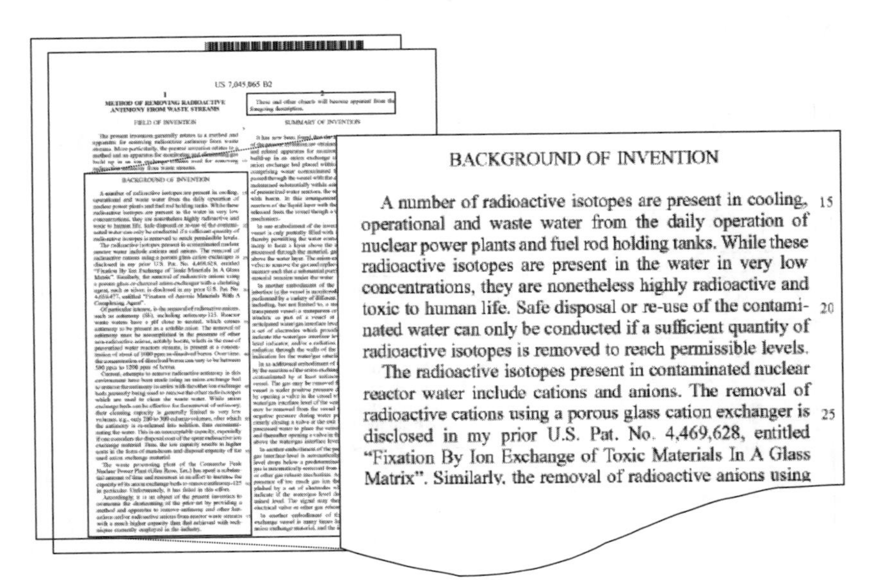

BACKGROUND OF INVENTION

A number of radioactive isotopes are present in cooling, operational and waste water from the daily operation of nuclear power plants and fuel rod holding tanks. While these radioactive isotopes are present in the water in very low concentrations, they are nonetheless highly radioactive and toxic to human life. Safe disposal or re-use of the contaminated water can only be conducted if a sufficient quantity of radioactive isotopes is removed to reach permissible levels.

The radioactive isotopes present in contaminated nuclear reactor water include cations and anions. The removal of radioactive cations using a porous glass cation exchanger is disclosed in my prior U.S. Pat. No. 4,469,628, entitled "Fixation By Ion Exchange of Toxic Materials In A Glass Matrix". Similarly, the removal of radioactive anions using

FIGURE 7.10 Background of Invention.

Practice Note:

The "Background of Invention" section may be included in a U.S. Patent to provide context for the disclosed invention and to identify problems with the prior art.

7.5 Summary of Invention

Each patent also includes a section called the "Summary of Invention." (*See* Figure 7.11.) The Summary of Invention section is intended to summarize the invention. Typically, patent practitioners repeat at least the independent claims of the patent application as originally filed in a sentence format in this portion of the patent application.

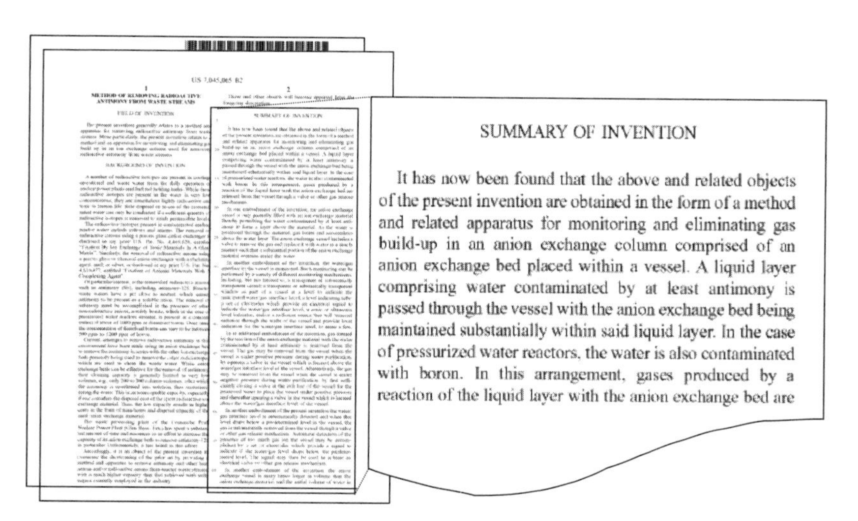

SUMMARY OF INVENTION

It has now been found that the above and related objects of the present invention are obtained in the form of a method and related apparatus for monitoring and eliminating gas build-up in an anion exchange column comprised of an anion exchange bed placed within a vessel. A liquid layer comprising water contaminated by at least antimony is passed through the vessel with the anion exchange bed being maintained substantially within said liquid layer. In the case of pressurized water reactors, the water is also contaminated with boron. In this arrangement, gases produced by a reaction of the liquid layer with the anion exchange bed are

FIGURE 7.11 Summary of Invention.

Practice Note:

"Summary of Invention" generally describes briefly the invention.

7.6 Figures and Description of Figures

While every patent does not necessarily include drawings or figures, it is common for patents to include one or more figures. U.S. Patent Rules require that an application include figures or drawings when necessary to understand the invention.[7] Typically, a representative figure is included on the cover of the patent (*See* Figure 7.12), and all figures will follow thereafter. The selection of which figure should be repeated on the cover page of the patent may be made by the applicant at the time of filing the patent application, or else the USPTO will make the selection.

Usually, a "Brief Description of Figures" section follows the "Summary of Invention" section of a U.S. Patent. (*See* Figure 7.12.) This brief description will generally identify, for example, the objects shown in each figure and the perspective of the drawing. For example, in the exemplary patent in Figure 7.12.

> FIG. 1 is a schematic diagram of a substantially transparent anion exchange column made in accordance with the invention.

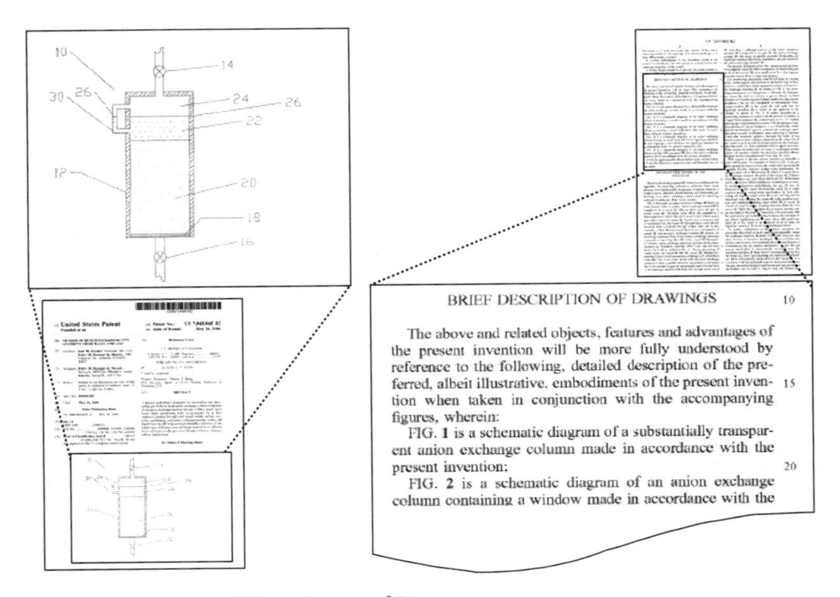

FIGURE 7.12 Figures and Description of Figures.

Practice Note:

Figures are often be included in a patent to illustrate the invention, as appropriate.

7.7 Detailed Description of Invention

The "Detailed Description of Invention" section of a U.S. Patent describes the invention, its operation, and how its benefits are achieved. This description must be sufficient so a person having a relevant technical background and experience can understand and practice the claimed invention. U.S. patent law refers to such a person as "a person of ordinary skill in the art." The description should be complete to the extent that a person with some knowledge of the field reading the description can make and use the equipment described or practice the process revealed without undue experimentation.

Practice Note:

"Detailed Description" provides sufficient details of embodiments of the invention to enable a person of ordinary skill in the art to practice the claimed invention.

The detailed description is usually made with reference to one or more figures. Typically, numbers or letters are used in the figures to indicate the significant components, so that these components may be located and their functions easily appreciated. The same numbers or letters are used throughout the detailed description and in the figures to refer to the same components.

The Detailed Description should include not only a detailed description of the components involved in a particular invention, but also how the components cooperate to solve the problem or produce the beneficial results, using the same reference numbers used in the drawings.

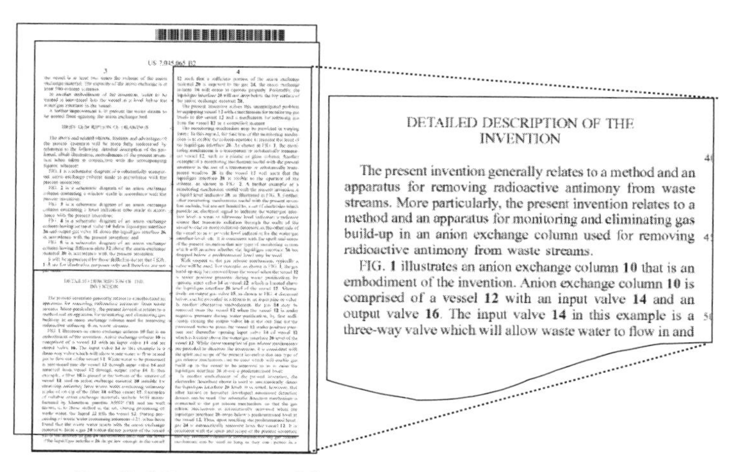
DETAILED DESCRIPTION OF THE INVENTION

The present invention generally relates to a method and an apparatus for removing radioactive antimony from waste streams. More particularly, the present invention relates to a method and an apparatus for monitoring and eliminating gas build-up in an anion exchange column used for removing radioactive antimony from waste streams.

FIG. 1 illustrates an anion exchange column 10 that is an embodiment of the invention. Anion exchange column 10 is comprised of a vessel 12 with an input valve 14 and an output valve 16. The input valve 14 in this example is a three-way valve which will allow waste water to flow in and

FIGURE 7.13 Detailed Description of the Invention.

Sometimes, the detailed description may also include examples of the invention. Such examples typically include information associated with particular embodiments or experiments associated with the invention. Examples can provide context as to what the invention is or is not.

7.8 The Claims

The claims define the invention and thus are the key part of a U.S. Patent. The claims define for the public the rights that are owned by the patentee during the term of the patent.

Practice Note:
The "claims" define the invention and are the key part to a U.S. Patent.

The claims are located at the end of the patent and usually begin with phrases such as: "What is claimed is:"; "I claim:"; or "We claim:."

As will be discussed below in Chapter 11, it is important to read and understand the claims to know whether a patent can affect your rights. This process of interpreting a claim can at times be complex (*see* Chapter 11), and a competent patent practitioner should be consulted to determine if a particular claim is an issue for the organization's products or services.

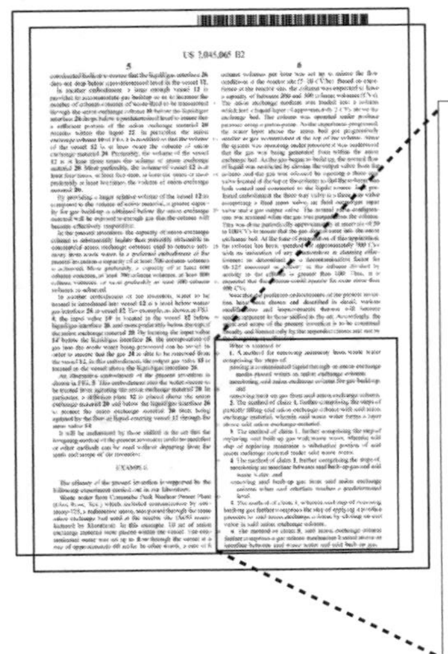

What is claimed is:

1. A method for removing antimony from waste water comprising the steps of:

passing a contaminated liquid through an anion exchange media placed within an anion exchange column;

monitoring said anion exchange column for gas build-up; and

removing built-up gas from said anion exchange column.

2. The method of claim **1**, further comprising the steps of partially filling said anion exchange column with said anion exchange material, wherein said waste water forms a layer above said anion exchange material.

* * *

5. The method of claim **1**, wherein said step of removing built-up gas further comprises the step of applying a positive pressure to said anion exchange column by closing an exit valve in said anion exchange column.

6. The method of claim **5**, said anion exchange column further comprises a gas release mechanism located above an interface between said waste water and said built-up gas.

FIGURE 7.14 The Claims.

It is important to recognize that there are different kinds of claims. Some claims are "independent," in that the claim stands on its own. Other claims are "dependent," in that the claim depends upon one or more other claims. Dependent claims include all of the limitations of the claims from which they depend plus whatever additional claims are further provided in the dependent claim.

In the exemplary patent as shown in Figure 7.14, Claim 1 is independent, and Claim 2 is dependent. Since Claim 2 depends from "claim 1" to meet the limitations of Claim 2, it is necessary to have all of the limitations of Claim 1, plus the additional limitations of Claim 2. Dependent claims may depend from other dependent claims. For example, Claim 6 in the exemplary patent depends from Claim 5, which in turn depends from Claim 1. Thus, in order to meet Claim 6, all the limitations of Claims 1 and 5 must be met in addition to the additional limitations of Claim 6.

CHAPTER 8

What Is Prior Art?

In Chapter 3, the requirements of patentability are discussed, including the requirements that a claimed invention be new and not obvious. In order to make such a determination, the scope and content of the relevant prior art must first be identified and understood. In this chapter, different kinds of prior art are generally discussed.

The focus of this chapter is not intended to be an exhaustive discussion of the details regarding how to determine if something is prior art under U.S. patent law; but instead, this chapter provides guideposts on how to determine what might be prior art which could impact on the patentability of a particular invention. Further, since the concept of what constitutes prior art differs from patent system to patent system, the present discussion is geared toward discussing the potential prior art in the context of U.S. patent laws.

Under U.S. patent law,[1] a valid patent cannot be obtained if the invention to be claimed is already known and disclosed in the prior art. U.S. patent law defines prior art to include the following:

- an invention that was described in a patent or printed publication anywhere in the world;[2]
- an invention that was known or used by others in the United States;[3]
- an invention that was commercially used, sold, or offered for sale in the United States;[4]
- an invention that was made by someone other than the persons claiming to be the inventors.[5]

To the extent that any of these activities occurred more than one year prior to the earliest effective U.S. filing date of the patent application at issue, these activities can act as an absolute bar to obtaining a patent on the invention.[6]

8.1 Patents and Printed Publications

Perhaps the most intuitive kind of prior art is a patent which issues or is filed earlier than the claimed invention. It makes sense to most people that an applicant should not be entitled to a new patent if someone else came up with and disclosed the same invention earlier.

Prior art patents can include not only issued U.S. Patents, but also

- Published U.S. Patent Applications;
- Patents issued or registered by other governmental authorities (e.g., issued Japanese Patents, registered Singapore Patents, issued European Patents, etc.); or
- Published patent applications by other governmental authorities (e.g., Japanese Laid Open Patent Applications, PCT Published Applications, European Published Applications, etc.).

The prior art status under U.S. patent law of each of these different kinds of patents and published applications is slightly different, depending upon the kind of patent or published application it is.

Practice Note:

Issued and Registered Patents and Published Patent Applications can be prior art, even if from another country.

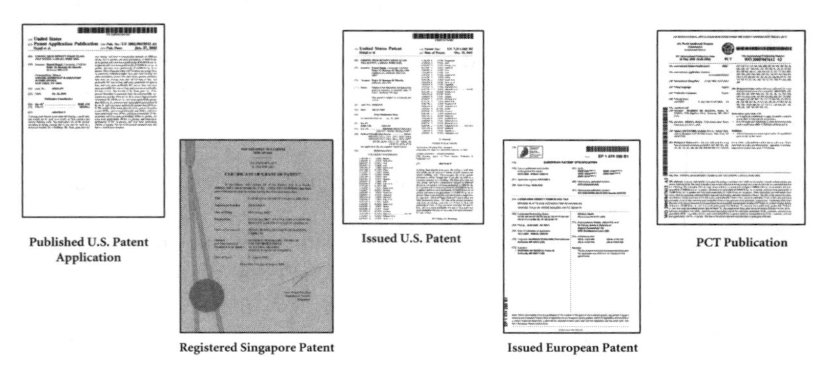

FIGURE 8.1 Examples of Different Types of Patents and Patent Publications that can be Prior Art.

Any patent (U.S. or otherwise) issued more than one year before the earliest effective filing date of a claimed invention must be considered under the assumption that the information disclosed in the earlier patent is prior art. In most cases, the earliest effective filing date is the earliest U.S. filing date or PCT filing date on applications designating the U.S., to which a claimed invention is entitled to priority.[7]

Likewise, any published application (U.S. or otherwise) published more than one year before the earliest effective filing date of the claimed invention must also be considered under the assumption that the information disclosed in the earlier patent or publication is prior art.

In the United States, prior art which is published more than one year before the earliest effective filing date of the claimed invention is referred to as "statutory" prior art because it must always be considered as prior art.[8]

Practice Note:

Patents which issue and published patent applications which are published more than one year before the earliest effective filing date of a claimed invention are called "statutory" prior art.

A U.S. Patent which issues prior to the earliest effective filing date of the claimed invention, even if less than one year prior, can still be prior art under U.S. patent law. It can be prior art either as of its issue date or, alternatively, as of its earliest effective filing date. However, unlike statutory prior art, at least in the United States, if an applicant can establish inventing the claimed invention earlier than the prior art date, then such prior art can potentially be overcome, as briefly discussed above in Chapter 5, Section 5.6.[9]

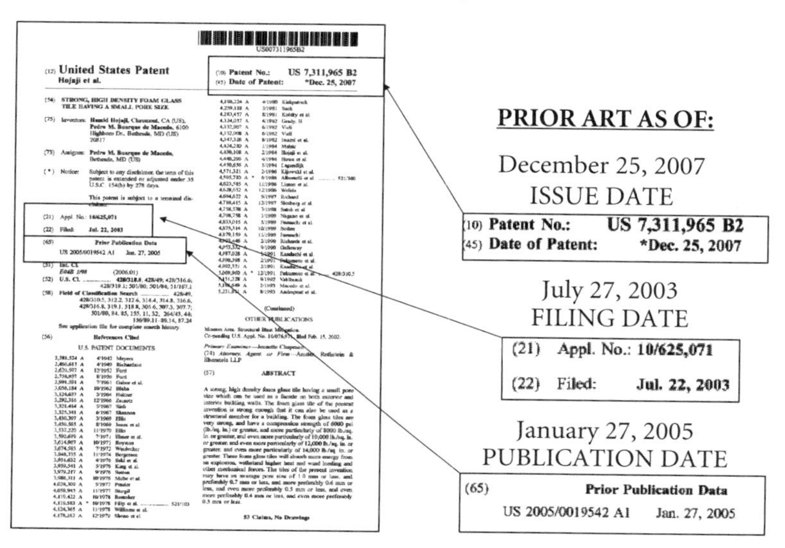

FIGURE 8.2 Prior Art status of issued U.S. Patent.

Even before a patent issues, or even if a patent never issues, a U.S. Patent Application can become prior art as of

- Its publication date;[10] and/or
- Its earliest effective filing date once it is published.[11]

If the U.S. Patent Application is published more than one year prior to the earliest effective filing date of the claimed invention, the published application will be statutory prior art.[12]

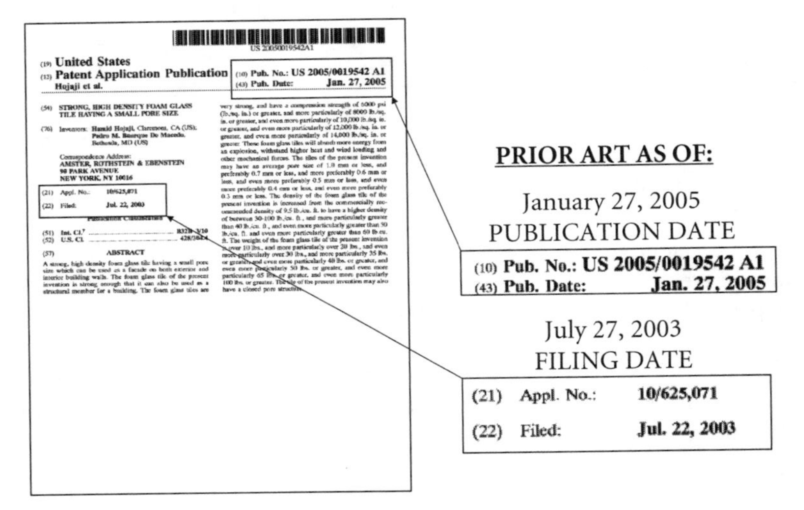

FIGURE 8.3 Prior Art status of published U.S. Patent application.

Another type of patent publication which can potentially be used as prior art is a PCT Publication. As discussed above in Chapter 6, Section 6.8.1, the World Intellectual Property Organization ("WIPO") has set up a procedure by which a single patent application may be filed in accordance with the Patent Cooperation Treaty ("PCT") in most of the countries of the world. A PCT Patent Application will be published approximately 18 months after its priority date in what is referred to as a PCT Publication. A PCT Publication becomes prior art as of its publication date, whether the United States is designated or not. If the United States is included among the "designated states," then the PCT Publication also becomes prior art as of the PCT filing date.

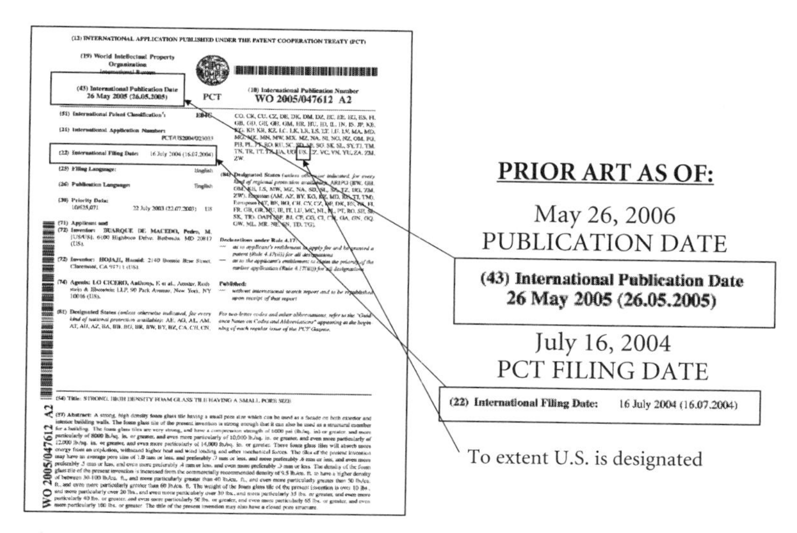

FIGURE 8.4 Prior Art status of published PCT Patent application.

Other non-U.S. Patent Publications also become prior art under U.S. patent law as of their publication date. However, once a non-U.S. Patent Application becomes "laid open" (made available for public inspection), U.S. patent law has recognized that the material found in that patent application file can also become prior art.[13]

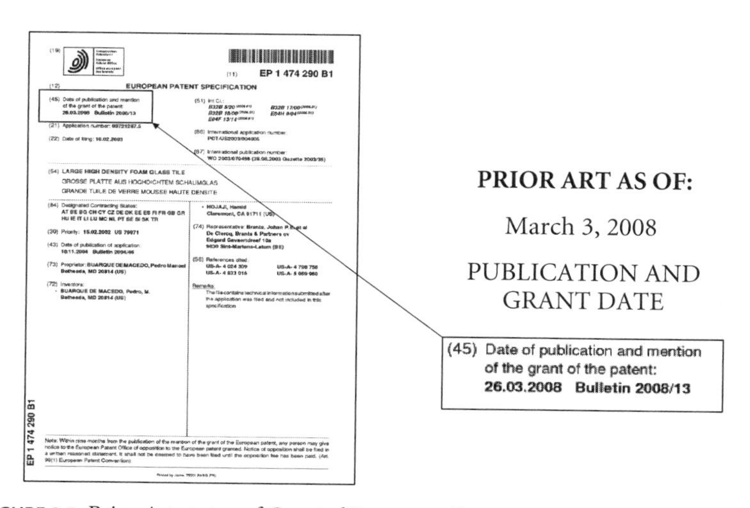

FIGURE 8.5 Prior Art status of Granted European Patent.

However, it is worth noting that the language in which a prior art reference is published does not affect its prior art status. Thus, the fact that a Japanese Laid Open Publication is only published in Japanese does not preclude it from being prior art. However, that does not mean that it is not necessary to obtain and use an English language translation to determine the patentable merits of the claimed invention.[14] It just means that the original prior art does not need to be published in English for it to be considered prior art.

Practice Note:

A patent or published patent application does not need to be published in the English language in order for it to be considered prior art under U.S. patent law.

Furthermore, U.S. patent law recognizes that other kinds of printed publications beyond patents and published patent applications can be used as prior art. For example, other kinds of items that can constitute printed publications and thus "prior art" include:

- Product brochures, advertisements, marketing materials, instruction manuals, service manuals, technical guides;[15]
- Data sheets and specifications;[16]
- Photographs when distributed;[17]
- Draft or published submissions to standard setting bodies (e.g., IEEE, VESA, etc.);
- PhD Thesis (at least when sufficiently cataloged);[18] and
- Textbooks, articles, lecture notes (when published), recorded presentations.[19]

The touchstone of whether a particular document is a printed publication, and thus prior art, is whether the document is generally "available to the public without restriction."[20] Phrased another way, was the document publicly accessible to the interested public? It does not matter how many copies of the document are available as long as the document is publicly accessible.[21] Thus, for example, a single copy of a doctorate dissertation can be a printed publication as long as it is cataloged by at least the library on whose shelf it is maintained.[22] Similarly, it does not even matter if anyone ever looked at or opened the document, as long as it is publicly available by the critical date.[23] On the other hand, even if 100 copies of a document existed early enough, if these copies are not publicly available (to at least the relevant public) and are maintained in secret, then they may not be considered prior art.[24] Further, as with patents, it also does not matter if the reference is written in English.[25]

In the world of the Internet, a document posted on an Internet Web site can also be prior art, once it is accessible to the public.[26] Archived Internet postings can be found on the "Way Back When Machine" at www.archive.org, going as far back as 1996.

8.2 Prior Knowledge or Use

Prior art under U.S. patent law also encompasses that which was publicly known or used before the claimed invention. Prior knowledge or use can come in many forms. Examples of prior knowledge or use which can constitute prior art include:

- Public demonstrations at a convention;[27]
- Laboratory procedures which are open to public view;[28]
- Video demonstrations;[29] and
- Demonstrations to the press.[30]

The touchstone to whether a prior use constitutes prior art under U.S. patent law is not a question of whether the public actually sees or understands the workings of the prior art.[31] Rather, the issue is whether there was "any use of the claimed invention by a person other than the inventor who is under no limitation, restriction, or obligation of secrecy to the inventor."[32]

Practice Note:

Prior public knowledge or use of an invention by others in the United States where there is no obligation of secrecy to the inventor is prior art.

This distinction traces back to the 1880s, when the U.S. Supreme Court considered whether a corset, provided by an inventor to a woman to wear in public, albeit under her outer clothing, was "public use." In that case, the U.S. Supreme Court recognized that the fact that the corset in question was provided to a third party to wear and use without any restriction, and was so worn, was sufficient to constitute a "public use" and preclude patentability. The U.S. Supreme Court explained its reasoning as follows:

> [S]ome inventions are by their very character only capable of being used where they cannot be seen or observed by the public eye. An invention may consist of a lever or spring, hidden in the running gear of a watch, or of a ratchet, shaft, or cog wheel covered from view in the recesses of a machine for spinning or weaving. Nevertheless, if its inventor sells a machine of which his invention

> forms a part, and allows it to be used *without restriction* of any kind, the use is a public one.[33]

In reaching this decision, the U.S. Supreme Court also recognized that whether a use constitutes a public use did not depend upon how many articles were used or how many persons had knowledge of it. Rather, the critical question is whether there was a use of the invention without restriction so that the public could learn about the invention.

However, it was recognized that when the use, even if in public view, was merely "experimental," it would not constitute a "public use" for purposes of determining if it was prior art.[34]

8.3 Prior Sale

Prior art can also come in the form of a product or device which is sold or offered for sale more than one year before the earliest U.S. effective filing date of a patent application.[35]

Practice Note:

A product or device which was sold or offered for sale more than one year before the earliest U.S. filing date is prior art.

An invention is sold or offered for sale under U.S. patent law if

- The invention must have been the subject of a commercial offer for sale more than one year before the patent application was filed; and
- The invention must have been ready for patenting more than one year before the filing of the application.[36]

Under the first prong of the test, the patented invention must have been subject to a commercial offer for sale more than one year prior to the filing of the patent application. In other words, if a patent application is first filed on January 1, 2008, then products or devices which are sold or offered for sale more than one year prior (e.g., before January 1, 2007) would meet this part of the test.

The determination of whether a transaction is a commercial offer for sale is fairly straightforward. Normal principles of contract law are applied.[37] All that is required is "a single sale or offer for sale" to create a bar to patentability.[38] This bar can be met even if the product sold is not scheduled to be delivered until after the critical date.[39] It also does not matter whether the sale is by the patentee or someone else unrelated. In either case, the prior sale or offer for sale is prior art and can render a patent claim invalid.[40] Thus, whether the product sold was invented by the patentee, some third party, or even a business partner, it can still be prior art. Even when a sale is consummated as part of a joint development agreement, as long as the parties to the sale are separate entities, a bar to patentability can still be created.[41] The critical issue is whether one side offered to sell to the other side of the transaction the patented invention before the critical date. If so, the first part of the test is met.

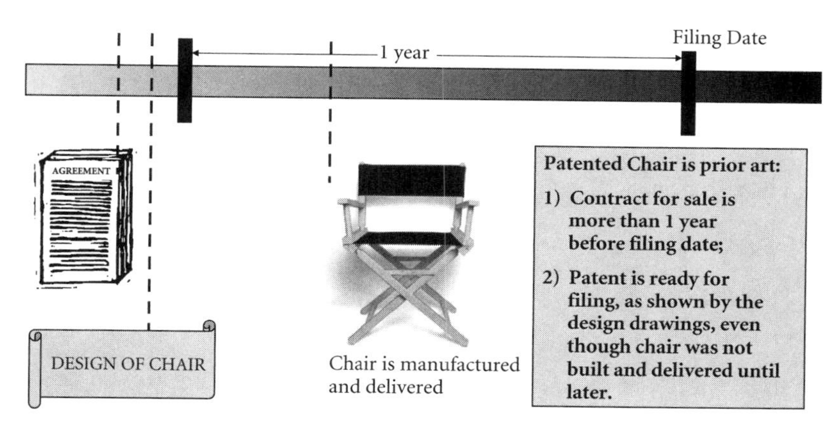

FIGURE 8.6 Time Line Relating to "On Sale" Bar to Patentability.

In addition to a commercial offer for sale, the invention must have been ready for patenting more than one year before the filing of the application. An invention is ready for patenting if it is reduced to practice (i.e., actually made) before the critical date or it is at least the subject of drawings and other descriptions which are sufficient to enable someone skilled in the art to build it.[42]

8.4 Derived from Another

U.S. patent law only grants patents to "Inventors," which is understood to mean the "first and true" inventors. This requirement comes from the U.S. Constitution, which grants to Congress the power to grant patent rights to "Inventors."[43] Thus, if an invention is derived from someone else, then the persons who derived the invention are not entitled under U.S. patent law to a patent.[44] However, in order for derivation by another to bar patentability, it must be a complete derivation. In other words, the *entire* invention (i.e., all the elements of a claim) must be derived from another to preclude an applicant or patentee from being entitled to a patent claim.[45]

CHAPTER 9

What to Disclose to the Patent Practitioner

In order to get an appropriate and useful patent, the patent practitioner preparing and prosecuting the patent application needs to be informed of all relevant information. The purpose of this chapter is to identify the different kinds of information the inventor or organization should gather and disclose to the patent practitioner so he can prepare the best possible patent application and ultimately obtain the best possible patent protection available.

9.1 Complete and Accurate Details of the Invention

Obviously, the most important information to disclose to a patent practitioner who is drafting a patent application is the complete and accurate details about the invention and how it works. Without a full understanding of the invention, it is unlikely that any patent practitioner can obtain the most effective patent protection available. However, in drafting a patent application, a patent practitioner must understand not only the basic details of the invention (at least as to the aspects for which claim coverage is being sought), but also the ways in which the invention can be modified to achieve a comparable (even if less satisfactory) result by others. This will better enable the patent practitioner to consider ways to ensure that the patent that ultimately issues will also cover such alternatives.

Practice Note:

Provide the patent practitioner with complete and accurate details of the invention.

This section discusses the different kinds of information about the invention that an applicant and/or inventor should provide the patent practitioner.

9.1.1 The Intended Operation of the Invention

A good starting point for any patent disclosure is a complete and accurate explanation of how the invention is intended to operate. This includes a description of the necessary and optional components of the invention and how those components interact with and relate to each other. This description should be made with references to flow charts, drawings, sketches, and/or reports as appropriate, copies of which should be provided to the patent practitioner.

Practice Note:

Provide the patent practitioner with a complete explanation of how the invention is intended to operate and how its components interact and relate to each other.

Referring to the chair example discussed in Chapter 3, the components of the invention include each of the components of the chair: arms, seat, back, and legs. The description could include a written narrative which identifies and describes each of the components and how they interact with each other. The description may also be made in conjunction with one or more drawings (such as Figure 9.1 below) that illustrate each part and how the parts are put together. In this example, the chair itself and each of the different parts of the chair are identified by different numerals. Thus, Figure 9.1 has labeled the chair as "10," and each of its separate components with separate numbers, e.g., arms 20, a seat 30, a back 40, and two pairs of crossed legs 50. Within the figure, both of the arms should be labeled with the same number (20) to show they are comparable structures. Similarly, each pair of the crossed legs (50) is likewise labeled with the same number. However, different numbers are used for the arms (20) and legs (50), since they represent different structures.

Patent practitioners often avoid using consecutive numbers (e.g., 1, 2, 3, 4, 5, etc.) when labeling a figure and drafting a description so that if additional parts are later identified for inclusion, interim numbers can be used.

It is also useful to identify in the description the material(s) each of these components is made of. For example, the arms 20 may be made of wood or a tempered wood. The seat 30 and back 40 are made out of cloth, such as treated wool cloth.

Additional unclaimed elements, like the supports 22 of the arms 20, and cross-supports 52 of the legs 50 should also be identified and labeled. These additional unclaimed elements may ultimately be claimed in dependent claims or perhaps be added after prosecution begins with respect to the independent claims.

Optional components should also be identified. For example, the chair may include an optional seat cushion (not shown). The optional seat cushion may be included as a feature of a dependent claim. The fact that the seat cushion is an optional feature, rather than a necessary feature of the invention, should be clearly identified to the patent practitioner to avoid the inclusion of unnecessary limitations in the independent claim.

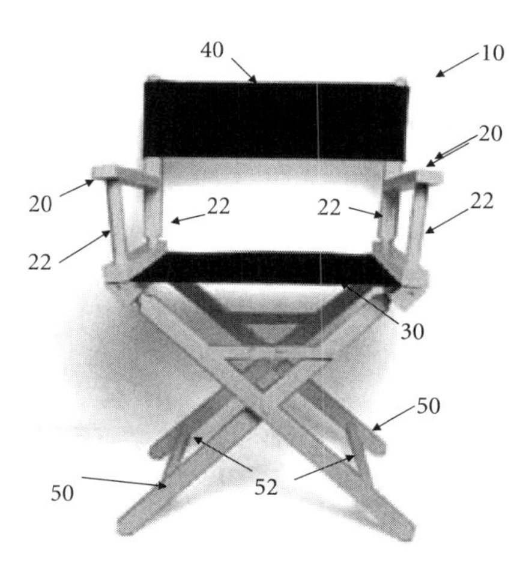

FIGURE 9.1 Sample Patent Figure.

Other important characteristics, like the dimensions, should also be identified. For example, the disclosure may specify the arms 20 should be between 30 and 35 inches long and between 1 and 3 inches wide. If there is a special reason for the selection of these dimensions, it should be provided to the patent practitioner. For example, the length of the arm 20 is based on the average length of an adult's arm, and the width is based on the fact that narrower arms would likely break when used. If there are any special materials to be used in connection with the invention, the source, supplier, brand name, and/or generic name of such materials should also be provided to the patent practitioner.

The relationship between components should also be described. Thus, in the chair example, in the case that the chair is a folding chair, how the chair folds should be described. In this case, the patent practitioner may want to draft a method claim directed to the method of folding the chair. (*See* Chapter 10, Section 10.4.)

Ultimately, the more details that are provided to the patent practitioner, the more likely it is that the patent practitioner will be able to obtain useful patent protection. Of course, it may not be necessary or appropriate to include every detail in a patent application, and an experienced patent practitioner, with input from the applicant, should be responsible for determining which details are appropriate or inappropriate for inclusion.

9.1.2 Potential Construction and Operation of Competitor's Products or Services in the Context of the Invention

As part of the patent drafting process, the patent practitioner should consider not only how the inventor plans to practice the invention, but also how others may practice the invention. (*See* Chapter 6, Section 6.3.) Thus, continuing with the chair example, it is also important to consider not only how the inventor plans to make the chair, but also how others may modify the chair and yet maintain the spirit of the invention. For example, as shown in Figure 6.5 above, the inventor may intend to make the chair with arms having a top bar and two vertical bars. However, a competitor may prefer using an arm with an additional central bar. The inventor should also consider and disclose these types of variations to the patent practitioner.

Practice Note:

Provide the patent practitioner with details of how competitors' products or services might be constructed and/or operate in the context of the invention.

Likewise, it is important to think about and disclose to the patent practitioner potential variations on the selected materials, dimensions, and relative operability of the components for potential inclusion in the patent application. Inventors should also disclose if any particular feature, material, etc., is necessary to make the invention work, as opposed to merely being desirable. This type of information informs the patent practitioner on how to draft claims to maximize their effective coverage.

9.1.3 Potential Future Modification of the Invention

In considering what patent protection should be sought, it also is important to consider how the product at issue may be modified at a later date to account for future developments and customer demands. For example, returning to the chair example, at the time the patent application is being prepared, the new chair's arms may be expected to be made out of wood. Thus, wood should be disclosed and possibly claimed as a material out of which the arms are to be made. However, if, in the future, the chair industry might begin using a new synthetic wood material (such as composites of wood fibers and recycled plastic), then this alternative material should be disclosed and possibly claimed.[1] At a minimum, to the extent that it can be anticipated, this kind of development should be included in the disclosure to the patent practitioner. It is important to remember that a patent, if issued, can last for up to twenty years. To be effective, it should take into account expected developments likely to occur during the life of the patent.

Practice Note:

Provide the patent practitioner with details on how the product may be modified in the future.

9.1.4 Best Mode of Practicing the Invention

U.S. patent law also requires including the best mode of practicing the invention known by the inventors in the description of the invention when the application is prepared and filed.[2] This requirement is part of the underlying rationale for granting patents.

The best mode requirement precludes inventors from applying for patents while at the same time concealing from the public preferred embodiments of their inventions which they have in fact conceived.[3]

In particular, the obligation to disclose the best mode of practicing the invention is limited to the best mode for practicing the claimed invention, and does not necessarily extend to unclaimed subject matter included in the disclosure.[4] However, best practices would have applicants disclose to the patent practitioner who is responsible for drafting the patent application more—not less—on the operation of the invention so that the practitioner can determine what should be included.

The scope of the claims may change during the course of the proceedings before the USPTO; therefore it is best to include all the details relating to the best mode of whatever subject matter may ultimately be included as the claimed invention.

Practice Note:

Provide the patent practitioner with the best mode(s) of practicing the invention known at the time.

9.1.5 Historical Record of the Invention

The patent practitioner should also be provided with an historical record of the development of the invention. In other words, the development of the invention includes details of who and when the invention was first conceived, built, disclosed, and/or sold.

Practice Note:

Provide the patent practitioner with an historical record of the development of the invention.

The historical record of the invention would include such information as

- The approximate or exact date when the concept of the invention first occurred to the inventors, along with details on how the inventors came up with the invention;
- Copies of any documents or electronic files that illustrate the invention, and the date on which they were prepared;
- Whether the invention has been disclosed to others, and, if so, where, when, and whether those disclosures were made under a non-disclosure agreement;
- Whether the invention is to be disclosed or sold in the near future, and, if so, when and to whom; and
- Whether the invention was developed under any government contract, and, if so, details of such contract.

This type of information assists the patent practitioner in determining the earliest "date of the invention" in the event that the same invention is independently made by a third party and there is a dispute as to who was the first inventor. In the case of a dispute over whose invention came first, the date on which the invention was conceived (e.g., the date on which the inventors came up with the invention) and reduced to practice (e.g., built) is important information in determining who will win such a dispute. (*See* Chapter 5, Section 5.6.) U.S. patent law requires corroboration of this information,[5] thus it is useful to collect it early on, so that if a dispute arises later, either in the context of the proceedings before the USPTO or in litigation, it will be ready and available.

The historical record of the invention is also useful to the patent practitioner to identify if there are any potential so-called "bar" dates, which would preclude the patent from issuing. A patent application in the United States must be filed within one year of any commercial exploitation or publication of the invention. (*See* Chapter 8.) In many foreign countries, there is *no* grace period at all, and the filing of a patent application must precede any public use or disclosure. This information can therefore be used to determine whether there is any time left and, if so, how much, within which to prepare and file a patent application, as well as to determine if patent protection outside the United States is potentially available.

Practice Note:

Provide the patent practitioner with a historical record of the invention to assist in drafting the patent application and developing a record for future use, if necessary.

9.2 Prior Art

Publications or acts ("prior art," *see* Chapter 8), even if not identical to the invention, may nonetheless be relevant to patentability because a valid patent can only be obtained if the differences between the invention and the prior art are not obvious, e.g., are more than a matter of the routine application of basic knowledge in the field.[6] (*See* Chapter 3, Section 3.2.)

U.S. patent law requires that inventors and individuals working with them disclose fully to the USPTO all prior art which could reasonably be considered as having a bearing on whether a patent should be granted.[7] Failure to make such disclosures can render a patent unenforceable, irrespective of its inventive merit, and expose the applicant to other serious consequences.[8] Of course, it is not necessary to disclose cumulative prior art, e.g., 15 different brochures of substantially the same product. One of such brochures would be sufficient. However, best practices dictate that all literature, patents, prior uses, etc., that an inventor has considered or used in the course of the events leading to the invention (whether deemed cumulative or not by the inventor) should specifically be identified to the patent practitioner, even if those publications do not disclose the invention. The patent practitioner can then determine which references should be submitted to the USPTO.

It is a popular misconception that patent protection can be obtained while simultaneously maintaining details of the invention as a trade secret.

This is contrary to established legal principles which require that the patent application must disclose the best mode of practicing the invention known to the inventor at the time the patent application is filed.[9]

Practice Note:

Provide the patent practitioner with copies of all prior art known to the inventors and others involved with the prosecution of the patent.

Thus, it is important that all of the inventors, and others who are involved with the patent prosecution, identify and disclose all the relevant prior art they are aware of to the patent practitioner. Such information includes all known prior art (such as disclosures, articles, systems, patents, publications, product brochures, products, etc.; *see* Chapter 8) that is closest to the invention.

In particular, the prior art should be identified both descriptively and through proper citation to the literature and patents. For example:

> The organization sold Model XYZ Widgets in 2005, which were first put on display at the January 2006 Widgets Show East. *See* John Smith, *New Widget Display Dazzles All*, WIDGET SHOW EAST TODAY, Jan. 10, 2006, p. 15.

In addition, problems with this prior art and how the invention overcomes such problems or otherwise improves upon the prior art should also be disclosed. For example:

> Model XYZ had elements A, B, and C, but did not include E. The present invention adds in element E. Without element E, widgets cannot achieve the speed and stability that customers desire. Prior to our invention, it was conventional wisdom that element E would make widgets slower and less stable.

Where the invention has resulted from combining elements or concepts from different fields, disciplines, or publications, all of the sources of information which may have been directly or indirectly referred to or relied upon in developing the invention should be identified. An explanation of why others would not make a similar combination should also be provided.

To the extent the organization has developed related work, that work should also be identified with sufficient detail so that the patent practitioner can take this other work into account when developing the patent application.

9.3 All Potential Inventors and Their Contributions

All persons who potentially may be considered inventors should be identified to the patent practitioner so it can be determined who should be identified as a named inventor. All inventors should be listed on the patent application.

Practice Note:
Provide the patent practitioner with the names of all persons who contributed to the invention and explain their contribution.

Sometimes applicants confuse the individuals who are inventors and the individual(s) who merely assisted, supported, and/or supervised the actual inventor. An inventor is someone who comes up with one or more elements of the claimed invention. This includes not only the features that are part of any independent claims, but also the features included in the dependent claims.

However, someone who is merely the "hands of the inventor" is not an inventor. In other words, someone who is asked to build what the inventor came up with is not an inventor, unless in the process of building the invention, he or she adds to the elements of what is ultimately the claimed invention.

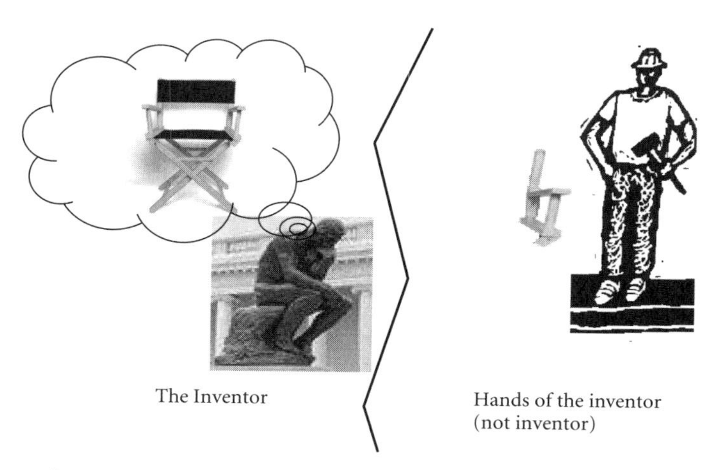

FIGURE 9.2 Inventor vs. Not the Inventor.

Similarly, someone who is merely in charge of the person who is an inventor, and to whom the inventor reports, is not an inventor unless he or she also contributes to the elements of the claimed invention. While the supervisor may be responsible for the project, that, in and of itself, does not make the supervisor an inventor. Of course, when the claimed aspects of the project are also conceived by the supervisor, then the supervisor should be listed as an inventor too.

Also, someone who contributes to the disclosure, but not the claimed invention is not an inventor. The determination of who is the inventor is based on who contributed *to the claims*, not merely who provided technical details which helped explain someone else's invention. Of course, if the details are used to expand upon the claimed invention, then the person who provided the added details would also be an inventor.

Consider again the chair invention from Chapter 3. Assuming Mr. A came up with the concept of the structure of a chair having a flexible rectangular seat, a flexible rectangular back, two arms, and two pairs of crossed legs, as shown in Figure 9.2. Then, Mr. A asked Mr. B to make the chair. In the process of making the chair, Mr. B decided the arms and legs should be made of tempered wood, and the flexible seat and flexible back should be made of a treated wool cloth.

Mr. A, and not Mr. B, would be the only inventor for the following claim:

What is claimed is:

1. A chair, comprising:
    a. a flexible rectangular seat;
    b. a flexible rectangular back;
    c. two arms; and
    d. two pairs of legs, wherein each pair of legs is crossed.

This would remain true, even if the disclosure included a description of the chair being made from the materials selected by Mr. B. However, if a further set of dependent claims directed to these materials, like claims 2 and 3 below, was also included in the application, then Mr. B would also be an inventor:

2. The chair of claim 1, wherein the arms and the legs are comprised of tempered wood.
3. The chair of claim 1, wherein the seat and the back are comprised of treated wool cloth.

FIGURE 9.2 Multiple Inventors.

Further, in the example, if Mr. C owns the organization and charged Mr. A with the task of coming up with a new chair design (and provides no details about what the design should be), and Mr. B with the task of building it, Mr. C would not be an inventor. Mr. C may ultimately be responsible for the chair project, and may even be the owner of the organization that will own the resulting patent, but unless Mr. C came up with at least part of the invention as claimed, he should not be identified as an inventor.

FIGURE 9.3 Inventors vs. Mere Supervisor.

In addition to identifying each of the potential inventors, it is a best practice to identify at least one contribution of each such inventor at the time the patent application is being prepared. This way, the decision to include or exclude particular individuals as inventors can be appropriately defended down the road, if necessary.

Practice Note:
Inform the patent practitioner of the contribution(s) of each inventor.

It is always easier to obtain cooperation and more accurate memories from co-inventors at the time of filing a patent application than it may be down the road after the patent is filed, prosecuted, and/or being implemented.

In determining who should be identified as a named inventor, it is a best practice to consider not only the contributions of each individual involved, but also the contributions of partners and agreements with partners as to who owns the invention.

Failing to include a necessary inventor early on may lead to costly outcomes. Consider, for example, the case *Ethicon, Inc. v. U.S. Surgical Corp.*, one of the leading cases which define the types of contributions that make someone a joint inventor.[10] In *Ethicon*, one of the inventors who was not named at the time the application was prepared and filed was subsequently found to be a joint inventor on the application. Since he had not assigned his patent rights to Ethicon, the accused infringer, U.S. Surgical, was able to enter into a separate licensing agreement with the missing inventor (for substantially less money than Ethicon wanted). This separate agreement was subsequently upheld by the court and resulted in the dismissal of Ethicon's patent suit against U.S. Surgical.

CHAPTER

10

Type of Claim Coverage to Seek

Claims can come in many forms. Understanding what type of claim to seek and how to draft such a claim are important aspects of patent drafting. This chapter discusses

- The parts of a claim;
- Different kinds of objections to claims;
- Common terms used in claims; and
- Different kinds of claims.

10.1 The Parts of a Claim

A claim defines the invention to be protected by the patent. A claim is a single sentence. Sometimes, it can be a very long sentence.

Practice Note:
A claim is a single sentence that defines the invention.

The beginning of the claim is called the "preamble." The preamble generally describes the purpose or intended use of the invention. For example, in the chair claim discussed in Chapter 3, the preamble is the part of the claim that states "A chair, comprising." While limitations found in a preamble can become limitations to a claim, in many instances the preamble may not be considered a limitation of a claim.[1] It is only when terms appearing in a preamble give meaning to the claim and properly define the invention that such terms are deemed limitations of the claim.[2]

The remainder of the claim following a transition word or phrase like "comprising," "consisting of," "consisting essentially of," "having," "including," etc. is referred to as the "body" of the claim.

The core substance of the claim is found in the "body" of the claim. Since the terms in the preamble may not be considered to be limitations, care should be taken to make sure ***all*** the limitations that are thought to be necessary to distinguish the prior art are found in the body of the claim.

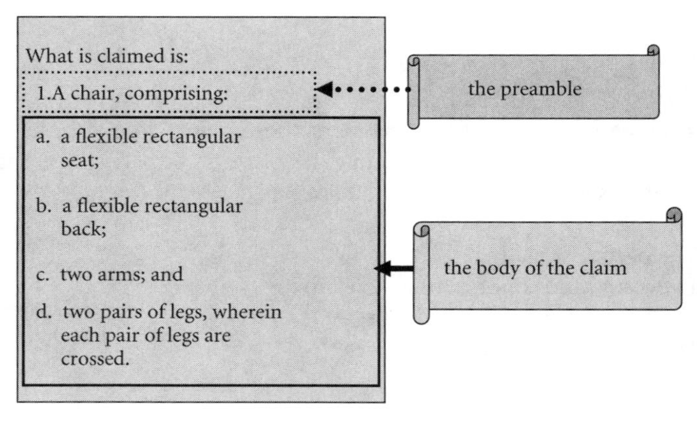

FIGURE 10.1 Parts of Claim.

Practice Note:
The parts of a claim include the preamble, the transition, and the body of the claim.

10.2 Different Kinds of Objections to Claims

As grammar rules exist to govern the proper construction of a sentence in a work of literature, an analogous set of rules exists to govern the structure of a claim in a patent. Thus, when these rules are not followed, there are certain typical "objections" that an examiner can make regarding the form of the claim. These objections to the claim are generally mere formalities which can normally be easily remedied. This section discusses examples of some of the more typical objections that might arise during patent examination of a particular claim including

- Indefiniteness and lack of antecedent basis;
- Not statutory subject matter; and
- Lack of support in the specification.

10.2.1 Indefiniteness and Lack of Antecedent Basis

U.S. patent law requires that a claim particularly point out and distinctly claim the subject matter which the applicant regards as his invention.[3] When the claim does not meet this requirement, it is said to be "indefinite." Examiners will object to claims which are indefinite.

Practice Note:
A claim that fails to particularly point out and distinctly claim an invention is said to be "indefinite."

One type of indefiniteness objection that examiners often make is that a claim term "lacks antecedent basis." In a claim, the same term is supposed to have the same meaning throughout the claim. Thus, the first time a claim term is introduced, that particular claim term should be preceded by an indefinite article like "a," "an," or a number like "one," "two," etc. Each time the same term is referred to thereafter, that claim term should be preceded by a definite article like "the" or "said."

For example, when a claim first refers to "a pair of legs," as in a claim to a chair, the indefinite article "a" is used. Thereafter, when referring to the same pair of legs in the same claim or one of its dependent claims, "*the* pair of legs," or "*said* pair of legs" should be used to indicate that it is the *same* pair of legs as those referred to earlier in that claim or the claim from which it depends.

Sometimes this can lead to awkward-sounding but correctly worded claim terminology. For example, if a claim provides for "at least one arm," a subsequent reference to that element would be "*the* at least one arm" or "*said* at least one arm." Although this may sound odd, such language is intended to make clear that the "arm" (or "arms") being referenced is the same "arm" (or "arms") referenced earlier.

When a claim refers to an item for the first time using a definite article (such as "the" or "said"), the examiner can properly object to the claim for its failure to provide an "antecedent basis" for that claim term.

Similarly, when a claim refers to an item twice with an indefinite article (such as "a" or "an"), it would be proper for the examiner to object to the claim as being "indefinite." For example, if the claim refers twice to "a leg" in the chair example, that reference would be indefinite because it is not clear if there is one "leg" referred to twice or there are two different legs. If there was only intended to be one "leg" claimed, then a definite article like "the" or "said" should be used to refer to the "leg" element the second time "leg" is stated. If there are supposed to be two different legs, then the first time "a leg" is referred to, it should be phrased as "a *first* leg," and the second time "a leg" is referred to it should be phrased as "a *second* leg." Subsequent references to the "first leg," would be preceded by the definite article "the" or "said," like "*the* first leg" or "*said* first leg," and additional or new legs would be referred to as "a *third* leg" and "a *fourth* leg."

However, where the claim refers to "a first leg" and "a second leg," a later reference to "the leg" would also be subject to an objection based on indefiniteness or lack of antecedent basis, since it would be unclear if "the leg" is referring to "the first leg" or "the second leg."

Proper use of definite and indefinite articles insures that the claim is clear and unambiguous.

Practice Note:
Proper use of definite and indefinite articles helps insure that the claim is clear and unambiguous.

10.2.2 Not Statutory Subject Matter

As discussed in Chapter 3, Section 3.4, a claim must be drafted to cover patent-eligible subject matter in order to be patent-eligible subject matter.[4] In recent years, the USPTO has become more vigilant in objecting to claims on the grounds that a claim is not directed to "statutory subject matter" under 35 U.S.C. § 101 (in other words, when the subject matter of the claim is not considered to be patent-eligible). If a claim is not directed to one of the appropriate statutory classes of subject matter (processes, machines, manufactures, and compositions of matter), the examiner will likely object to the claim as being directed to non-statutory subject matter. For many claims, addressing this objection usually requires redrafting the claim. However, for some types of claims, it may not be possible to overcome this objection and still obtain meaningful patent protection.

10.2.3 Lack of Support in the Specification

U.S. patent law further requires that the specification contain a written description of the invention and of the manner and process of making and using it.[5] This means that each element in a claim should be supported by the description found in the specification. When an applicant attempts to present a claim which covers subject matter that is outside the original disclosure of the specification, the examiner is likely to object to such a claim as not being supported by the specification or lacking "written description." This type of form objection, when properly made by the examiner, may be difficult to overcome without removing the new subject matter from the claim, or filing a new patent application covering the new subject matter, and thus losing the benefit of the original filing date.

10.3 Common Terms Used in Patent Claims

While the choice of potential claim terms is as varied as the English language itself, there are certain common terms patent draftsmen use which have commonly accepted meanings when found in a claim. This section provides a brief explanation of some of these commonly used terms and their judicially espoused meanings in the ordinary course of patent practice, including

- "Comprising" versus "composing" versus "including";
- Numbers;
- "First," "second," "third," etc.;
- "The" and "said"; and
- Terms of degree.

While the meanings of these terms discussed here are the presumptive meanings, claim construction, as discussed Chapter 11, is always based on the context of the particular patent claim at issue. Thus, it is possible in a given context, that although the ordinary meaning of a term like "a" may mean "one or more," in the context of a particular patent claim, that term may nonetheless be limited to a particular meaning such as "one."[6]

10.3.1 "Comprising" versus "Composing" versus "Including"

Between the preamble of a claim and the body of a claim, there is usually a transition word like "comprising," "composing," "including," "containing," "having," "characterized by," etc. When used in patent claims, these transition words generally have well-understood meaning.

Some transition words, like "comprising," are understood to mean the concept of including, but not limited to. Thus, the elements of a claim that are found after the word "comprising" are generally understood to be essential elements necessary to meet the claim, but do not preclude the addition of other elements.[7] Thus, for example, in the chair claim, when the claim is for "a chair, *comprising* four legs, a seat, and a back," this claim language would require each of those elements to be present in an infringing chair, but would not preclude an infringing chair from also having a seat cushion or some other structure. The transition term "comprising" is thus referred to as an "open-ended" transition word. Other words that are typically construed as open-ended transition words are "including," "containing," "characterized by," and "mixture."[8]

Practice Note:
An "open-ended" transition, like "comprising," is understood to mean including at least the listed elements, and perhaps others.

A claim may also be drafted to be closed-ended by using a transition phrase such as "consisting of." This transition conveys the concept that the claim requires that the listed elements be present, and that no other elements can be present.[9] Thus, in the chair example, a claim which reads "A chair *consisting of* four legs, a seat, and a back," would not read on a chair that also had a seat cushion.

Practice Note:
A "closed-ended" transition, like "consisting of," is understood to mean including *only* the listed elements, and no other elements.

Sometimes a claim intends to be generally, but not absolutely, closed-ended. This is particularly true for claims that are directed to chemical compositions. In such circumstances, transition phrases like "consisting essentially of" are used to convey the concept that all of the elements are necessary and that only trace or minimal presence of other elements can be present.[10] Thus, in the salt example, "A table salt, *consisting essentially* of 40%–60% mol. weight sodium and 40%–60% mol. weight potassium," would require an infringing table salt to have sodium and potassium in the designated mole weights, but would allow for trace elements of other elements or compounds (such as iodine perhaps) to be present.

Practice Note:

Some transitions, like "consisting essentially of," are understood to mean including the listed elements, and no other significant elements.

Certain terms, such as "having," may be construed as either open-ended or closed-ended, depending upon the context in which the term is used.[11]

Although these transition terms in patent claims are generally understood to have the meanings as discussed in this section, every claim must be read in the context of the patent in which it is contained and the prosecution history which led to the issuance of the particular claim. In that context, courts have recognized that even these well-understood meanings could be inapplicable for a particular claim or in a particular context.

10.3.2 Numbers

Typically, when a claim uses a numerical term, it can have one of two different meanings, depending upon the transition word or phrase used in the claim and the context of the numerical term.

- The claim could be limited to the specific number identified, and no more. For example, "a chair consisting of four legs" has four legs, not five legs, and not merely three legs;[12] or
- The claim could be interpreted to require that at least the specific number of items is present, but more items could also be present and still meet the claim. Thus, for example, "a chair, comprising four legs," may have four legs, five legs, six legs, etc., but would not have merely one, two, or three legs.

A claim in which a specific number has been identified, such as "four" in the first example, is typically closed-ended when using a closed-ended word like "consisting of," as in the first example.

Conversely, a claim in which a specific number has been identified, such as "four" in the second example, is typically open-ended when using an open-ended word like "comprising," as in the second example.

However, if the intrinsic record (e.g., the claims, the specification, and the prosecution history, *see* Chapter 11) requires otherwise, a court may reach a different interpretation.[13]

Typically, when a claim refers to an item with an indefinite article like "a" or "an," it is interpreted to mean "one or more" items. However, when the intrinsic evidence requires it to mean "one and only one" item, courts have adopted such constructions.[14]

Finally, another common numerical term used in patent claims is "plurality," which generally means "more than one" or "two or more."[15]

10.3.3 "First," "Second," "Third," etc.

As discussed above, when a claim contains multiple different elements that are the same kind of thing, like a chair with four legs, and each element (e.g., each leg) is specified separately in a claim, patent draftsmen use the adjectives like "first," "second," "third," etc. to distinguish between different specific elements being referenced.[16]

Thus, in a case when a court was faced with a claim providing "a safety razor blade unit comprising a guard, a cap, and a group of *first, second* and *third* blades," the court recognized that reference to "first," "second," and "third" blades in the claim was not used to show a serial or numerical limitation but instead was used to distinguish or identify the various members of the group.[17]

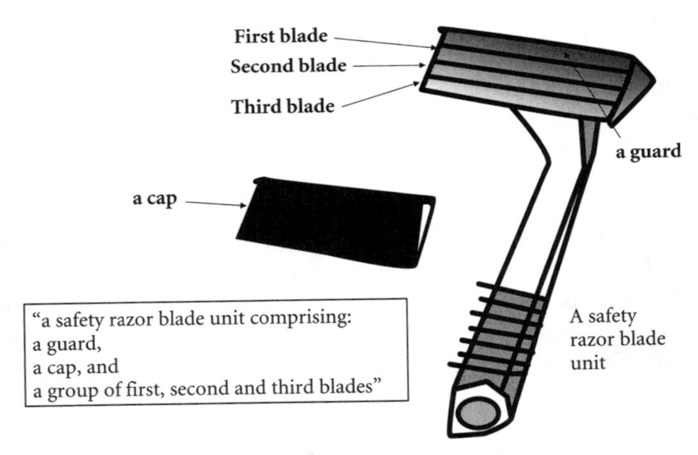

FIGURE 10.2 Use of "First", "Second", "Third", etc., in a Claim.

10.3.4 "The" and "Said"

Definite article, like "the" and "said," are used to refer to an item that has already been specified earlier in the claim. The first time the item is referred to, as discussed above, it should be identified with an indefinite article, like "a" or "an." Every additional reference to that item should be made with a definite article, like "the" or "said." Patent claims are intended to rigidly follow this grammar rule.

10.3.5 Terms of Degree

Claims draftsmen often do not want to be limited to precise ranges or features. Thus, terms of degree may be used as adjectives.

For example, instead of saying a range of "5 cm to 10 cm," the range may be qualified by the term "*about* 5 cm to *about* 10 cm." The qualifier "about" would add a degree of leeway, which could result in 4.9 cm or 10.1 cm coming within the claimed range.[18]

Similarly, instead of referring to a surface as being "flat," a draftsman might refer to the surface as being "*substantially* flat" or "*generally* flat." The term "generally," like the term "substantially," is a term of approximation.[19] It means the surface is approximately, rather than perfectly, flat.[20] Often, absent specific teaching in the intrinsic record, these terms are construed as not requiring a specific numerical limitation.[21]

10.4 Different Kinds of Claims

Claims can come in different forms. As discussed in Chapter 3, there are various statutory classes of patent-eligible subject matter:

- Processes;
- Machines;
- Manufactures; and
- Compositions of matter.[22]

These different classes of patent-eligible subject matter transcend into different types of claims:

- Method claims, including methods of manufacture and methods of use claims;
- Device or apparatus claims;
- System claims; and
- Composition claims.

Thus, "processes" may be claimed as "method" claims. Method claims can come in different forms. For example, one type of method claim may be a "method of manufacturing" something. In the chair example, a claim could be directed to "a method of manufacturing a chair, wherein the method comprises" a series of specific steps involved in building a chair.

Another type of method claim is a "method of using" claim. In the razor blade example discussed above, a claim could be directed to "a method of using a razor blade to shave, wherein the method comprises" a series of steps involved in using the razor blade.

"Machines" and "manufactures" can be claimed as "apparatus" claims or "system" claims.

An "apparatus" claim claims a particular type of apparatus. In the chair example, a claim could be directed to "a chair, comprising" various parts.

When many different parts or devices are put together in a system, like a computer system, these elements can be claimed collectively in a "system" claim, like "a computer system, comprising. . . ."

Another more unusual form of claim is a so-called "product-by-process" claim. This type of claim claims a particular product made by a particular process, such as "a chair, comprising a seat and four legs *glued* to the seat." In this exemplary claim, the chair to which the legs are attached by a method other than gluing, like nailing the legs to the seat, would not infringe the claim literally.[23]

Compositions may also be claimed. In the "table salt" example above, a claim could be drafted as "a table salt consisting essentially of" various chemical components.

Finally, another type of claim, which is borrowed from European Patent practice, is the so-called "*Jepson*" claim.[24] It is named after the legal case[25] that said the Jepson format is an appropriate claim format in the United States. A *Jepson* claim recites in the preamble all the elements that were present in the prior art and uses as the transition phrase "the improvement comprising," followed by the elements that would not be present in the prior art. When claims are drafted in *Jepson* format, U.S. patent law takes that form of claim as an implied admission that the subject mater of the preamble is the prior art work of another.[26] However, this implication may be overcome where an applicant gives another credible reason for drafting the claim in *Jepson* format.[27]

Ultimately, a patent application (or family of related patent applications) may include one or more of these different types of claims to maximize the patent protection in different implementations of an invention.

CHAPTER

11

How to Construe a Patent Claim

A patent is defined by its claims. To understand what a patent covers, it is important to understand what the claim covers. In other words, how a claim is read and interpreted (or "construed")?

U.S. patent law recognizes that the first step in determining whether a claim is valid or infringed is for a court to properly determine the meaning and scope of the claims at issue.[1] Thus, it is important to understand how to read a claim. Likewise, it is important to understand that the same meaning or "construction" of a claim applies whether the analysis being performed is a determination of validity or infringement.[2]

Practice Note:

Determining the meaning of a claim is the first step in a validity or infringement analysis.

It is a "bedrock principle" of U.S. patent law that "the claims of a patent define the invention to which the patentee is entitled the right to exclude."[3] In interpreting patent claims, U.S. patent law directs that publicly available sources should be examined to define what a person of ordinary skill in the art would have understood the disputed claim language to mean.[4] Publicly available sources include:

- The words of the claims themselves;
- The remainder of the specification;
- The prosecution history; and
- Certain extrinsic evidence concerning relevant scientific principles, the meaning of technical terms, and the state of the art.[5]

The words of the claims, the remainder of the specification, and the prosecution history are often called the "intrinsic" evidence, because this information is part of the patent itself and is publicly available so that everyone has access to it. This type of information is considered the most relevant information.

Practice Note:

The best sources for claim construction are "intrinsic" evidence, which includes the words of the claims, the remainder of the specification, and the prosecution history.

Evidence from outside the patent itself and the other intrinsic evidence are referred to as "extrinsic evidence."[6] Some kinds of extrinsic evidence may also potentially be considered, but U.S. patent law prefers objective forms of extrinsic evidence, such as

- Relevant scientific principles;
- The meaning of technical terms, preferably from objective learned treatises; and
- The state of the art, which is usually defined by analyzing the relevant prior art.

Practice Note:

Some forms of "extrinsic" evidence may also be considered, but objective forms are preferred.

The process of construing a claim can at times be very complex and may not give each kind of evidence discussed in this chapter the same weight in every circumstance. However, it is useful to understand what kinds of evidence may be considered to construe a claim limitation in general, so that when faced with claim construction, issue-spotting can be more effectively performed. Nonetheless, it should be kept in mind that this Guide only presents general guidelines to assist in the issue-spotting process, and that particular application of these principles (and other principles not discussed herein) requires the assistance of an experienced and competent patent practitioner.

11.1 Intrinsic Evidence

11.1.1 The Claim Itself

The starting point for determining the meaning of a patent claim is the claim language itself.[7] U.S. patent law recognizes that the claims themselves provide "substantial guidance" as to the meaning of particular claim terms.[8] Thus, in construing a particular claim term, U.S. courts may look to

- The context of a claim term's use within the claim; and
- The use of the same claim term or similar claim terms in other claims.[9]

First, U.S. patent law recognizes that other terms used in conjunction with a particular claim term can be useful when construing a claim term's meaning.

Practice Note:
The way a claim term is used in conjunction with other terms in the claim is useful in construing the claim term's meaning.

For example, in one case, the court was tasked with construing the term "ingredients" as it was used in the phrase, "a mixture of solid and lipid *ingredients*." The dictionary definitions recognize that the term "ingredient" can refer to either

- The *starting* materials, as in a recipe, for example; or
- The components of a mixture *after* they have been combined.

It was also recognized that the term "mixture" means "a portion of matter consisting of two or more components in varying proportions that retained their own properties." In other words, a mixture refers to a combination of ingredients after they had been combined. Thus, the court in this context found the surrounding claim language to "strongly suggest[] that 'ingredients' refers to the components *after* they have been combined to form that 'mixture.'"[10]

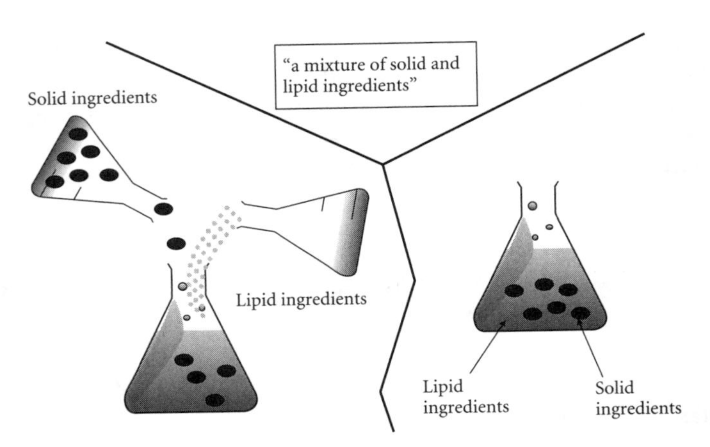

FIGURE 11.1 Interpreting "Mixture" using Context of Claim.

In another case, the court was tasked with construing the phrase "along a line" as that phrase was used in a claim for a method of using a catheter which provided that "the catheter body engages the opposite wall of the aorta *along a line* having a length of about 1.5 cm or greater." The accused infringer argued that "along a line" required that "a line" be inherently "straight," relying on the ordinary meaning of the term "line." The court rejected this construction because, in the context of the claim language quoted above, this phrase "refers to the position of the catheter as it is being used in the human body rather than the shape of the catheter in its rest state." Thus, the court found that "[b]ecause 'along a line' describes the contact portion of the catheter in its engaged state, [the claim] does not inherently require the contact portion of the catheter to be straight in its rest state."[11]

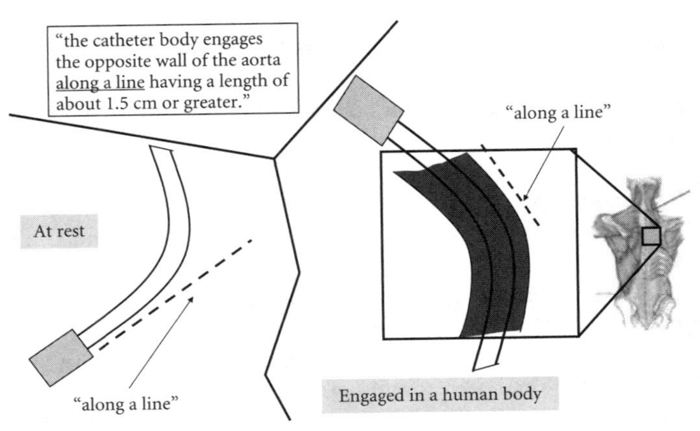

FIGURE 11.2 Interpreting "Along a Line" using Context of Invention.

Similarly, U.S. patent law also recognizes that the relationship of the use of a claim term to other claims, both asserted and unasserted, can be used to construe the meaning of the claim term.[12] Thus, U.S. patent law presumes that claim terms are "normally used consistently throughout the patent," and assumes that "differences among claims" raise "a presumption" that the different terms mean different things.[13] Further, U.S. patent law is reluctant to adopt claim constructions of terms which would contradict the use of that term in other claims.[14]

Practice Note:
The way the claim term is used in other claims helps to construe the claim term's meaning.

For example, a court was tasked with interpreting the phrase "*partially* hidden from view." The court rejected a construction of "*generally* hidden from view" or "*at least* partially hidden from view," when the patentee used the terms "generally" and "at least" elsewhere in the claims. The court's reasoning was that if the patentee wanted to cover the concept of "*generally* hidden from view" or "*at least* partially hidden from view," in this instance the patentee knew what language to use to do so. The failure to use such language in one limitation, while using it in others, suggested that the claim was not intended to have such a meaning.[15]

However, these presumptions are not rigid rules. Therefore, one of these presumptions can be overcome by a definition that is otherwise clear from the claim language, description, and/or prosecution history.[16]

Practice Note:
Claim construction maxims are not intended to be rigid rules, but merely guideposts to claim construction.

11.1.2 Patent Specification

The patent specification is the portion of the patent that contains a written explanation of the invention and teaches the public how to make and use the invention.[17]

U.S. patent law recognizes that the patent specification is also relevant to the determination of a disputed claim term's meaning.[18] Thus, U.S. patent law instructs that a claim should be construed "not only in the context of the particular claim in which the disputed term appears, but in the context of the entire patent, including the specification."[19]

Practice Note:
The patent specification should be considered as part of the claim construction process.

In particular, U.S. patent law examines the specification to determine whether

- A special definition has been provided for a claim term;[20]
- Any disclaimers or disavowals as to scope of patent protection were provided; [21] and
- A proposed construction is consistent with the preferred embodiments disclosed.[22]

While words and terms used in a claim are generally given their ordinary and customary meaning as understood by one of ordinary skill in the art,[23] a patentee may choose to be his or her own lexicographer and use terms in a manner different from their ordinary meaning, provided that the patentee's definition is clearly set forth in the specification.[24] Thus, "it is always necessary to review the specification to determine whether the inventor has used any terms in a manner inconsistent with their ordinary meaning."[25] "The specification acts as a dictionary when it expressly defines terms used in the claims or when it defines terms by implication."[26] After all, the specification "is the single best guide to the meaning of a disputed term."[27]

While it is not proper to read a limitation into a claim from the written description, it is proper to look to the written description to define a term already found in a claim limitation.[28] Thus, with this rule in mind, courts have adopted interpretations of claim terms using seemingly uncommon definitions based on the context of the disclosure and the relevant prosecution history.

For example, in one case, a court was tasked with construing the term "board," as used in a claim directed to "A decking *board* for use in constructing a flooring surface for exterior use. . . ." Although the claim did not include other language that limited the term "board" to boards made from "wood cut from a log," the specification itself and the prosecution history made it clear that the term "board" was limited to wood cut from a log. Further, throughout the written description, the context of the invention was limited to the situation where the boards are made from wood cut from a log. This context was reinforced by arguments made during prosecution.[29]

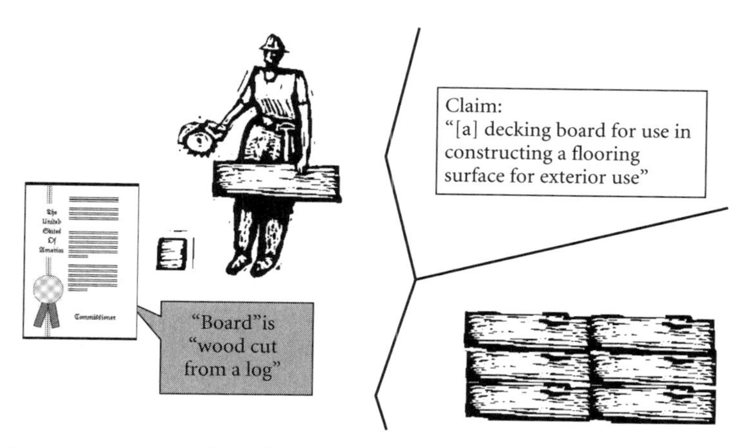

FIGURE 11.3 Interpreting "Board" using Written Description.

Finally, while U.S. patent law will generally not limit a claim term to a preferred embodiment in the specification,[30] it likewise will try not to adopt a claim construction which would not read on a preferred embodiment from the specification.[31] Nonetheless, exceptions to both of these guidelines can be found in the case law.[32]

11.1.3 Prosecution History

The "prosecution history" is the contemporaneous back and forth between the patent applicant and the USPTO.[33] U.S. patent law recognizes that the prosecution history of a patent should be considered in determining the meaning of a claim.[34]

Practice Note:
The prosecution history should be considered as part of the claim construction process.

For example, in one case, a court was tasked with interpreting the term "downwardly" in the claim phrase "each of said driving surfaces extending *downwardly*." The accused infringer argued that the driving surface could only be planar surfaces (as shown in the patent) and not curved surfaces (as was used in the accused device). The court agreed because the patentee distinguished prior art based on this distinction in arguments before the USPTO to get the patent.[35]

Even non-dispositive statements made during prosecution have resulted in claim constructions which have limited the meaning of claim terms extensively.

This is illustrated by the case where a court was tasked with construing what the "outer surface" meant in the context of a claim limitation that read "drive collar . . . having an *outer surface* defining a drive head that accepts a driving mechanism." The accused infringer argued that the "outer surface" was required to be the exterior outer surface of the drive collar, rather than an interior outer surface, as was used in the accused device. During the prosecution, the patentee made the *unsuccessful* argument that the prior art "appears to be cylindrical *on the outside*, thus impractical for being rotated by a mine roof bolting machine." Although this argument was ultimately not relied upon by the examiner in granting the claims, the court nonetheless used this argument to support its construction that the patentee during prosecution disclaimed a construction of the claim which did not limit the "outer surface" to the "exterior" outer surface.[36]

11.1.4 Prior Art

U.S. patent law also recognizes that the state of the art, which includes the cited prior art (and potentially uncited prior art), may play a role in claim construction.

Practice Note:
Prior art may be considered as part of the claim construction process.

Based on the state of the art, courts have used the prior art to assist in construing terms that might otherwise be considered imprecise.

For example, in one case, a court was tasked with interpreting the claim term "pharmaceutically effective amount." Ultimately, the court adopted a construction which required 2.5 to 15 mg/day based on what one of ordinary skill in the art would understand to be the FDA approved dosage, even though this range was not explicitly disclosed in the specification.[37]

Likewise, in another case, a court was tasked with interpreting the phrase "relatively small." Using the prior art to specify ranges that should not be construed to be within the scope of the claim, the court adopted a construction which included the range "about .015–.040."[38]

11.2 Extrinsic Evidence

U.S. patent law will also consider certain types of extrinsic evidence in claim construction. Extrinsic evidence is all evidence external to the patent and prosecution history, including

- Dictionaries and learned treatises;
- Expert testimony;
- Inventor testimony; and
- Prosecuting attorney testimony.[39]

These sources may be used as long as the court assigns the source an appropriate weight.[40]

11.2.1 Dictionaries and Treatises

One source outside of the patent itself that U.S. patent law recognizes may be appropriate to rely upon in order to understand what a claim term means is a dictionary or a learned treatise. The use of a dictionary is particularly appropriate when the patent itself and its prosecution history do not define a particular claim term.[41]

Practice Note:

Dictionaries and learned treatises may also be considered as part of the claim construction process.

Thus, for example, courts have turned to dictionaries like the OXFORD ENGLISH DICTIONARY to inform their understanding of how to interpret the ordinary meaning of words in a claim. In one case, the court turned to such a dictionary to help it interpret the word "hold" in the phrase "*hold*ing a wafer" in a claim.[42] In another case, a different court turned to a dictionary to help it interpret the word "opener" in the phrase "housing part *opener*."[43] Similarly, in the example above regarding "*partially* hidden from view," that court looked to several dictionaries which confirmed its meaning "to some extent."[44]

Ultimately, U.S. patent law allows the use of dictionaries since they are considered an objective, third-party source which can help inform the court as to what someone of ordinary skill in the art would understand a particular phrase or term to mean.

Of course, courts are not supposed to use dictionaries blindly, or to adopt meanings of claim terms that contradict the teachings of the specification or prosecution history.[45] In this regard, U.S. patent law cautions against the overuse of dictionaries as follows:

> The main problem with elevating the dictionary to such prominence is that it focuses the inquiry on the abstract meaning of words rather than on the meaning of claim terms within the context of the patent. Properly viewed, the 'ordinary meaning' of a claim term is its meaning to the ordinary artisan after reading the entire patent. Yet heavy reliance on the dictionary divorced from the intrinsic evidence risks transforming the meaning of the claim term to the artisan into the meaning of the term in the abstract, out of its particular context, which is the specification. . . . The use of a dictionary definition can conflict with that directive because the patent applicant did not create the dictionary to describe the invention.[46]

Thus, it is important to be informed of what a dictionary may say about a particular term's meaning, but not to over-rely upon such a definition.

11.2.2 Experts

U.S. patent law allows a court to look to a technical expert in order to gain a general understanding of the background of the art as a backdrop to claim interpretation.[47] Such an expert must be one of ordinary skill in the relevant art.[48] However, when an expert provides "only conclusory legal opinions . . . rather than evidence of how that term is commonly used and understood in the art," that testimony cannot be used to alter the definition in the specification and prosecution history, which controls.[49] The use of experts in the claim construction process is generally confined to a very limited role.

Practice Note:
Experts should play only a limited role in the claim construction process.

11.2.3 Inventor Testimony

An inventor's testimony is often sought in patent litigation. Such testimony, in certain circumstances, may be relevant extrinsic evidence. Generally, U.S. patent law is not interested in an inventor's "subjective intent," since, if it is not part of the public record, it should not be part of a claim construction analysis.[50] But, an inventor's testimony may be relevant to provide a background as to the claimed invention and its development.[51] Further, an inventor's admission of what the invention is or is not, when it is counter the litigation assertion, can be relevant testimony.

Practice Note:

An inventor's testimony should only play a limited role in the claim construction process.

11.2.4 Prosecuting Attorney Testimony

A prosecuting attorney's testimony is also often sought in patent litigation. Prosecuting attorneys can help explain facts that occur in the prosecution of a patent before the USPTO, which might not otherwise be readily available in the prosecution history. Like an inventor's testimony, a prosecution attorney's "subjective intent" as to a meaning of a claim term is considered by U.S. patent law to be entitled to "little or no weight" in determining the scope of the claims, except as documented in the prosecution history.[52]

Practice Note:

A prosecuting attorney's testimony should only play a limited role as part of the claim construction process.

11.3 Claim Construction Maxims

When a claim is otherwise ambiguous based on a review of the intrinsic evidence, a court may look to one or more claim construction maxims to help guide it in selecting the proper claim construction.

Practice Note:

Courts may use claim construction maxims as guideposts to assist in the claim construction process.

One such maxim provides that claim terms should be interpreted consistently in different claims, if possible.[53] This maxim has even been applied, in certain circumstances, to provide that the same terms, as used in different claims and in different, but related patents, should be interpreted to mean the same thing.[54]

Practice Note:
Claim terms should be interpreted consistently, if possible.

Another claim construction maxim provides that meaning should be given to all words in a claim, if possible.[55]

Practice Note:
Meaning should be given to all words in a claim, if possible.

On the one hand, a construction that does not read on a preferred embodiment from the specification is "rarely, if ever, correct."[56] On the other hand, without more,[57] the court will not limit claim terms to a preferred embodiment described in the specification.[58] Nonetheless, exceptions to both of these guidelines can be found in the case law.

Practice Note:
Claims should be construed to read on preferred embodiments, but not necessarily be limited to preferred embodiments.

Another claim construction maxim often invoked is the so-called "doctrine of claim differentiation." This doctrine has been summed up as follows:

> There is presumed to be a difference in meaning and scope when different words or phrases are used in separate claims. To the extent that the absence of such difference in meaning and scope would make a claim superfluous, the doctrine of claim differentiation states the presumption that the difference between the claims is significant.[59]

The Federal Circuit has also gone on to caution, "[h]owever, the doctrine of claim differentiation *does not serve to broaden claims* beyond their meaning in light of the specification and *does not override clear statements of scope in the specification and the prosecution history.*"[60] This same caution applies to each of these maxims.

Practice Note:
Differences between claims are presumed to be significant.

A further corollary to the doctrine of claim differentiation is that a properly stated dependent claim should be narrower in scope than the claim from which it depends. Thus, without more, a construction of a term in an independent claim which does not also encompass the limitations of its dependent claims is presumptively incorrect.[61]

Another construction maxim is, when there is a choice between two constructions, and one construction would invalidate the claim, and the other construction would preserve the validity of the claim, the construction which preserves the validity of the claim should be adopted.[62] However, this does not mean that a court will read a limitation into a claim that is not otherwise present.[63]

Practice Note:
If otherwise ambiguous, a narrower interpretation that preserves validity should be chosen over a broader interpretation that does not.

A corollary of this maxim is:

> Where there is an equal choice between a broader and a narrower meaning of a claim, and there is an enabling disclosure that indicates that the applicant is at least entitled to a claim having the narrower meaning, we consider the notice function of the claim to be best served by adopting the narrower meaning.[64]

This corollary has also been restated as:

> [W]here a claim is ambiguous as to its scope [the Court has] adopted a narrowing construction when doing so would still serve the notice function of the claims.[65]

However, it is important to recognize that none of these claim construction maxims are absolute. Each of them can be overcome by the intrinsic record.

CHAPTER

12

How to Determine Infringement of a Patent Claim

In order to determine whether a claim is infringed by a particular product or process, U.S. patent law provides for a two-step process to be followed.

- The claim must be construed as discussed in Chapter 11;
- Each of the elements of the claim, as properly construed, must be found in the accused device or process, either literally or under the doctrine of equivalents.

The U.S. Supreme Court has confirmed that the first step (construing the claim) is a question of law, to be decided by a judge. By contrast, the U.S. Supreme Court has confirmed that the second step (applying the claim to the accused device or process) is a question of fact to be decided by the fact finder, which in most patent infringement actions will be the jury.[1] This chapter addresses the second step, i.e., how to determine if a claim has been infringed.

12.1 All Elements of the Claim Must Be Present Literally or by Their Equivalents

In the second step of an infringement analysis, the properly construed claim must be compared to the accused device or method to determine whether each and every limitation of the claim is met by the accused device or process.[2]

In this analysis, in order to establish infringement, it is necessary to establish that each of the limitations of the asserted claim is present, either literally or by substantial equivalents, in the accused device or process.[3] The U.S. Supreme Court has made it abundantly clear that the failure of an accused device or process to include even one element required by the claim is fatal to an assertion of patent infringement.[4]

Practice Note:
Each of the limitations of an asserted claim must be present, either literally or by substantial equivalents, in an accused device or process.

A claim limitation is literally met when that limitation, as written and properly construed, can be met by a particular element in an accused device or process.

Practice Note:
A limitation is literally met when the limitation, as written and properly construed, is met by a particular element in an accused device or process.

Assume the chair claim were to read as follows:

What is claimed is:
1. A chair, comprising: a. a flexible rectangular seat; b. a flexible rectangular back; c. two arms; and d. two pairs of legs, wherein each pair of legs is crossed.

In order to determine if the chair in Figure 12.1 in literally infringed, each of the elements of the chair claim, above, would need to be compared and matched with a corresponding structure in the chair.

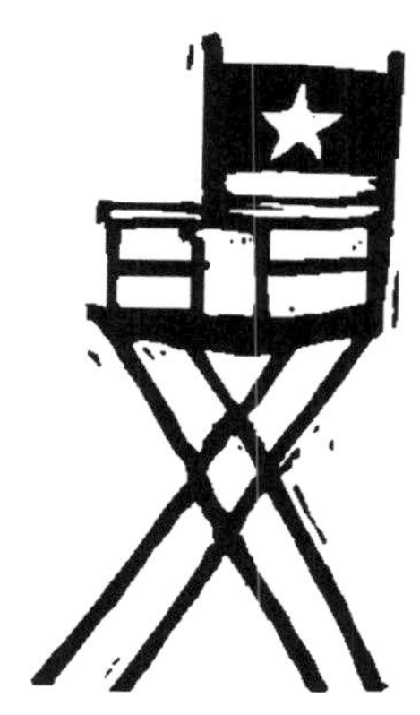

FIGURE 12.1 The Accused Chair.

In this case, it is a relatively simple process as the following diagram shows:

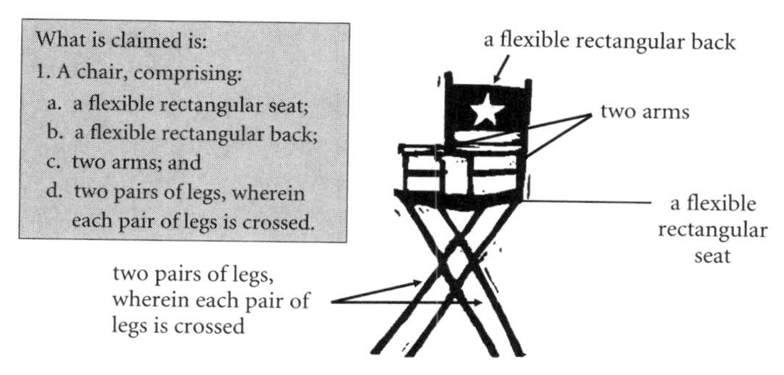

FIGURE 12.2 How the Accused Chair Infringes Claim 1.

Since each of the limitations in the claim, i.e., "a flexible rectangular seat," "a flexible rectangular back," "two arms," and "two pairs of legs, where each pair of legs is crossed" is each found in the accused new chair, the accused new chair would be found to "literally" infringe this claim.

Sometimes there are minor, insubstantial differences between a claim term as written and an accused device or process. U.S. patent law recognizes that if the differences are merely insubstantial, and the accused device contains an "equivalent" of the missing element, then the claim would still be infringed under the "doctrine of equivalents."

Practice Note:

A claim element which is not literally present may still be met if the substantial equivalent of the missing element is present in an accused device or process.

One way to determine equivalency is by analyzing whether the accused element performs the same function, in the same way, to achieve the same result as that called for by the allegedly corresponding claim element. This type of analysis is referred to as the "Function-Way-Result" test. The point of the Function-Way-Result test is to determine whether there is a substantial difference between the asserted claim element and the alleged equivalent.[5]

Practice Note:

One way of showing that an allegedly corresponding structure is not substantially different is the "Function-Way-Result" test.

The application of the doctrine of equivalents is exemplified by a case where a jury was asked to determine whether a catheter with a "curved portion" was the equivalent of a claimed catheter which required a "straight" and "substantially straight" portion. The jury found the claim to be met by the doctrine of equivalents, and the trial court and appellate court sustained the verdict.

The Federal Circuit found that this verdict was supported by expert testimony which established that differences in shape between the curve portion of the accused XB catheter and the straight or substantially straight portion of the asserted claims was "insubstantial" and met the Function-Way-Result test.

- *Insubstantial differences* were established by evidence that cardiologists (i.e., persons of ordinary skill in the art) would have difficulty distinguishing the two during use.

The *Function-Way-Result* test was also shown to be met by expert testimony as follows:

- *Function:* The curve portion of the accused "XB" catheter and the straight and substantially straight portions in the claims provide backup support for the catheter during use. Indeed, the name "XB" stands for "extra backup." Also, while the curve portion made the product easier to manufacture, it did not alter the XB catheter's functionality.

- *Way:* The curve portion of the accused XB catheter and the straight and substantially straight portions in the claims both engage the wall of the aorta at a particular location for a substantial length during use. The length of engagement by the curve portion during use was explained to be indistinguishable from the length of engagement in the claims.
- *Result:* The curve portion of the accused XB catheter and the straight and substantially straight portions in the claims both achieve the same *result* by making it difficult to dislodge the guide catheter from its desired orientation during use.[6]

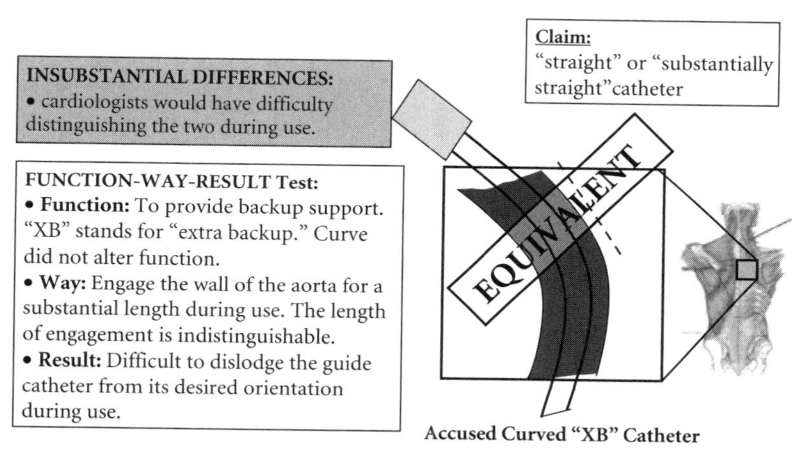

FIGURE 12.3 Infringement under Doctrine of Equivalents.

However, there can be *no* infringement under the doctrine of equivalents in instances where the inventor has already given up the right to cover such a product during the prosecution of the patent.[7] This principle is known as the "doctrine of prosecution history estoppel." Application of this principle is a question of law to be decided by a court.[8]

Practice Note:
The doctrine of equivalents cannot recapture what was given up during prosecution.

To determine the scope of prosecution history estoppel, U.S. patent law objectively examines whether a competitor would reasonably conclude that an applicant's conduct during prosecution surrendered the disputed subject matter.[9] An estoppel can be created either by an amendment to a claim during prosecution or by arguments made about a claim during prosecution.[10]

Indeed, allowing a jury to find infringement in the face of prosecution history estoppel is a reversible error.[11]

When an amendment is made to a claim during prosecution for reasons related to patentability, absent certain special circumstances, U.S. patent law will preclude the doctrine of equivalents from being used to read a claim element on those activities which would have been within the scope of the claim prior to amendment, but were thereafter excluded as a result of the narrowing amendment.[12]

In the chair example above, assuming that the original claim presented in the application merely recited as an element of the claim "a seat," and that in response to the USPTO's citing the flyer prior art against the claim it was amended to recite "a *flexible* seat," then the patentee would be precluded from asserting that a seat that was rigid is the equivalent of a "flexible" seat due to prosecution history estoppel.

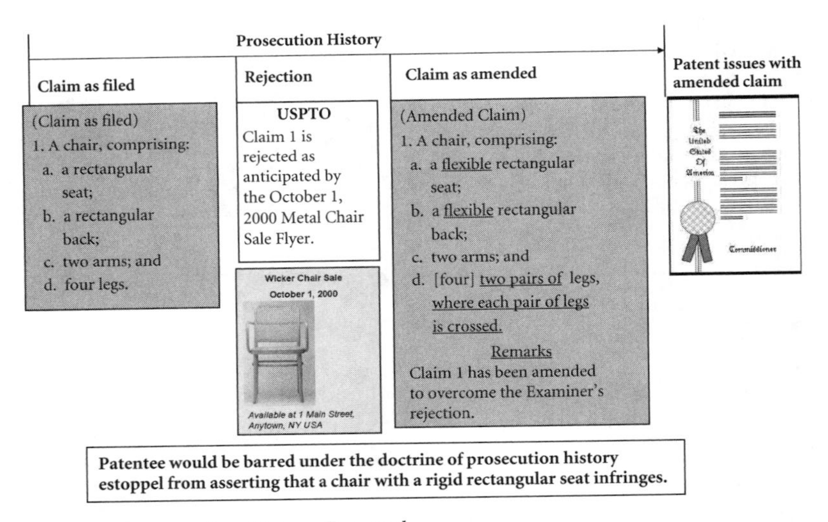

FIGURE 12.4 Prosecution History Estoppel.

U.S. patent law recognizes that a narrowing amendment only raises a presumption to preclude a claim of infringement under the doctrine of equivalents.[13] This presumption does not apply when the amendment in question is not narrowing. It also does not apply, when

- The equivalent was unforeseeable at the time of the amendment;
- The rationale behind the amendment bears no more than a tangential relationship to the asserted equivalent; or
- There exists some other reason as to why the patentee could not have reasonably been expected to describe the asserted equivalent.[14]

Practice Note:

The presumption against asserting equivalents when amendments are made during prosecution may be overcome in certain circumstances.

Another way that U.S. patent law restricts the doctrine of equivalents is that the doctrine cannot expand the scope of a claim so as to encompass subject matter that was disclosed in the specification, but not claimed.[15] The rationale behind this limitation is that it would not have been unforeseeable for the claims draftsmen to anticipate the features disclosed in the specification and draft a claim to cover it. By not drafting a claim that clearly read on the embodiment disclosed, U.S. patent law presumes that the patentee should not be entitled to later assert that the narrowly drafted claim should encompass the broader subject matter.

In addition, the scope of equivalents is determined in the light of prior art. The doctrine of equivalents cannot expand the scope of a claim so as to encompass what is already disclosed in the prior art.[16] Thus, as part of an inquiry under the doctrine of equivalents, U.S. patent law requires that the prior art be examined to assure that the range of equivalents asserted by the patentee does not encompass the prior art.[17]

Finally, under the "All Elements Rule," the doctrine of equivalents cannot be used to write a limitation out of a claim.[18] Thus, when a claim requires a "majority," the doctrine of equivalents cannot make the claim read on a "minority."[19] Similarly, when a claim requires that a slot "extend over" the top, the doctrine of equivalents cannot make the claim read on something with a slot that is "under" the top.[20]

Practice Note:

The Doctrine of Equivalents cannot be used to read elements out of a claim under the "All Elements Rule."

To the extent it is determined that an independent claim of a patent is not infringed, it is unnecessary to consider the dependent claims. As a general rule in U.S. patent law, a dependent claim cannot be infringed by an accused device or method which does not infringe the claims from which it depends.[21]

Practice Note:

If an independent claim is not infringed, then by definition, neither are its dependent claims.

12.2 Direct Infringement

A claim of a U.S. Patent is said to be directly infringed when someone, without authority and during the term of the patent, makes, uses, offers for sale, or sells, within the United States, or imports into the United States, a product or process encompassed by that claim.[22]

Thus, U.S. patent law recognizes the following activities as potentially infringing activities:

- Manufacturing an infringing product in the United States;
- Using an infringing product or process in the United States;
- Offering to sell or selling an infringing product or process in the United States; or
- Importing into the United States an infringing product or a product made by an infringing process.

Practice Note:

A patent claim is directly infringed when one makes, uses, sells, offers for sale in the United States, or imports into the United States a product or process which is encompassed by one or more claims of a valid, unexpired U.S. Patent.

Under U.S. patent law, neither copying nor intent, is required for a finding of direct infringement.[23] In other words, someone can be found to be an infringer whether he or she knew about the patent or intended to infringe the patent. However, the fact that an infringer copied the invention or intentionally infringed may affect the damages to be awarded. (*See* Chapter 15, Section 15.4.) Further, in certain circumstances where a patentee practices a claimed invention, but does not mark its products, the failure of the patentee to provide notice of a patent can limit the period of damages which might otherwise be available. (*See* Chapter 15, Section 15.5.)

Practice Note:

Generally, intent and copying are not required to directly infringe a patent claim.

12.3 Contributory Infringement

U.S. patent law recognizes that even if someone does not practice all the elements of a claim, if that actor contributes to an act of infringement by another, he or she may nonetheless be found liable for contributory patent infringement.[24]

Practice Note:

U.S. patent law does not allow someone to contribute to the infringement of another.

In order to establish any theory of *indirect* infringement (including contributory infringement discussed in this section, or inducing infringement as discussed in Section 12.4), U.S. patent law requires in the first instance that someone else in fact *directly* infringes a claim of a patent.[25] In other words, one cannot indirectly infringe a patent claim by another if there is not also a direct infringer of the patent claim in the first place.

Further, in order to prove direct infringement, a patentee must show either that

- The accused device necessarily infringes the patent claim; or
- Specific instances of direct infringement.[26]

When a device can be used in different manners, some of which directly infringe and some of which do not infringe, then the accused device does not *necessarily* infringe the patent claim. Thus, in such circumstances, the patentee must point to *specific* instances of direct infringement and the patentee's damages will be limited to the damages associated with those specific instances of direct infringement.[27] Vague, hypothetical references are not enough.

Practice Note:

Indirect infringement (like contributory infringement and inducing infringement) requires that someone actually directly infringe.

In addition to establishing direct infringement by others, a patentee must also establish the following elements of a claim for contributory patent infringement:

- The defendant sold a component for use in practicing the patented process or combination;
- The component constitutes a material part of the invention;
- The defendant knew that the item it sold was especially made for or adapted for use in infringing the patented combination; and
- The item sold is not a staple article or commodity of commerce suitable for substantial non-infringing use.[28]

Each of these elements must be met to establish a claim for contributory infringement.

12.4 Inducing Infringement

Another kind of "indirect" infringement recognized by U.S. patent law is "inducing infringement." A claim for inducement to infringe is a separate and independent cause of action.[29] In other words, someone can be liable for inducement without incurring liability for contributory infringement.[30]

To sustain an action for inducement, the plaintiff must show that "the alleged infringer's actions induced infringing acts *and* that he knew or should have known his actions would induce actual infringements."[31]

Thus, as with a claim for contributory infringement, it is a prerequisite of a claim for inducement of infringement that there is direct infringement of the patent claims.[32]

In addition, proof of "actual intent" to cause the acts which are the infringement is required.[33] This requires that the alleged infringer's actions induced infringing acts and that he "knew or should have known" his or her actions would induce actual infringements.[34] At a minimum, this requires that the alleged infringer was aware of the patent.[35]

Proof of such intent may be inferred from circumstantial evidence; direct evidence is not required.[36] Circumstantial evidence may include "giving a direct infringer instructions on how to use a patented process or designing a product to infringe."[37] This point is illustrated in the Rubix Cube case. The patent claim at issue there required that the cube puzzle device actually be solved in order to infringe. The defendant sold the device with instructions on how to solve the puzzle. The court found the defendant liable for inducement.[38] However, providing instructions by itself is not necessarily enough to establish inducement. For example, one court denied summary judgment to the alleged infringer on the issue of inducement where the instructional manual by the alleged infringer described both potentially infringing and admittedly non-infringing configurations for the products it sold.[39]

CHAPTER

13

How to Enforce a Patent

It is important to understand the general steps on how to enforce a patent. In this chapter, the focus is on the pre-litigation steps to enforcing the patent. In other words, what steps should be taken before commencing a patent litigation.

13.1 Goals

The first step in deciding to enforce a patent, as with any other litigation or business decision, is to understand what the organization hopes to obtain by enforcing a patent. Unless the ultimate goals are framed at the beginning of the process, and refined throughout the process, it will be difficult and unlikely that the ultimate goals of the organization will be met in a timely and efficient manner, if at all.

As discussed in Chapter 2, there are many different reasons an organization may want to obtain patent protection. Some of those same goals also apply to patent enforcement actions. For example, one goal in enforcing a patent may be to stop competitors. Alternatively, another goal in enforcing a patent may be to obtain appropriate compensation for the use of the organization's patented technology.

When the ultimate goal is to shut down a competitor, or at least to limit a competitor's ability to compete, the resources required to commit to an enforcement program may be substantially greater than when the ultimate goal is merely receiving a reasonable royalty for the infringements by the competitor. Of course, the higher the royalty payment demanded, the more expensive it will likely be to obtain the desired royalty.

For example, a competitor is less likely to agree to go out of business than a competitor would be willing to pay money. Thus, a competitor who is fighting to stay in business is more likely to devote greater resources to litigation, and less likely to resolve the litigation, than one who merely has to pay a modest sum of money.

Of course, sometimes, the demands of a patentee may be so high that it would be the equivalent of demanding that the target go out of business. In such circumstances the patentee should be prepared to devote enough resources to engage in an extended litigation.

When a patentee is only seeking a modest monetary payment to resolve a patent dispute, it is more likely that the patent dispute will be resolved in a prompt and efficient manner. Of course, that is not always the case.

A prime example of this principle is the Lemelson Medical, Education and Research Foundation licensing program. In this program, the Lemelson Foundation would seek only a nuisance value royalty (e.g., approximately 0.1 percent of sales) so that most potential licensees would find that paying the royalty was cheaper than litigating the matter. Using this technique, the Lemelson Foundation collected over $1 billion in licensing revenue before the patents were eventually found to be unenforceable under the doctrine of prosecution laches.[1]

Sometimes, a patent dispute, like any other dispute, may be about hurt feelings, or some other grudge. These cases are very difficult to resolve since the resolution of such cases tends to be divorced from the merits of the dispute.

It is important that the decision makers involved in developing and implementing a strategy for a patent enforcement action understand and be kept abreast of the organization's goals for the action, so that the strategy implemented can be appropriately tailored to address such goals.

13.2 Demand Letters

One of the difficult strategy questions involved in patent disputes is how to begin the process of raising a dispute. As discussed in Chapter 5, Section 5.8, it was a common practice that patentees would send prospective targets "notice" letters which would put them on notice of the patents at issue, but, at the same time, might not subject the patentee to a lawsuit by the accused infringer seeking a declaration that the patent was invalid or not infringed. However, with the subsequent change in U.S. patent law after the *MedImmune* case,[2] this practice became substantially curtailed. As a result, patentees more often now bring lawsuits first and write letters later.

To begin the clock on damages, a notice letter must

- Be from the patent owner;
- Be to the accused infringer;
- Identify specific patent numbers;
- Identify the accused products; and
- Be an affirmative communication of a specific charge of infringement.

When all of these elements are not present in a notice letter, there is a risk that the notice letter will be deemed ineffective in starting the damages period.

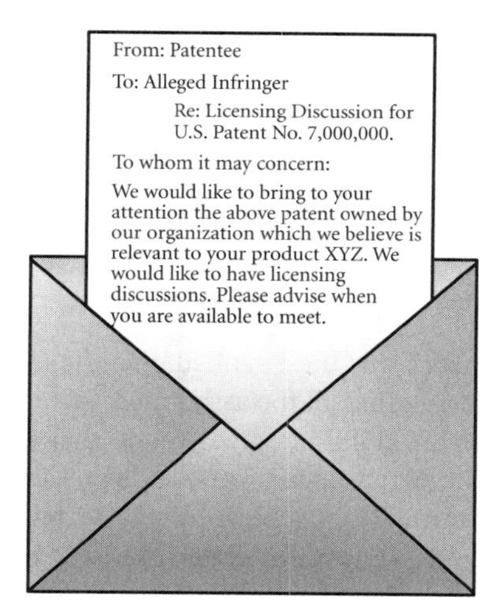
From: Patentee

To: Alleged Infringer

Re: Licensing Discussion for U.S. Patent No. 7,000,000.

To whom it may concern:

We would like to bring to your attention the above patent owned by our organization which we believe is relevant to your product XYZ. We would like to have licensing discussions. Please advise when you are available to meet.

FIGURE 13.1 Notice Letter.

13.3 Confirm the Assertion Prior to Starting a Lawsuit

In preparing to bring a patent infringement action, the pre-suit investigation should include the steps of identifying and understanding

- The patent(s) to be asserted;
- The infringing product(s);
- The infringing actor(s);

- The potential risks; and
- The ultimate goal.

Only when all of these items are addressed can an appropriate strategy be formulated and implemented.

13.3.1 The Patent(s)

A pre-suit investigation should include identifying and understanding the patent(s) and claim(s) to be asserted.

This step includes not only identifying the patent or patents which are to be asserted, but also identifying all of the patents and patent applications that relate to the asserted patents. The collection of patents that are related to each other is called a "Patent Family." A chart showing the relationship of such patents is called a "Patent Family Tree." Each of the patents, patent applications, and prosecution histories for the patents in the Patent Family should be reviewed to see what impact they might have on the interpretation and assertability of the patent which is intended to be enforced.[3]

Practice Note:
Identify all related patent(s) and patent applications.

It is important to insure that the intended plaintiff actually has the right to bring a lawsuit. This means that all the assignments which were made leading to the plaintiff's ownership should be reviewed to make sure they are correct and complete, and have been properly recorded with the USPTO. In addition, to the extent that any licenses (exclusive, or otherwise) have been granted, those licenses should be reviewed to confirm that the intended target has not already been granted rights to the patent. Failure to properly address these issues before commencing a lawsuit can impact the efficiency and results of litigation.[4]

Practice Note:
Confirm that patent ownership issues are addressed ahead of time.

The patent and its claims should also be reviewed for any typographical errors or other errors. Specific procedures have been set up by the USPTO to correct errors in a prompt and efficient manner. Certificates of correction can be issued in a matter of weeks to address minor typographical errors.[5] While in the context of litigation it is possible that a court may correct a typographical error, taking care of the error ahead of time can eliminate a lot of costly litigation fees and expenses and uncertainty surrounding such errors.

In some cases, a court's reluctance to make corrections that patentees should have made at the USPTO can have severe consequences. For example, in a case involving a patent for baking a dough product into a "light and fluffy" pastry, the patentee was severely impacted by failing to correct this kind of error early on. The claim in question provided: "heating the resulting batter-coated dough ***to*** a temperature in the range of about 400°F to 850°F."

While the patentee probably intended the claim to cover heating the batter-coated dough "at" a temperature in the range of about 400°F to 850°F, rather the "to" such a high temperature, the court nonetheless refused to "correct" the claim. Significantly, the court chastised:

> Even "a nonsensical result does not require the court to redraft the claims of the . . . patent. Rather, where as here, claims are susceptible to only one reasonable interpretation and that interpretation results in a nonsensical construction of the claim as a whole, the claim must be invalidated."[6]

Similarly, other more time-consuming procedures can be used to correct more substantive errors, if necessary. The choice of which procedure to follow may depend upon the scope of the error and the time it is likely to take to correct the error using that procedure.

Practice Note:

Review and correct all errors in the patent claims or disclosures before starting an action.

The entire prosecution history (back and forth between the patent applicant and the USPTO) should also be examined ahead of time to see if there are any statements that might be used to limit the scope of the claims. As discussed in Chapter 11, Section 11.1.3, the prosecution history is one of the sources to which a court will turn in order to construe claim terms. In addition, as discussed in Chapter 12, Section 12.1, statements to the USPTO about what the invention is and is not can preclude a patentee from later asserting that a claim covers that which was given up to get the patent. This is called "prosecution history estoppel."

Practice Note:

Analyze the prosecution history to be sure to address any statement which could affect the scope and coverage of a patent claim.

Each prior art reference which has been identified should be studied carefully to understand what is new and different about the claimed invention. This study should include both

- The cited prior art (i.e., prior art provided to or identified by the USPTO during examination of the patent application); and
- Any other uncited prior art which may have been identified at a later date relating to the claimed invention.

Understanding what the prior art does and does not disclose can help in understanding the merits of the patent assertion.

Practice Note:
Understand and evaluate all the cited and uncited prior art.

Finally, any relevant secondary considerations of non-obviousness should be identified, and evidence substantiating such arguments should be gathered and developed. As discussed in Chapter 3, Section 3.2, these secondary considerations include:

- The invention's commercial success;
- Long-felt but unresolved needs for the invention;
- The failure of others to come up with the same solution;
- Skepticism by experts;
- Praise by others;
- Teaching away by others;
- Recognition of a problem; and
- Copying of the invention by competitors, etc.

Thus, for example, if the claimed invention has been particularly successful in the marketplace, sales records, advertising literature, and customer testimonials should be gathered and made available to counsel. Similarly, if the patented invention has been the subject of any industry awards or favorable press, such documents should likewise be gathered. Objective recognition of the merits of an invention by third parties can be very powerful evidence that a particular invention is not obvious.[7]

Practice Note:
Identify any relevant secondary considerations and gather evidence to support such considerations.

In sum, in making the choice of which claims of which patents to assert, all of the above should be kept in mind. Ideally, the claims should read clearly on the accused product, read on only one actor (and the right actor) (as discussed below), have no mistakes, and be simple and clear to understand. Claims should be clear of the known prior art (cited and uncited) and include dependent claims which still read on the accused device, so that the dependent claims can be relied upon in the event that the broadest independent claim is found to be invalid.

13.3.2 The Accused Product(s) or Service(s)

It is also important to investigate the potentially infringing product. This begins with gathering and analyzing all of the available information about the potentially infringing product. For example, to the extent a product can be bought in the marketplace, at least one sample should be purchased and tested to see if it conforms to the claims. Also, if product brochures or literature are available, such documents can be useful in understanding whether a particular product infringes. Of course, sometimes not all of the information that may be necessary to definitively understand an accused product may be readily available.

All of the information obtained should then be used to apply the claims on an element-by-element basis against the accused product as discussed in Chapter 12. This type of analysis is an important precursor to bringing a patent infringement lawsuit in the United States.

It is also useful to try to obtain an estimate of the total infringing sales in order to understand what the case is worth. Failure to consider the actual value of a positive outcome has caused many litigants to waste a lot of time and resources over very little potential recovery.

Practice Note:
Identify and understand the infringing product(s) or service(s).

13.3.3 The Infringing Actors

Next, it is important to identify and understand who are the infringing actors. Conduct an investigation to identify the potential targets who may be infringing the patents-in-suit. If the potential targets are competitors, as opposed to non-competitors, then the potential scope of damages may be different. These factors are discussed in Chapter 15 and Chapter 17.

It is important to understand the number of necessary actors involved in a potential target's acts of infringement. For example, a method claim cannot be directly infringed unless a single actor performs all of the acts required by the claim. Yet, "a defendant cannot thus avoid liability for direct infringement by having someone else carry out one or more of the claimed steps on its behalf."[8]

The case of *Muniauction v. Thompson* illustrates the problem of the multi-actor infringers. In the claim in question, there was no dispute that no single party performed every step of the asserted claims. For example, the claim included an "inputting step" that would be completed by a user, and many of the other steps were to be performed by the auctioneer's system. The court was thus faced with the issue of "whether the actions of at least the bidder and the auctioneer may be combined under the law so as to give rise to a finding of direct infringement by the auctioneer."[9] In *Muniauction*, the court found that it did not. Thus, a $35 million jury verdict, which was doubled with interest to result in a $76.4 million judgment, was reversed, even though all of the steps of the claim were found to be performed![10]

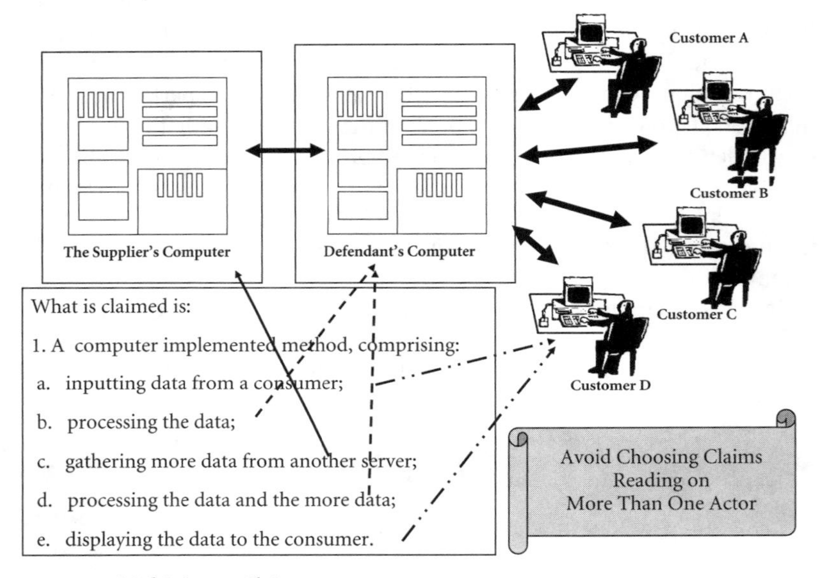

FIGURE 13.2 Multi-Actor Claim.

Practice Note:

Identify and understand who the infringing actor(s) are and how many are necessary to infringe the claim.

When there are numerous potential targets that can be selected to be the subject of a patent enforcement strategy, a variety of considerations may be relevant in selecting which, if any, should be pursued. For example, the organization's resources may limit how many targets should be addressed at a time, in which case the targets must be prioritized.

In some instances, patentees choose to go after the largest target first to bring the other targets in line. In other instances, patentees instead choose to develop a war chest by going after smaller or medium-sized targets which may be more vulnerable to settling the dispute quickly.

Another consideration that may affect which target to pursue is the target's role in the infringing product's manufacture, sale and use. For example, in the Lemelson Foundation patent enforcement program, discussed above, the patentee limited its enforcement activities to end-users of the patented product, rather than the supplier of the allegedly infringing machines. The theory behind this strategy was that by licensing the organizations that use the machines that manufacture the chips, the damages the patentee would be seeking would be on a larger product market (i.e., of the allegedly infringing chips), rather than the smaller market for the manufacturing equipment that allegedly practiced the claimed invention. Thus, greater licensing revenue would be available to be collected. If Lemelson licensed an equipment manufacturer at 1.0 percent of the sale price of the equipment sold, it would be a lot less than licensing the purchaser of that equipment at a rate of 0.1 percent of the entire production made with a machine.

Another consideration that might affect the selection of the target is whether one or more of the potential targets is a strategic business partner with the patentee. In such case, it may be prudent to avoid an aggressive patent enforcement program against an organization's suppliers or customers.

Another consideration would be the patent portfolio of each of the various targets. The issue of counter-patents is discussed in Section 13.4, below.

Identifying and evaluating the potential venues (or places) where the targets can be sued is another important consideration. Some jurisdictions are considered more "patentee-friendly," and some jurisdictions are considered more "accused infringer-friendly." PriceWaterhouseCoopers, in its *2008 Patent Litigation Study: Damages Awards, Success Rates and Time-to-Trial*, reported interesting statistics on the variances in outcomes for various particular courthouses, as shown in the Figure below.

Location Matters

Patentee-Friendly (1995-2007):

	Patentee Success Rate	Median Time to Trial (Years)
M.D. Fla.	66.7%	1.71
E.D. Tex.	54.6%	1.79
C.D. Cal.	51.0%	1.71
E.D. Va.	50.0%	0.88
W.D. Wisc.	50.0%	0.91

Defendant-Friendly (1995-2007):

	Patentee Success Rate	Median Time to Trial (Years)
D. Conn.	15.8%	4.66
E.D. Mich.	18.5%	
S.D. Fla.	25.0%	
S.D.N.Y.	30.6%	2.10
N.D. Cal.	33.0%	2.87

Source: *PricewaterhouseCoopers 2008 Patent Litigation Study: Damages Awards, Success Rates and Time-to-Trial.*
A "success"included instances where a liability and damages (if included) decision was made in favor of the patent holder, either at trial or by summary judgment. Study only included jurisdictions with a minimum of 15 patent cases.

FIGURE 13.3 Significance of Choice of Court Venue.

It is also a good idea to choose a target where the information about the infringing product or service is more easily available. This will enable the investigation to confirm early on the quality of the potential assertion.

Finally, assuming the patent enforcement program is about raising revenue, it is a good idea to investigate the target's available assets to satisfy a potentially favorable judgment and prior litigation history. Unless the point of the litigation is to put a potential target out of business, a target which is on the verge of filing for bankruptcy would not be a good choice for a patent enforcement program which is seeking to raise funds.

Practice Note:
The first target(s) of the patent enforcement program should be carefully selected.

13.3.4 The Risks

Prior to commencing a patent enforcement program, it is also beneficial to identify and understand the potential risks of implementing such a program, such as:

- Cost;
- Counter-patents;
- Economic harm caused by defendants in the marketplace;
- The size of the defendant's war chest; and
- Running out of resources to finish the program.

Practice Note:
Identify and understand the potential risks of starting a patent action.

First, can the organization afford a patent enforcement program? Besides the obvious drain on an organization's financial resources, an enforcement program also requires employee time and effort and can disturb the normal operation of the organization in its primary business. On the other hand, the question may also be whether the organization can afford not to enforce its patents against a fierce competitor.

Practice Note:
Risk: Patent litigations can be expensive and time-consuming.

Second, the target may have one or more relevant counter-patents. (*See* Section 13.4.) The risk of starting a patent enforcement program against such a competitor may be an invitation to the target to commence its own patent enforcement program against the organization.

Practice Note:
Risk: Counter-patents.

Some targets may be able to cause economic harm to the organization in the marketplace and should be avoided for that reason. For example, if one of the targets is a major customer or supplier of the organization, that target may cause significant economic harm to the organization by deciding not to do business with the organization as a result of the patent enforcement program.

Practice Note:
Risk: Economic harm in the marketplace caused by the defendant.

If raising revenue is the goal of the program, it is also best to choose first the targets that would most likely enter into a license agreement. It is also best to avoid targets which have a large war chest and an incentive to fight the assertion.

Practice Note:
Risk: Defendant with a large war chest.

Finally, make sure the organization can afford to see the enforcement program through to the end before it starts. Nothing can be worse than getting into a situation where the organization commences an assertion and/or lawsuit, causing a financial drain on the organization without enough resources to finish the job and obtain the ultimate recovery being sought.

Practice Note:
Risk: Not having sufficient resources to carry out the enforcement program to completion.

13.3.5 The Goal

Finally, as this chapter began, always keep the ultimate goal in mind, and make sure the strategy being developed and implemented is focused on achieving that goal.

Practice Note:
Always keep your ultimate goals in mind in developing, implementing, and reformulating your patent assertion strategies.

13.4 Address Counter-Patents

Before beginning a lawsuit against any party, it is important to consider what type of assertion(s) that party can bring against the organization. In the context of patent infringement assertions, one of the most important considerations is whether the target has its own "counter" patents, i.e., its own patents to assert to counter the organization's assertions.

Thus, before bringing a patent infringement suit against a particular target, all the relevant patents and pending applications the target owns or controls should be identified and analyzed. Nothing can be more upsetting to management than to authorize a lawsuit to raise funds for the organization, only to get stuck making a large payout to the target for infringing the target's own counter-patents.

13.5 Set Up Procedures for Gathering and Preserving Documents and Electronic Evidence

At the beginning of any litigation, it is important to set up appropriate document retention procedures. These procedures start before the litigation begins, with the organization having an appropriate document retention policy in place and making sure it is followed. There are standard document retention policies available which can be tailored to an organization's needs. When implemented, the organization should consider the necessity and desirability of maintaining different kinds of documents as well as the practicality and costs. A document retention policy should also consider potential risks associated with not retaining the types of documents one would normally expect an organization to maintain.

Practice Note:

Set up appropriate procedures within the organization to identify and preserve relevant documents and information.

Once litigation has been commenced, the organization should issue a so-called "Litigation Hold," which advises its employees to maintain documents that would be relevant to the organization. A Litigation Hold should provide a brief summary of the litigation and the nature of the dispute, and identify with sufficient particularity and specificity the types of documents that should be maintained for purposes of the litigation. (When the litigation is over, it is also a good idea to let the organization know that the Litigation Hold has been lifted and that the normal document retention policy is put back in effect.)

Thereafter, in-house counsel and outside litigation counsel should educate each other on the relevant facts and issues and types of evidence which need to be identified and gathered for the lawsuit. These documents should be gathered and reviewed for production in the most efficient manner possible. The temptation to simply produce everything without reviewing it in order to save on the cost of a document review (which can be substantial) should be resisted. It is dangerous to have only the other side in litigation knowing what the organization's documents say. It is like walking around steep cliffs with a blindfold on.

Over the course of litigation, the scope of documents and information being sought in discovery is likely to be expanded by the demands of the opposing party.

In recent years, U.S. courts have brought home to organizations the serious consequences of failing to take serious a litigant's duty to gather and produce documents and other information. For example, in a patent litigation,[11] a court sanctioned an organization and its in-house and outside attorneys for failing to search for and produce key electronic documents such as the relevant e-mails of employees who testified on behalf of the organization. The sanction was millions of dollars and included the attorneys' having to attend classes.[12]

13.6 Select and Obtain an Appropriate Venue

A part of the pre-suit investigation includes identifying the correct court in which to bring the lawsuit. The various options of location (or "venue" as U.S. patent law calls it) are discussed in Chapter 14. The point of the present discussion is more focused on the fact that the appropriate courthouse in which the action should be brought should be identified ahead of time.

In selecting a particular venue, factors like the convenience of the courthouse to the parties and witnesses should be considered. Other factors that are often considered are the likely reception that the court and the juries in a particular district will have to the organization as a litigant and the case to be presented. These types of considerations are often included in the pre-suit analysis. Available venues in which to bring a lawsuit may affect which one of multiple potential targets should be selected, when other factors are otherwise equal.

Practice Note:

Consider ahead of time in which courthouse it is best to bring a lawsuit.

13.7 Steps to Take Pre-Lawsuit to Prepare for Litigation

Before jumping into litigation, it is prudent to get all your ducks in a row and make sure you are prepared to bring a lawsuit. In this regard, there are certain aspects of bringing a patent litigation that can be anticipated.

For example, many district courts and judges with a significant amount of patent experience have established procedures or special rules for patent cases which can be identified ahead of time, and care can be taken to develop the proofs necessary to meet those requirements. For example, the Northern District of California developed a set of "Patent Rules," which have been adopted in varying forms in many of the more patent-friendly courthouses, including, for example, the Eastern District of Texas and the Northern District of Georgia.

Under these Patent Rules, near the beginning of the case, the patentee is expected to serve a set of preliminary infringement contentions which require the patentee to

- Identify the patents being asserted;
- Identify the claims being asserted;
- Identify the accused instrumentalities; and
- Provide a breakdown, element-by-element, of how each of the claim limitations read on each of the accused instrumentalities.[13]

One step that a patentee can perform before bringing a patent litigation is to prepare a draft of such initial disclosures (at least in substance) so that the patentee will be in a position to quickly and promptly satisfy this requirement.[14]

In turn, the defendant(s) will be required soon thereafter to provide their own invalidity contentions[15] and, in some courts, even non-infringement contentions.[16] By acting quickly, a patentee can potentially limit the defenses that an accused infringer may be able to develop.

It is also important to develop at least a preliminary view of how the claims should be interpreted ahead of time in order to read on the accused products, and in order to avoid known prior art. This knowledge can prevent misstatements about the claim scope early on in the litigation. Of course, as the facts develop in litigation, it may be necessary to modify these preliminary views.

Similarly, before the litigation commences, it is a good idea to identify all the commercial embodiments of the asserted claims by the organization and its licensees. The patentee in litigation will be expected to identify this information.[17]

The patentee should also have available the prosecution histories and cited prior art, since this too is expected to be disclosed as part of the initial disclosures.[18]

It is useful to identify ahead of time the witnesses who may be necessary or desirable to take discovery from and/or call at the time of trial. It is also important to understand which witnesses are undesirable, too. Typical types of witnesses in a patent infringement lawsuit include:

- The inventors of the patents;
- Persons who worked with the inventors;
- The attorneys and others who worked on prosecuting the patent with the USPTO;
- Business people who implement the patented invention;
- Individuals involved in licensing; and
- Experts and/or consultants to support the infringement and/or damages contentions.

It is also prudent to obtain commitments from necessary experts and/or consultants before the litigation begins. Examples of such experts/consultants include:

- Technical experts/consultants;
- Damages experts/consultants (reasonable royalty and economists);
- Licensing experts (if appropriate);
- Prosecution history/willfulness experts;
- Graphics consultants;
- Jury consultants; and
- Translators (if one of the parties is from outside the United States).

The failure to perform this simple task could result in the first choice expert/consultant being retained by an opponent or being not otherwise available.

Finally, in considering the pre-suit investigation, if preliminary injunctive relief is to be sought, then it will be necessary to act quickly, and get all of the proofs of the case prepared before the action commences. In such a case, the anticipated court's treatment of such motions should also be considered when deciding in which courthouse to bring the lawsuit.

Practice Note:
Do your homework, and get all your ducks in a row before starting a lawsuit.

CHAPTER

14

Where to Resolve a Patent Dispute

When a patent dispute arises, a patentee or accused infringer has several choices when selecting a place to resolve the dispute. The place where a dispute is to be resolved is known as the "venue."

In some instances, a party may desire to engage in business or settlement discussions before entering into formal legal proceedings. Unfortunately, such discussions may not always be an option, and thus, it may be necessary to involve a third party to assist in resolving the dispute.

Different venues for resolving patent disputes include:

- U.S. Federal District Courts;
- U.S. International Trade Commission;
- USPTO, in the context of a Reexamination Proceeding;
- A private arbitration or mediation; or
- Another country's court of law over a related patent.

A brief overview of the advantages and disadvantages associated with each of these alternative venues is set forth in this chapter.

14.1 Courts

A federal judge in a court of law is one example of an objective third party who can resolve a patent dispute. In the United States, the federal court system has exclusive jurisdiction over patent litigation disputes.[1] In other words, only federal courts (in contrast to state courts) can hear and resolve disputes over whether a patent is infringed.

Practice Note:
Federal courts have exclusive jurisdiction to hear patent disputes in the U.S.

The U.S. federal court system has three distinct levels:

- U.S. District Courts;
- U.S. Court of Appeals; and
- U.S. Supreme Court.

A patent infringement suit is brought and decided in the first instance in a U.S. district court. This is where a trial will be conducted, if necessary. After the district court enters judgment, either party may appeal to a U.S. Court of Appeals. In patent cases, all appeals are heard by the U.S. Court of Appeals for the Federal Circuit ("Federal Circuit"). In some cases, a party may further appeal to the U.S. Supreme Court.

This section reviews the general procedure in a typical patent case, assuming that the procedural options available have been fully exhausted. Because litigation (and patent litigation in particular) can be very complex, this overview is not intended to cover every possible contingency. Rather, this section addresses some of the more common procedural situations used to identify and deal with different issues that may arise.

For present purposes, a patent infringement action must be brought in one of the many U.S. district courts. Every state and territory in the United States has at least one district court. Many states, especially larger states, like New York, California, and Texas, have more than one district court. New York, for example, has four district courts, including

- The U.S. District Court for the Southern District of New York;
- The U.S. District Court for the Northern District of New York;
- The U.S. District Court for the Eastern District of New York; and
- The U.S. District Court for the Western District of New York.

Practice Note:
A patent infringement action must be brought in a U.S. district court.

Further, each U.S. district court can have one or more U.S. district judges that preside over cases brought in that court. Each district court also may have one or more U.S. magistrate judges who assist the district court judges in handling procedural matters like discovery disputes or supervising mandatory settlement discussions between the parties. Sometimes, magistrate judges, with the consent of the parties, may be assigned to conduct all proceedings in a case, including trial.

A patent dispute is commenced in a U.S. district court when the plaintiff files a complaint. The complaint is a legal document which identifies the parties, states the different causes of action being asserted by the plaintiff(s), and sets forth the relief which is being requested. The filing of a complaint commences the pleading stage of litigation.

Practice Note:

A patent dispute is commenced in a U.S. district court through the filing of a complaint.

In a patent infringement suit, the complaint should identify

- The patents being asserted;
- At least one claim of each patent being asserted; and
- The accused products with sufficient detail to apprise the defendants of what the charge of patent infringement is about.

When an accused infringer raises a patent dispute, the action is called a "declaratory judgment" action because the accused infringer is seeking a declaration that he or she has not infringed the claims of one or more patents and/or that the patent claims are invalid and/or unenforceable.

Practice Note:

An accused infringer may bring an action seeking a declaration that a patent is not infringed, invalid, and/or unenforceable.

After a party files its complaint in district court, the party must properly serve the complaint on each of the defendants. U.S. law limits the specific district court in which a particular defendant can be sued. Some of these limits are absolute, and some of them are discretionary. The particular district court in which an action is filed must be one in which both jurisdiction and venue are appropriate.

With respect to jurisdiction, the district court must have jurisdiction over the type of action being brought ("subject matter jurisdiction") and over the person or entity being sued ("personal jurisdiction"). As noted before, all U.S. district courts have subject matter jurisdiction over patent infringement lawsuits. A detailed discussion of subject matter jurisdiction and personal jurisdiction is beyond the scope of this Guide.

Practice Note:
A U.S. district court must have jurisdiction both over the "subject matter" of the dispute and the parties involved in the dispute.

With respect to venue, U.S. patent law limits the U.S. district courts in which a particular patent action can be brought based on factors of convenience, such as

- Where all the plaintiffs are located;
- Where all the defendants are located; or
- Where the acts of infringement occurred.

Some of these limits are absolute limits, and some of these limits are discretionary. If a party brings a patent infringement action in an inappropriate U.S. district court, the party being sued can bring a motion to the court seeking to dismiss or transfer.[2]

Practice Note:
The U.S. District Court must also be an appropriate "venue" (or location) for the dispute.

Once the complaint is served on a defendant, the defendant must prepare and file an answer to the complaint, answering each of the assertions in the complaint. In addition, if the defendant has any affirmative defenses he or she wants to assert, these defenses should be plead at this time, to the extent known. Typical affirmative defenses which may be plead in a patent infringement action include:

- The complaint fails to state a claim on which relief may be granted;
- The claims of the patent are not infringed;
- The claims of the patent are invalid;
- The claims of the patent are unenforceable, due to some equitable doctrine like inequitable conduct;

- The defendant is authorized to practice the patent by a license or the doctrine of patent exhaustion; and
- The patentee is barred from asserting a claim for infringement under an equitable doctrine like laches or estoppel.

These and other affirmative defenses, to the extent they are available, may be plead at this time. Certain affirmative defenses may be plead generally, while other defenses which are based on fraudulent acts. like inequitable conduct, need to be plead with particularity. In other words, sufficient factual support for these later kinds of affirmative defenses must be set forth in the pleadings so that the responding party has adequate notice of the basis for the affirmative defense.

Often, especially in patent cases, a defendant may assert one or more counterclaims. For example, a defendant may counterclaim, seeking a declaration that the patents being asserted are not infringed, invalid, and/or unenforceable or asserting that the plaintiff infringed one or more claims of patents owned by the defendants. Sometimes, a defendant may assert that the patentee violated some other law, like antitrust or tort law, by an improper assertion of the patents in question.

Practice Note:
A defendant may assert affirmative defenses and counterclaims in response to a complaint

When a defendant asserts a counterclaim, the plaintiff must file an answer or reply to the counterclaim which responds to the assertions made in the counterclaim, much as the defendant's answer to the complaint responds to the assertions made in the complaint.

Sometimes it may be necessary for a defendant to bring in additional parties, like a missing owner or licensee of the patents-in-suit, or one of defendant's suppliers whom the defendant believes should be responsible for any alleged patent infringements. These additional parties may be joined in the action in a third-party complaint. The defendant then becomes the third-party plaintiff, and the additional parties become third-party defendants. The same type of jurisdictional and venue concerns that govern a complaint also govern third-party complaints.

Practice Note:
A defendant may also bring third parties into the action by way of a third-party complaint.

After third-party complaints have been served, third-party defendants are expected to file answers, which may include affirmative defenses, in the same manner as any other defendants.

At some point, after all the complaints and third-party complaints have been filed, served, and answered, and all counterclaims have been responded to, the court will schedule a Scheduling Conference during which the court adopts a schedule which will govern the case and its timetables. A Scheduling Conference usually marks the end of the initial pleading stage in litigation.

Practice Note:
The pleadings stage in litigation is the initial stage, where the parties and their contentions are identified.

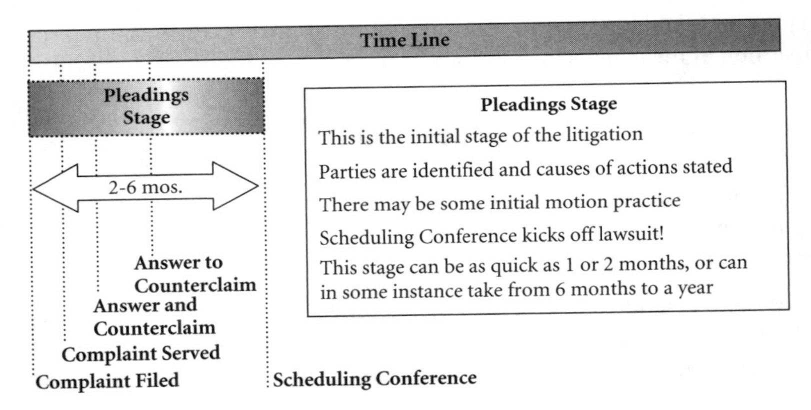

FIGURE 14.1 Pleading Stage in Litigation.

Once the preliminary pleadings are done and the court has entered a Scheduling Order, the discovery stage usually commences. Discovery is the procedure by which the parties can ask each other for documents, testimony, and other information that is necessary to prepare their respective cases and to understand the other side's contentions. Different methods of discovery include

- Documents requests;
- Interrogatories (written questions);
- Request for admissions; and
- Depositions (oral questions to witnesses).

Third-party discovery may also be served, in which the parties may seek information, documents and perhaps depositions from nonparties. Other than trial, the discovery stage can be the most expensive and burdensome part of litigation.

Practice Note:

The parties exchange documents and information during the discovery stage of litigation.

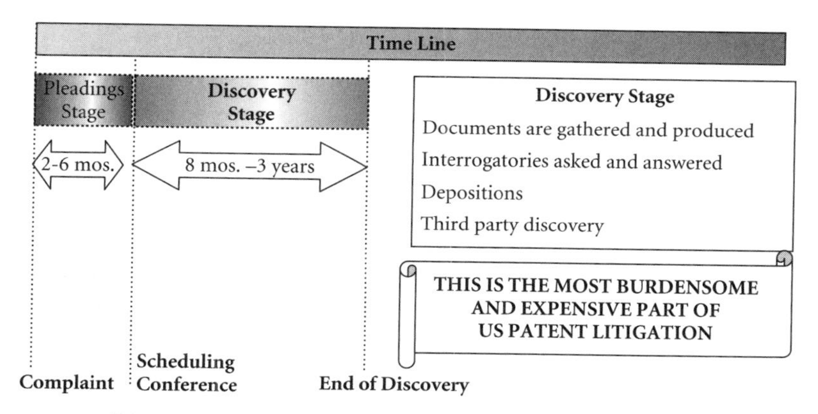

FIGURE 14.2 Discovery Stage in Litigation.

In many of the more active U.S. district courts which hear patent disputes, special rules have been adopted which govern the procedures used in patent litigations. For example, the district courts in the Northern District of California, Eastern District of Texas, District of New Jersey, and Northern District of Georgia all have adopted special patent rules. These procedures provide a mechanism by which parties provide certain timed, mandatory disclosures, with the goal of identifying claim construction disputes early and in an efficient manner, to be resolved by the court. These special procedures typically include the following steps:

- Infringement contentions;
- Identification of accused products;
- Invalidity contentions;
- Exchange of terms to be construed and proposed constructions;
- Briefing; and
- Claim construction hearing.

Many patent litigations are resolved by the parties after a claim construction hearing.

Practice Note:
Special rules to facilitate a claim construction hearing are followed for patent cases in certain U.S. district courts.

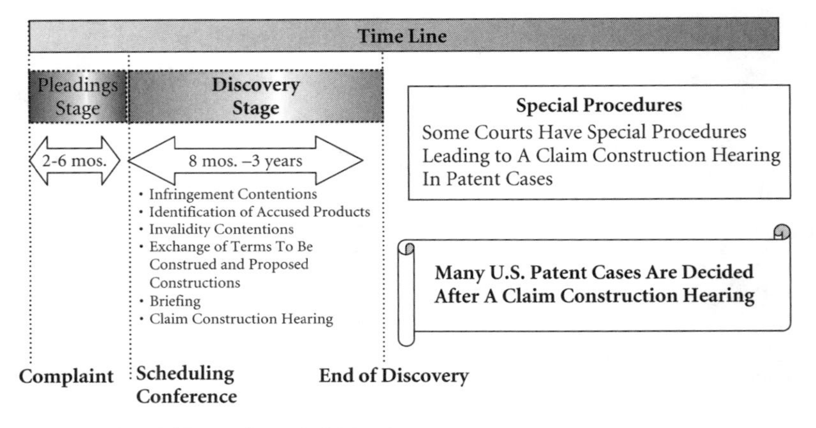

FIGURE 14.3 Special Procedures in Litigation.

After the claims have been construed, the parties complete discovery and exchange their respective expert reports. Typically in patent cases, experts are hired to provide their opinions on issues relating to infringement, validity, enforceability, and damages. Courts allow parties to present expert testimony at trial, if it is considered legitimate science and will help a jury or the court as fact finder resolve a disputed issue of fact.

Once the claims have been construed, all the parties' contentions exchanged, and expert opinions provided and tested with discovery, the court's schedule usually provides the parties with an opportunity to file one or more dispositive motions in an effort to resolve the case, such as motions for summary judgment or partial summary judgment. This is often called the dispositive motion stage of litigation. Dispositive motions may also be brought earlier in the case. However, if a motion is brought before appropriate discovery has been taken, the party opposing the motion may be entitled to conduct discovery before responding.

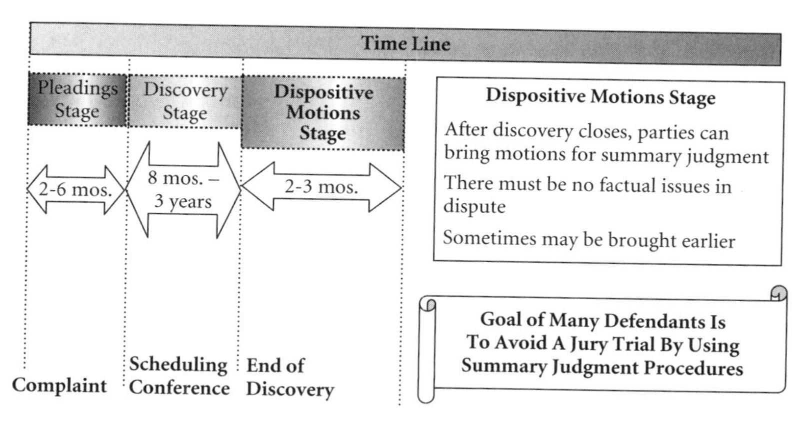

FIGURE 14.4 Dispositive Motions Stage of Litigation.

Practice Note:

Many patent litigations may be resolved by dispositive motions.

If the case is not resolved by dispositive motion(s), the parties will then begin to prepare for and conduct a trial. Most patent cases involve jury trials. This means that a jury (usually consisting of at least six people) will decide the factual disputes between the parties, and a judge will resolve the legal disputes. An example of a legal dispute is how the claim should be construed (*see* Chapter 11). An example of a factual dispute is whether the accused device possesses each of the elements of the claim as construed by the court (*see* Chapter 12). Assuming that there are facts in dispute, at the completion of the trial, the jury is expected to issue a verdict indicating whether any valid claims have been infringed, and if so, determine the amount of damages, if any, to be awarded to the patentee.

Practice Note:

In a jury trial the district judge will decide questions of law, and the jury will decide questions of fact.

After trial, the party that does not prevail usually files motions challenging the jury's verdict. In the event that the patentee prevailed at trial, there might also be motions to enhance damages and grant an award of attorney's fees, and perhaps pre-judgment interest. After all the issues raised during litigation are resolved by the court, the judge then enters a final judgment, effectively ending the proceedings before the U.S. district court.

It can take at least a year, if not years, for a patent infringement action to proceed from the filing of the complaint to entry of final judgment.

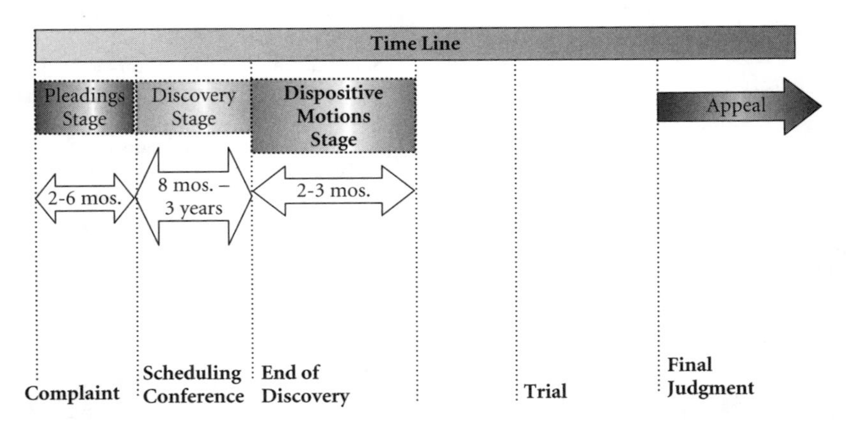

FIGURE 14.5 Litigation Time Line.

A final judgment may be appealed to the U.S. court of appeals once it is entered. In patent cases, the U.S. Court of Appeals for the Federal Circuit ("Federal Circuit") has exclusive jurisdiction over all appeals in cases arising under U.S. patent law.

Practice Note:
In patent litigation, the Federal Circuit hears all appeals from the various district courts.

Once an appeal is filed, the record from the proceedings before the district court will be transmitted to the Federal Circuit. However, before this is done, the parties may be required to make sure the record is complete and accurate.

To do so, the parties work on preparing an Appendix which will include all of the potentially relevant documents which the Federal Circuit judges who will be deciding the appeal may want to review.

Thereafter, the parties brief their appeals.

- The Brief of the Appellant(s) (which is to have a *blue* cover);
- The Brief of the Appellee(s) or Respondent(s) (which is to have a *red* cover); and
- The Reply Brief of the Appellant(s) (which is to have a *gray* cover).

In some cases, third parties may want to submit briefs as friends of the court ("amicus curiae") or as a third-party intervenor (which is to have a **green** cover).

Any supplemental briefs are to have *tan* covers.

The Appellate Court Rules dictate the color of the cover of the different briefs to make it easier for the judges to identify which brief is by which party.[3]

After the briefing is complete, the appeals court sets a hearing date, at which point the parties may address the panel deciding the case. If the parties chose not to present oral argument, the case will be submitted on the written record. Typically, absent extraordinary circumstances, the panel is composed of three judges. Thereafter, usually within three months, the panel issues its decision. Sometimes it may take longer (even substantially longer) for the panel to issue a decision.

Practice Note:

Most appeals in patent litigations are heard by three-judge panels of the Federal Circuit.

Surprisingly, the Federal Circuit does reverse many of the patent case decisions made by the district court. For example, some commentators have reported that approximately 30 percent of summary judgment decisions in patent cases are appealed, and approximately 60 percent of those decisions are modified or reversed by the appeals court. Similarly, approximately 40 percent of trial decisions are appealed, with almost 70 percent of those decisions being modified or reversed.[4]

Practice Note:

The Federal Circuit reverses a surprisingly large number of decisions by U.S. district courts in patent litigations.

When the Federal Circuit reverses or modifies a decision by a U.S. district court, the case will often be remanded to the district court for retrial, taking into account the reasons the Federal Circuit reversed the decision.

The panel decision may also be subject to review by all of the active judges of the Federal Circuit (called "en banc review") and by the U.S. Supreme Court. Neither of these events occurs very often.

The process before the Federal Circuit can take about a year from start to finish.

At any point during this procedure, the parties may settle the case, thereby ending the litigation with respect to those parties. As this simplified explanation demonstrates, the procedures involved in a patent infringement action brought in a U.S. district court can be complex, expensive, and time-consuming. However, because there are so many levels of review, there are also many opportunities for the system to correct errors that may occur along the way.

Practice Note:
A dispute may settle at any point during the litigation process.

The U.S. court system also provides an opportunity for obtaining damages and equitable relief like a preliminary and/or permanent injunction, which are designed to preclude continued infringement. The remedies available in the district court make it a desirable venue for many patentees.

Practice Note:
The court system can provide a wide range of remedies in a patent dispute.

In sum, patent litigation in the U.S. court system has the following features:

- It can be complex;
- It can take years;
- It can be expensive;
- It can be burdensome on an organization;
- It can lead to significant liability;
- It may stop infringers from continuing to infringe;
- It has available appellate review as a double-check on improper results; and
- Despite clear Rules of Procedure, juries, U.S. district court judges, and appellate judges can be unpredictable.

14.2 International Trade Commission

Besides the U.S. court system, there are other venues where patent disputes may be resolved. For example, when a patentee seeks to stop the importation of an infringing device by a competitor, another option may be seeking an exclusion order from the U.S. International Trade Commission ("ITC"). Thus, in addition to the ITC's broad mandate regarding issues related to international trade, its governing statute called "Section 337"[5] provides a cause of action before the ITC for unlawful importation of infringing goods which destroy or substantially injure an U.S. industry.

Practice Note:
The ITC is an alternative venue where a patentee can bring a patent dispute.

Damages are not awarded in ITC proceedings; only exclusion orders and cease and desist orders may be granted, including

- A "limited exclusion order," which applies only to infringing products sold by the accused infringer, who is called the "respondent" in an ITC proceeding;
- A "general exclusion order," which applies to all products that would infringe the patent claims, regardless of the source (a general exclusion order may thus affect customers and suppliers too, not just the respondents); and
- A "cease and desist order," which prevents the further sale in the United States of infringing products already imported into the United States.

Thus, if the goal in enforcing the patent is merely to collect money, and not to stop a competitor from bringing infringing items into the United States, an ITC proceeding may not be the appropriate venue for resolving that patent dispute.

The ITC may also issue a temporary cease and desist order during the pendency of the ITC proceeding. The standards governing the grant of such preliminary relief is comparable to the standards used in the U.S. court system for issuing a preliminary injunction in a patent action.

Practice Note:
While damages are not available, the ITC can issue Exclusion Orders and Cease and Desist Orders to stop the ongoing importation of infringing goods.

In addition, since an ITC proceeding may only stop importation of infringing products into the United States, unless the competitor is importing the infringing products from outside the United States into the United States, an ITC proceeding may not be the right venue for resolving a patent dispute.

Also, an ITC proceeding requires that the patentee (called the "complainant") be a domestic industry, e.g., makes the product in the United States. The domestic industry requirement has been interpreted relatively broadly.

A complainant may establish a domestic industry, for example, by showing that it is involved in activities such as

- Sales activities by the Complainant;
- Licensing activities to others in the United States;
- Investment in manufacturing facilities and equipment in the United States; and
- Investment in research and development, as well as employment of a large number of people in the United States.

Practice Note:

The complainant must meet the "domestic industry" requirement for an ITC enforcement action.

Further, an ITC proceeding is best used in cases where the patentee has a technically sound case, does not need much discovery, and is fully prepared before bringing the action. The complaint in an ITC action typically has substantially more detail than a complaint in litigation before a U.S. district court.

An ITC proceeding is presided over by an Administrative Law Judge ("ALJ"), who is usually more technically savvy than most U.S. district judges and juries. Thus, there will not be a jury deciding the case, who may be more swayed by emotion than technical merit.

Practice Note:

An ITC proceeding is decided by an ALJ, not a jury.

In addition to the ALJ, the Office of Unfair Import Investigation, and a staff attorney who represents the public interest and acts as an impartial third party, plays an important role in all ITC investigations. The ITC staff attorney may, among other things

- Issue discovery requests;
- Take depositions; and
- Examine witnesses at trial.

Practice Note:

The Office of Unfair Import Investigation and its staff attorneys play an important role in an ITC proceeding.

Because the ITC is an administrative agency and not a federal court, the decisions of the ITC do not have a preclusive effect as do decisions in a proceeding in a U.S. district court. However, because the remedies in certain circumstances are so powerful, an ITC proceeding may be an effective tool in resolving a patent dispute.

Practice Note:

Decisions of the ITC have no preclusive effect but may nonetheless be an effective tool in resolving a patent dispute.

Before commencing an ITC Investigation, the ITC must decide to issue a Notice of Investigation. This means that the ITC must be convinced, before the case even begins, that the complainant in an ITC proceeding has a strong enough case to be heard. Thus, as discussed in Chapter 13, Section 13.7, it is even more important for a patentee to do its homework before seeking to commence an ITC proceeding.

Practice Note:

A complainant must convince the ITC to commence an action.

This process begins with the complainant filing a complaint with the ITC. The ITC Rules set forth very specific content requirements for a proper complaint before the ITC, which must include

- A description of specific instances of alleged unlawful importations or sales;
- The name, address, and "nature of business" of each respondent;
- An indication of whether the infringement has also been the subject of a proceeding in a U.S. district court, and, if it has, must provide a summary of the proceeding;
- Identification of any licensees of the patent;
- A description of the domestic industry, including a description of complainant's business and its interests in the relevant domestic industry; and
- A claim chart comparing the patent claims to the accused products.

The ITC may refuse to commence an investigation if a complainant fails to include all of this information in its ITC complaint.

Thus, in order to make sure the ITC complaint meets its standard, prospective complainants often provide draft complaints to the ITC staff attorney and work with the ITC staff attorney to ensure the final complaint complies with the ITC Rules and sets forth sufficient evidence to justify issuing a Notice of Investigation and commencing an ITC proceeding. This process is usually informal and may be iterative.

An ITC proceeding moves along relatively quickly. As the sample time line for an ITC investigation in Figure 14.6 illustrates, an entire proceeding could be finished within a year and half from the time an ITC complaint is filed.

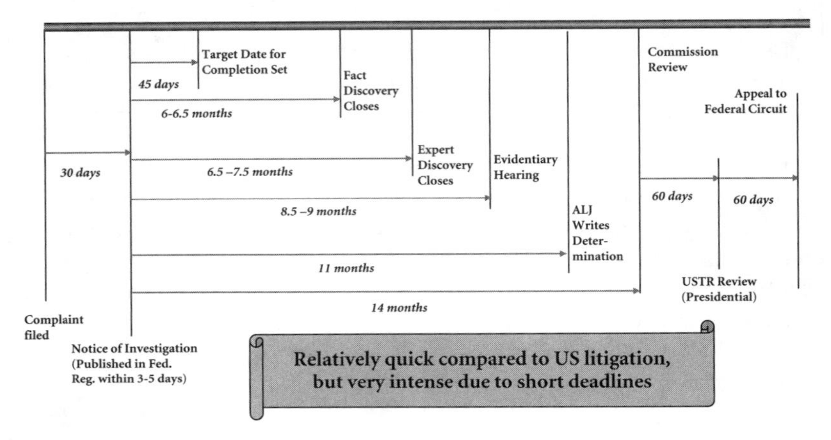

FIGURE 14.6 Sample Time Line of ITC Investigation.

ITC Investigations can be burdensome on the litigants because they are processed so quickly. In turn, the compressed schedule usually results in a higher monthly expense than litigation in U.S. district courts.

In sum, the features of an ITC proceeding include:

- It is relatively quick;
- Because it has short deadlines, it can be very intense;
- It allows for discovery, but tends to have less discovery than litigation in U.S. district courts;
- The remedy available is only an injunction, and not monetary damages;
- It is still expensive, although probably less expensive in the long run than a litigation in U.S. district courts;
- It is decided by an ALJ without a jury; and
- There is no preclusive effect to an ITC determination, regardless of outcome.

14.3 USPTO

An accused infringer may also seek to have the USPTO reconsider the patentable merits of a patent claim through one of a host of different procedures.[6]

Likewise, a patentee may use procedures at the USPTO to cure defects in an issued patent,[7] including reissue proceedings and reexamination proceedings.

14.3.1 Reissue

If a patentee determines that an issued patent is "defective," U.S. patent law provides a procedure by which a "defective" patent may be reconsidered, cured, and "reissued."[8]

Practice Note:

"Defective" patents may be cured in a reissue proceeding.

For purposes of seeking a reissued patent, a patent is deemed "defective" when the issued patent is "deemed wholly or partly inoperative or invalid,"[9] either by reason of

- A defective specification or drawing; or
- The patentee claiming more or less than he had a right to claim in the patent.

In other words, a reissue patent may correct errors in the written description of the invention including the specification and drawings, as well as in the claim scope (being too broad and/or too narrow). While a reissue patent may always narrow the scope of claims during the term of a patent,[10] it may only broaden the scope of the claims if it is filed *within two years* of the issue date of the original patent.[11] Of course, whatever is claimed in the reissue patent must have been within the scope of the original disclosure of the patent when it was originally filed. Thus, while a reissue patent may correct errors in the specification and figures, it may not add "new matter" (e.g., substance not originally included).[12]

Practice Note:

A reissue patent may always narrow the issued claims, but must be filed within two years of the issue date of a patent to broaden the claims.

A reissue patent is also only available when the error being corrected was made without any deceptive intent. Thus, the error could arise out of inadvertence, accident, or mistake.[13] On the other hand, a broadened reissue has generally been based upon a post-issuance discovery of attorney error in understanding and appreciating the scope of an invention, such that the original claims were too narrow.[14]

Practice Note:
Reissue patents may only address errors made without any deceptive intent.

Of course, a claim in a reissue patent must meet all of the requirements of patentability that a claim in any other patent is required to meet.

Generally, a reissue application requires the same parts that are required for an application for an original patent, including

- Specification;
- Claims;
- Drawings;
- Petition;
- Oath; and
- Fee.

Further, a reissue application is examined in generally the same manner as a non-reissue, non-provisional application.[15]

When a reissue patent is "reissued," the original patent is surrendered by the patentee, and the patentee may only enforce any new claims from the date of the reissuance. Thus, in order to reissue a patent with new claims, the reissued patent must be reissued before the original patent expires.[16]

Practice Note:
The USPTO will only reissue patents before the term of the original patent expires.

To the extent the USPTO reaffirms the patentability of any previously issued claims; those claims remain in force and are effective from the original issuance date of the patent containing those claims.

Practice Note:
Claims in a reissue patent that are substantively the same as the claims in the original patent are enforceable as of the original issue date.

14.3.2 Reexamination

Another procedure that can be used to reexamine the merits of an issued patent is a reexamination proceeding. The reexamination procedures offered by the USPTO may only be used to test the validity of claims in a patent based on certain kinds of prior art. Specifically, the USPTO will only consider printed publications and patents and will not consider any prior public use or sale defenses.

Practice Note:

A third party may test the validity of one or more claims of an issued patent in the USPTO based on prior art consisting of printed publications and patents using a reexamination procedure.

While a reexamination proceeding may result in the invalidation of one or more claims in an issued patent, it may also result in a claim being narrowed, yet still valid in light of the newly identified prior art. Depending on the way the claim is narrowed during reexamination, new non-infringement defenses may become available to an accused infringer. Alternatively, the claim could become a stronger claim which may still be infringed. Because claims can be "fixed," it is preferable from an accused infringer's perspective, in most cases, to only use a reexamination procedure when a patent is expired or will soon expire so that the new claims cannot be asserted.

Practice Note:

Instituting a reexamination proceeding may be a risky strategy.

There are two types of reexaminations proceedings than can be instituted in the USPTO:

- *Ex partes* Reexamination;[17] and
- *Inter partes* Reexamination.[18]

Ex partes reexamination may be commenced either by a patentee or a third party. However, when a third party commences an *ex partes* reexamination, it may not participate thereafter. *Inter partes* reexamination may also be commenced by a third party. However, in *inter partes* reexamination, the third party can participate in the entire proceedings.

Ex partes reexamination is a "one-shot" presentation that can be made by a named or anonymous third-party challenger in order to present previously unconsidered prior art, along with an explanation as to why the prior art renders one or more claims invalid. If the reexamined patent is found by the USPTO to be valid over the newly presented art, the challenger (and others) will have greater difficulty arguing that the claims are invalid over that prior art in future proceedings. Even though *ex partes* reexamination is a "one-shot" deal, multiple, successive *ex partes* reexamination requests can be filed to present different prior art as the proceedings progress.

For patents that are based on applications filed on or after November 29, 1999, *inter partes* reexamination procedures are available. To date, a relatively few number of *inter partes* reexaminations have been filed. One reason challengers tend to be reluctant to participate in *inter partes* reexamination proceedings is because participation in such proceedings precludes the challenger from using in litigation not only the defenses that were presented to the USPTO, but also other defenses that could have been brought to the USPTO as part of that proceeding. It does not preclude the challenger from making assertions of invalidity based on newly discovered prior art that was unavailable at the time of the *inter partes* proceedings.

Generally, either one, but not both, of these proceedings may be used. However, either of these proceedings may be used in conjunction with any of the procedures discussed in this chapter. For both kinds of reexamination proceedings, some courts are willing to stay an ongoing patent litigation to allow the USPTO to consider invalidity challenges raised in a reexamination proceeding.[19] Thus, by instituting a reexamination proceeding, a defendant in a patent litigation may be able to put off substantial litigation expenses in the hopes that the USPTO will declare the claims invalid or require the patentee to narrow the claims in a manner that would not be infringed by the defendant.

Figure 14.7 illustrates sample timelines of the two different kinds of reexamination proceedings available before the USPTO.

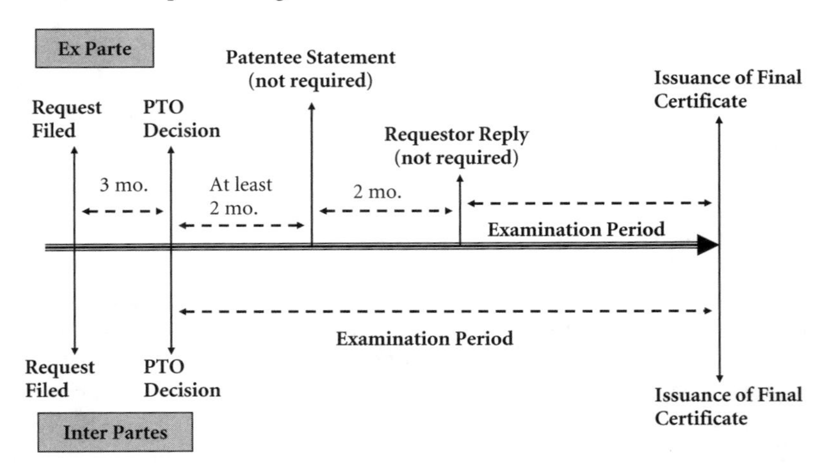

FIGURE 14.7 Reexamination Proceedings (before USPTO).

Generally, reexamination proceedings have the following features:

- It is a less expensive proceeding than litigation or an ITC proceeding;
- It can only address certain invalidity issues;
- At least *ex partes* reexamination can be anonymous;
- It is less burdensome on an organization than full-scale litigation;
- Seeking a reexamination may result in stay of litigation; and
- If unsuccessful, it can effectively eliminate best defenses.

14.4 Private Arbitration or Mediation

The parties may also elect to have a dispute resolved in a private proceeding by an arbitrator and/or mediator. The Federal Arbitration Act, U.S. patent law, and U.S. law in general, allows for parties to resolve or mediate their patent disputes in private, before a private arbitrator or mediator.[20]

In a private arbitration or mediation, the parties pay for the decision-maker(s), usually one or three arbitrators or one mediator, to resolve the dispute.

In mediation, the mediator usually only facilitates the parties in settlement discussions. The mediator is usually not given authority to bind the parties and may not require them to resolve a dispute. A mediation may be useful where the parties are not very far apart and just need help in reaching a creative resolution of the dispute.

Practice Note:
In mediation, a mediator facilitates the parties' settlement discussions.

In arbitration, it is intended that the arbitrator(s) will resolve the dispute. Usually, the result of an arbitration is binding on both parties. Because an arbitration is a voluntary proceeding, which the parties mutually decide to participate in, the parties are usually able to craft particular rules and procedures that will govern the proceeding.

Practice Note:
In arbitration, one or more arbitrators may decide the parties' dispute in a manner defined by the parties.

Thus, parties to arbitration may provide for

- How many arbitrators will preside over the proceeding;
- How the arbitrators are selected;
- Whether discovery will be available;
- The schedule for the proceeding;
- The length and location of the hearing; and
- The type of remedies which may be granted.

The arbitration process is very flexible. When properly planned out, arbitration can be a useful procedure for resolving patent disputes. However, if not properly planned, arbitration can be a burdensome, complex, expensive, and potentially unsatisfying proceeding.

Practice Note:
Arbitration procedures need to be properly planned out to be useful.

14.5 Courts and Patent Offices Outside the United States

Finally, a patent dispute may be resolved outside the United States, in a court or other patent office of another jurisdiction, if the dispute is framed in terms of the other jurisdiction's patents. While only U.S. courts can resolve disputes over U.S. Patents, and other jurisdictions can resolve disputes over their own patents,[21] a patentee may nonetheless seek to enforce non-U.S. Patents in an effort to resolve a patent dispute.

Practice Note:
Patent disputes may also be resolved using non-U.S. Patents in non-U.S. tribunals.

CHAPTER

15

What Is a Patent Worth?

In order to understand what a patent is worth, it is important to understand how damages are awarded in a patent infringement action. It is ultimately the potential for damages that will have the greatest impact in determining what a patent is worth.

For purposes of the present discussion, there are three types of potential damages that can be awarded in a patent infringement action:

- Pre-issuance damages;
- Post-issuance compensatory damages; and
- Enhanced damages, including treble damages and attorney's fees.

Generally, a patent does not become effective until the patent issues. However, in certain circumstances where a patent is infringed before a patent issues, a patentee may nonetheless be entitled to certain damages. This kind of damages is referred to as "pre-issuance damages." Pre-issuance damages are always limited to "compensatory" damages and are discussed in Section 15.2.

After a patent issues and throughout its term, if the patent is infringed, then a patentee may be entitled to damages to compensate it for infringements by others. These kind of damages are referred to as "post-issuance compensatory damages." There are a variety of different potential measures of such damages, some of which are discussed in Section 15.3. This is the most common form of damages.

Under certain circumstances, depending upon the conduct of the infringer, "enhanced damages" may also potentially be awarded. Enhanced damages can include:

- The entry of some multiple up to three times the compensatory damages awarded (often called "treble damages"); and/or
- An award of attorney's fees.

A brief discussion of the possible types of enhanced damages is provided in Section 15.4.

Finally, there are also certain limitations on the ability of a patentee to collect damages. These potential limitations are briefly discussed in Section 15.5.

15.1 Patent Term

As a preliminary matter, in order to understand the value of a patent, it is necessary to understand how long the claims of a patent have been in effect and enforceable and how long they will continue to be so. This period of time is referred to as the "patent term." A patent does not become effective until the patent issues. The USPTO issues patents every Tuesday.

Practice Note:
The term of a U.S. Patent is the period of time in which the claims have been and will continue to be effective and enforceable.

Once a patent expires, the contents of a patent are dedicated to the public, and the claims are no longer enforceable.[1]

A patent that issues based on a patent application that was filed after June 8, 1995 (absent some form of extension) will remain in effect for up to twenty years from its earliest effective filing date. Patents that issue based on applications filed prior to that date will remain in effect for up to twenty years from their earliest effective filing date or 17 years from the issue date, whichever is later.

Practice Note:

Generally, the term of a U.S. Patent begins when the patent issues, and ends approximately twenty years from the earliest U.S. filing date.

The earliest effective filing date for a given U.S. Patent in this context is the earliest filing date of a parent, non-provisional patent application to which priority is claimed in whole or in part. This point is illustrated in the diagram repeated below. In this example, Issued Patent 1 was filed on the filing date of Patent Application 1 and issued on the issued date of Patent Application 1. *The term of the Issued Patent will then be from the issued date of Patent Application 1 until twenty years from the filing date of Patent Application 1.* This period is shown as "Patent Term" for Issued Patent 1. Issued Patent 2, which claims priority to Patent Application 1, was filed on the filing date of Patent Application 2 and issued on the issue date of Patent Application 2. The filing date of Patent Application 2 is after the filing date of Patent Application 1, but before the issue date of Patent Application 1. The period between the filing date of Patent Application 2 and the issue date of Patent Application 1 is called the period of "overlapping pendency." *The Patent Term for Issued Patent 2, under these circumstances, will be from the issuance date of Patent Application 2 until the twenty years from the filing date of Patent Application 1.* In this example, the Patent Term for Issued Patent 2 is shorter than the Patent Term for Issued Patent 1.

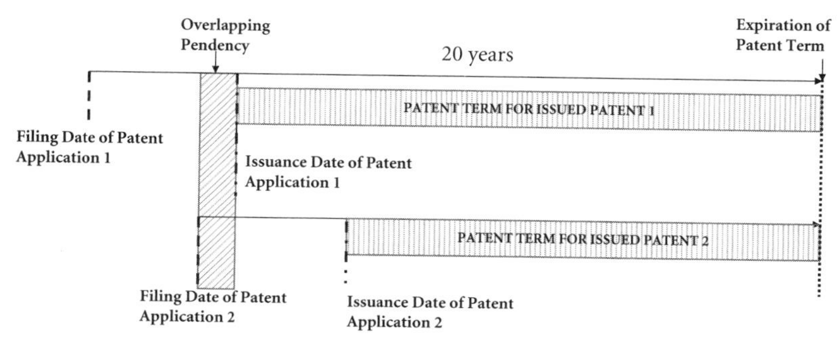

FIGURE 15.1 Example of Patent Term Calculation.

The patent term may also be *limited* for various reasons. For example, during prosecution, the claims of a patent application may be provisionally rejected for so-called "double patenting." A "double patenting" rejection may be issued because more than one patent and/or patent application claim patentably indistinct subject matter. In such a case, a patentee may overcome such a rejection by filing what is called a "terminal disclaimer." In a terminal disclaimer, the patentee gives up the part of the patent term in the disclaimed patent application that extends beyond the patent term of the other overlapping patents or patent applications which are the subject of the disclaimer.

Practice Note:
The term of a U.S. Patent may be shortened by a terminal disclaimer.

The patent term may also be *extended* for various reasons. For example, the term of patents filed after 2000 may be extended for any delay attributed to the USPTO, less any delay attributed to the applicant.[2] Similarly, the patent term can also be extended for certain types of patents, like those for drugs, when commercial exploitation of the patent is delayed by governmental review, by, for example, the Food and Drug Administration[3] or some other U.S. government agency.

Practice Note:
The term of a U.S. Patent may be extended under certain circumstances.

15.2 Pre-Issuance Damages

In the past, there were no remedies available against a potential infringer for actions taken prior to the issuance of a U.S. Patent.[4] However, in 1999, U.S. patent law was changed to allow, under certain circumstances, a patentee to recover damages for patent infringement that occurs prior to the issuance of a U.S. Patent.[5]

In particular, once a U.S. Patent Application has been published by the USPTO, a potential infringer can become liable for pre-issuance damages in the form of a "reasonable royalty" (*see* below, Section 15.3.2)[6] if

- The potential infringer infringes a claim published in the application;[7]
- The patent owner puts the potential infringer on actual notice of the published Patent Application;[8] and

- The patent issues with a valid and infringed claim that is substantially identical to the published claim which is infringed.

The right to pre-issuance damages is *only* available retroactively. If a U.S. Patent never issues, then there will be no remedy for infringement of a published U.S. Patent Application.

Practice Note:

Pre-issuance damages may be available for U.S. Patents that were published before the U.S. Patent is issued.

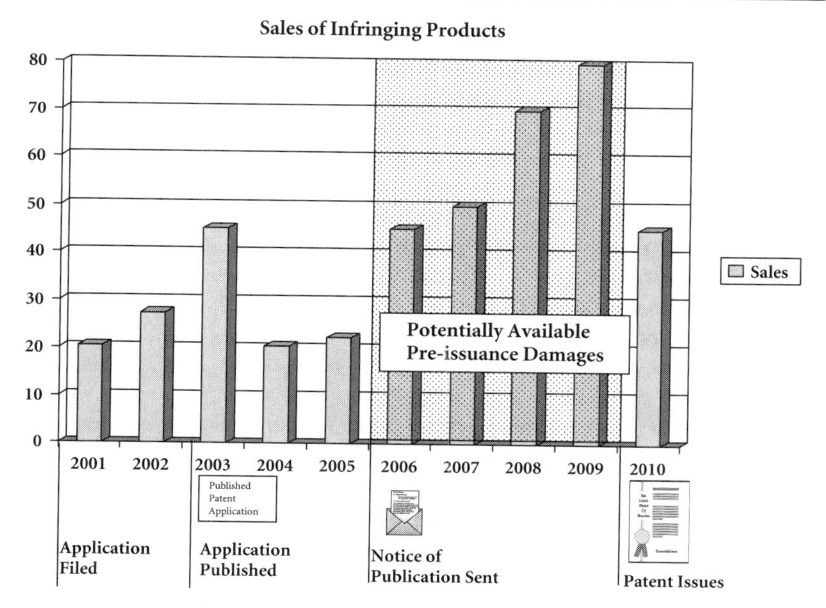

FIGURE 15.2 Potentially Available Pre-issuance Damages.

The only potential damages available during the pre-issuance period are "reasonable royalties." (*See* Section 15.3.2). There is no right to exclude (e.g., be issued an injunction) during this period.

Practice Note:

Pre-issuance damages are limited to a reasonable royalty.

The existence of this remedy may provide a patent applicant potential strategic opportunities for putting competitors on notice of a published Patent

Application, thereby putting the competitor in the risky position of potentially owing substantial patent damages, if and when the patent issues, if the Published Patent application is ignored.

15.3 Post-Issuance Compensatory Damages

Compensatory damages are the primary monetary remedy for patent infringement under U.S. patent law.[9] The goal of any compensatory damages theory is to make the injured party whole for the losses caused by the infringer's inappropriate activity.[10] Thus, compensatory damages are meant to put the injured party in the same position it would have been in "but for" the infringing activity.[11]

Practice Note:

Compensatory damages are available for post-issuance infringements of a U.S. Patent.

Depending upon the circumstances of the case, the appropriate measure of compensatory damages in a patent infringement case may be one of

- Lost profits;
- Established royalty rate; or
- Reasonable royalty.

In addition to determining the appropriate measure of compensatory damages, and regardless of which measure of damages is applied, a patentee may also recover based on the "entire market value" of what the patentee lost as a result of the infringer's sales of an infringing product or device or system, that includes an infringing component, rather than just the infringing component itself.

The elements necessary for establishing damages under each of these theories are generally discussed herein.

15.3.1 Lost Profits

A patentee that produces a patented item may be entitled to receive its lost profits due to infringing sales by a competitor. The logic behind this theory of damages is that if there had not been an infringement, the patentee would have made the sale, and thus the infringer harmed the profits of the patentee who lost that sale. This requires a patentee to show that there was a "reasonable probability" that, "but for" the infringement, the patentee would have made the sales that were made by the infringer.[12]

Practice Note:

Lost profits from sales of an infringing competitor is one form of compensatory damages that may be available for patent infringement.

Further, even if the patentee were to sell a product that did *not* practice the patented invention, but nonetheless competed against the infringing product, a patentee may be entitled to an award of lost profits.

U.S. patent law has devised various alternative ways to calculate lost profits, including

- The *Panduit* Test;
- Diverted Sales;
- Price Erosion; and
- Market Value Rule.

Each of these different ways is briefly discussed herein.

15.3.1.1 The *Panduit* Test

U.S. patent law recognizes that lost profits may be awarded where the so-called *Panduit*[13] test is satisfied. While this test may be used, U.S. patent law recognizes that other tests may also be used.[14]

Under the *Panduit* test, a patentee must establish

- Demand for the patented product;
- Absence of acceptable non-infringing substitutes;
- Manufacturing and marketing capability to exploit the demand; and
- The amount of the profit that it would have made, but for the infringement.[15]

Thus, the patentee must first show that there is a market for the patented product, in other words, that the patentee (or infringer) has customers for the patented product. Second, the patentee must show that there are no other products that consumers would find commercially acceptable which are available for purchase instead of the patentee's product. However, the mere existence of competing devices does not necessarily make the devices acceptable substitutes. A product on the market lacking the advantages of the patented product may not be an acceptable substitute.[16] Third, the patentee must show that it had the commercial capabilities to manufacture and market the additional patented products. Finally, the patentee must show the amount of profit that it would have made but for the infringement.

Generally, a patentee must be able to satisfy all four elements to be entitled to an award of lost profits.[17]

Once a patentee has established a reasonable inference that the lost profits claimed were in fact caused by the infringing sales, for example, by satisfying the *Panduit* test[18], the patentee "has sustained the burden of proving entitlement to lost profits due to the infringing sales."[19] "The burden then shifts to the infringer to show that the inference is unreasonable for some or all of the lost sales."[20]

Practice Note:

The *Panduit* test is one methodology used to determine whether to award lost profits for a patent infringement.

15.3.1.2 Diverted Sales

One way that lost profits may be measured is by the quantity of diverted sales. In other words, the patentee must show that *but for* the infringement, the patentee would have made the sale. This would not be the case if

- There were other licensed competitors who might have made the sale instead, without having to compensate the patentee; and/or
- There were non-infringing alternative products available which customers would have bought instead of the patentee's product.

The diverted sales could consist of all or a portion of the infringing sales that the patentee could have been expected to make had there not been infringement.

Practice Note:

A patentee may be entitled to an award of damages for its diverted sales to the infringer as a result of patent infringement.

Of course, when sales are diverted, the damages to a patentee may be more than just losing the sale itself. For example, if a patentee sells less product, the costs of manufacturing each product may be higher than if the patentee was able to achieve higher economies of scale by manufacturing and selling more product. Likewise, if no one else is selling a similar product, the patentee may also have been entitled to charge more for each product (as discussed in Section 15.3.1.3). Both of these types of damages may also be recovered as a result of diverted sales.[21]

15.3.1.3 Price Erosion

A patent owner may recover lost profits for price erosion by showing that the infringement caused the patent owner to charge lower prices than the market otherwise would have dictated.[22] In a market with only two viable competitors, a court may infer that the patentee would have charged higher prices but for the infringement. Price erosion damages can be described as "the difference between actual costs of goods and potential price—the price [that the patentee] could have realized had there been no competition from the infringers."[23]

Practice Note:

Price erosion damages may also be available for patent infringements.

As with lost profits for diverted sales, the patent holder must show that it would have been able to charge higher prices *but for* the infringement, and it must prove the amount of its loss.[24]

15.3.1.4 Market Value Rule

Regardless of the measure of damages accepted, when a patentee seeks damages on unpatented components sold with a patented apparatus, under limited circumstances courts may apply the "entire market value" rule to determine whether such components should be included in the computation of damages.[25] The entire market value rule permits "recovery of damages based on the value of a patentee's entire apparatus containing several features when the patent-related feature is the basis for customer demand."[26]

Practice Note:

Patent infringement damages may in certain circumstances be awarded based on the "entire market value" of the product containing the infringing component, not just the value of the infringing component.

In determining whether to apply the entire market value rule, courts primarily focus on whether the patented feature is the "basis for customer demand." Thus, in a case involving a patent claim for an elliptical port that eliminated noise and improved bass tones, the patentee was awarded damages based on the value of the entire speaker system, not just the port, since demand for the speaker system was based on the speakers producing desirable bass sounds.[27]

15.3.2 Reasonable Royalty

In the absence of provable lost profits, the minimum statutory recovery a patentee may receive for an infringed patent is a reasonable royalty on the sale of the infringing device.[28] The appropriate method for determining a reasonable royalty is to postulate a hypothetical negotiation between the parties as a willing licensor and willing licensee at the time the infringement began. The purpose of providing a "reasonable royalty" as an alternative measure of patent damages is not to direct the form of compensation, but rather "to set a floor below which damages may not fall."[29]

Practice Note:

Damages in the form of a reasonable royalty is the floor below which a damage award for patent infringement may not fall.

Back in the 1970s, the case, *Georgia-Pacific Corp. v. U.S. Plywood Corp.*, set out a series of factors (the "*Georgia-Pacific* factors") that should be considered when determining what should be a reasonable royalty.[30]

These factors include the following:

- Royalties received by the patentee which tend to prove an established royalty;
- The rates paid by licensees for other patents that are comparable to the one in suit;
- The nature and scope of any existing license, e.g., exclusive or non-exclusive, restrictions as to field of use, territory or customers;
- Whether the patentee has a policy of licensing to others;
- The commercial relationship between the patentee and the infringer, e.g., are the competitors in the same business or some other relationship;
- The extent that sales of other products, e.g., related products or supplies for a patented machine, are affected by using the patented technology;
- The duration and term left on the patent;
- The established profitability of the product made under the patents, e.g., its commercial success and current sales;
- The benefit of the patented invention over prior art that had achieved similar results;
- The nature of the patented invention, the character of its commercial embodiment as owned and produced by the licensor, and the benefits for those who have used the invention;

- The extent that the infringer has made use of the invention and any evidence probative of the value of that use;
- Customary royalty rates in the industry for analogous inventions;
- The portion of the profits for the infringing device that are attributable to the use of the invention rather than other elements, the manufacturing process, business risks or significant features, or improvements that are added by the infringer;
- The opinion of experts as to what a reasonable royalty may be under the circumstances; and
- The royalty that a *prudent licensee*, who, as a business proposition wants a license to manufacture the patented product and make a reasonable profit, and a *prudent patentee*, who was willing to grant a license, would have agreed upon if both had been reasonably and voluntarily trying to reach an agreement.

A detailed discussion of each of these factors is beyond the scope of this Guide.

Practice Note:

The *Georgia Pacific* factors may be used to calculate a reasonable royalty.

15.4 Enhanced Damages

In addition to being able to recover compensatory damages, in some circumstances the patentee can also recover enhanced damages. Enhanced damages can be in the form of attorney's fees[31] and/or multiple damages, up to treble (three times) any actual damages.[32] Historically, in many patent suits, these enhanced damages can be significant.

Practice Note:

Enhanced damages in the form of up to three times (treble) the compensatory damages may be available for willful patent infringement.

U.S. patent law allows for attorney's fees to be awarded in so-called "exceptional cases." The case law has found cases to be "exceptional" when an infringer has acted "willfully" with respect to the infringement. Thus, courts may inquire as to whether there has been "willful infringement." Alternatively, when the losing party in a patent infringement action acted inappropriately in the litigation, a court may also find a case to be "exceptional" and award attorney's fees to the prevailing party.[33]

Although the statute governing multiple damages does not state explicitly when a court is entitled to award such enhanced damages, the case law developed has found it appropriate to award enhanced damages when there has been "willful infringement."

For over two decades, U.S. patent law regarding "willful infringement" was based on the principle that receipt of notice of another's patent rights created a duty of due care to determine whether the recipient of such notice is infringing, either because it did not practice the claims, the claims were invalid, and/or the claims were unenforceable.[34] U.S. patent law went so far as to draw an adverse inference against an accused infringer if he or she did not obtain and produce in litigation a competent opinion of counsel concluding that the accused infringer did not infringe. Thus, in order to establish that this duty of care was met, accused infringers were often put in the untenable position of either waiving privilege and providing a copy of its counsel's legal analysis to the patentee, or risking a finding of willful infringement and paying treble damages and attorney's fees if the accused infringer lost the suit.[35]

Starting in 2004, U.S. patent law governing willful infringement began to evolve and address the problems associated with this problematic choice. As a first step, in 2004, the Federal Circuit reconsidered its decades of precedent on willful infringement. Although it chose at that time not to eliminate the duty to avoid infringement, the Federal Circuit in the *Knorr-Bremse* case eliminated the adverse inference that was being drawn when an accused infringer did not waive privilege and did not produce its opinion by counsel.[36]

While *Knorr-Bremse* began to address some of the concerns with the way U.S. patent law regarding willful infringement developed, it did not address all of the relevant concerns. Since the duty to avoid infringement still existed, the untenable choice still remained. Some accused infringers developed the practice of having two separate attorneys involved when a patent assertion was made: litigation counsel, who would be involved in the negotiations and actual litigation of the dispute with the patentee; and opinion counsel, who would be retained solely for the purpose of providing an opinion of counsel to be used as evidence of an infringer's good faith belief that it did not infringe a valid claim.

As a result, extensive disputes over the scope of waiver of privilege arose. In 2006, the Federal Circuit in *EchoStar*[37] held that when an opinion of counsel is relied upon to defend against a charge of willful infringement, there is a subject matter waiver of communications with counsel on the same subject, but the waiver did not extend to work product that was never communicated.

While this decision did reduce some of the risk of waiving privilege, it did not address whether the waiver included trial counsel in addition to the counsel that provided the opinion being relied upon.

Finally, in 2007, the Federal Circuit took the opportunity to reformulate U.S. patent law of willful infringement in *In re Seagate*.[38]

Under the new standard, U.S. patent law applies a two-part test to determine willful infringement:

- The infringer must have acted despite an objectively high likelihood that its actions constitute infringement of a valid patent; and
- The patentee must demonstrate that the objectively defined risk was either known, or was so obvious that it should have been known, to the accused infringer.[39]

This new two-part test presents a more stringent standard than the old test that was formerly applied by U.S. courts.

With respect to the first part of the new test, it is significant that it is an "objective" test, rather than a "subjective" test. In other words, the accused infringer's actual state of mind is irrelevant to this first inquiry.

Under the "objective recklessness" standard, courts look to the strength of the defenses and closeness of the case, and whether the defendants made efforts to avoid infringement by attempting to design around the patent. Of course, it is important to remember that the defenses do not need to be winners for these purposes, since the question of willful infringement only comes up when the accused infringer has already been found to infringe. In other words, the defenses have already failed. And now, the issue is whether the defenses were reasonable at the time in light of the circumstances.

A useful example of how the objective reasonableness standard has been applied by courts is *Abbott Laboratories v. Sandoz, Inc.*[40] In this case, Abbott held several patents for an antibiotic drug called clarithromycin. In June 2005, Abbott had brought a patent infringement lawsuit against Teva who was manufacturing a generic version of the antibiotic drug, and obtained a preliminary injunction. In November 2005, Abbott had brought a second patent infringement lawsuit against Andrx, another generic manufacturer of the same drug, and again obtained a preliminary injunction. On appeal in the *Teva* case, in June 2006, the Federal Circuit reversed the grant of the preliminary injunction on the grounds that there were substantial questions of validity that should have precluded the district court from granting the injunction. Thereafter, in December 2006, Sandoz launched its generic version of the drug, relying upon the appellate court's decision in *Teva*. In January 2007, the Federal Circuit upheld the preliminary injunction in *Andrx* without discussing the validity of the Abbott patents, and disavowed any preclusive effect of its prior decision in *Teva*. Ultimately, Sandoz was found by the jury to infringe and, in fact, even willfully infringe the Abbott patents. The district court rejected the finding of willful infringement in its application of the *Seagate* test on the grounds that there was only an "objectively low likelihood" that Sandoz would infringe a valid patent claim at the time it decided to launch the infringing product based on the appellate court's decision in *Teva*.

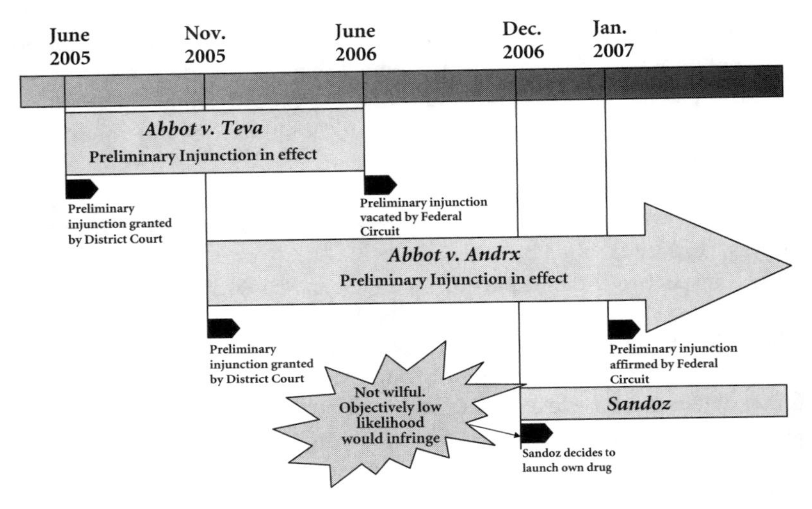

FIGURE 15.3 No Willful Infringement.

However, even if a patentee is able to establish that the infringer acted in an "objectively reckless" manner, the patentee must also establish that the objectively defined risk was known or so obvious that it should have been known to the accused infringer.[41]

One factor used to demonstrate that the second prong of the test is not met is when an accused infringer has performed its own testing and experimentation on accused products that shows non-infringement.[42]

One useful example of where an infringer was found to be willful under both prongs of the *Seagate* test is *Ball Aerosol v. Limited Brands, Inc.*[43] In *Ball Aerosol*, the district court found that the infringer acted objectively reckless when it received a notice letter. The court granted the patentee's motion for summary judgment earlier on in the case, finding that the patent claim was valid. The district court relied on the fact that the infringer had received a written notice of infringement to establish that the infringer knew or should have known of the obvious risk that it would infringe the patent. Curiously, this decision was ultimately vacated when the Federal Circuit on appeal found that the patent claim which the district court found to be valid and willfully infringed to be invalid and not infringed.

15.5 Limitations on Damages

U.S. patent law also places certain limits on a patentee's ability to collect damages. These limits are discussed in this section.

15.5.1 Notice and Marking

A patentee who practices a claimed invention has a duty to mark its products that practice one or more apparatus claims in a U.S. Patent with the patent numbers it practices.[44] This duty applies not only to the patentee, but to anyone who sells a patented article with authority of the patentee (such as licensees).[45]

Practice Note:

A patentee (and its licensees) has a duty to mark products that practice an apparatus claim in a U.S. Patent.

The purpose of the marking requirement is to provide the public with notice that a patented article is the subject of patent protection.[46]

This duty can be fulfilled by placing on the patented article the word "patent" or the abbreviation "pat.," together with the number of the patent. When, due to the character or nature of the article, this cannot be done on the article itself, it may instead be accomplished by placing a notice on a label affixed to the article or its packaging.

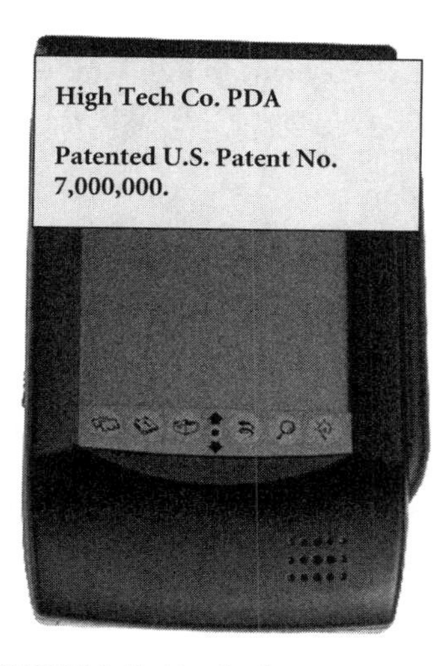

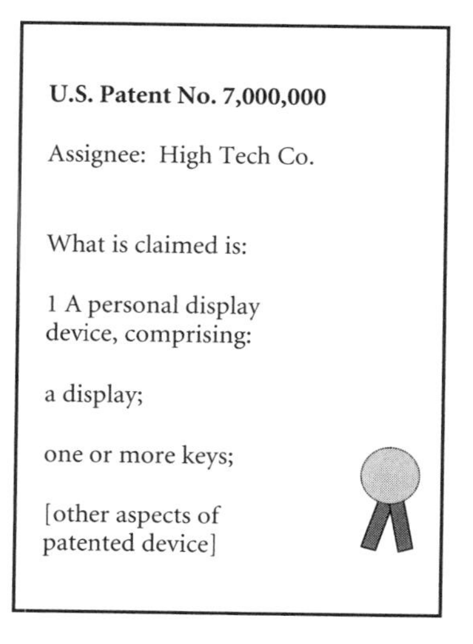

FIGURE 15.4 Marking Products.

One method used to test whether a patentee has a duty to mark a particular product is to ask "whether the product would infringe the patent if sold by an unauthorized party."[47] If it would, then the patentee has a duty to mark the product.

Once this duty arises, the patentee (or one acting with authority under the patent) must mark it in a "substantially consistent and continuous" manner to meet this duty.[48] When licensees or someone other than the patentee is involved, a more lenient "rule of reason" may be applied to determine if the marking has been sufficient since it is more difficult to control third parties.

If a patentee sells a patented product that is not marked, the patentee may nonetheless avail itself of the benefits of marking by starting to mark the patented products at a later date.[49] In such a case, the damage period would not apply during periods when the patentee did not mark its patented products which were being sold.

Practice Note:

Failure to properly mark products can result in a potential loss of recovery of pre-lawsuit damages, before the patentee places the infringer on notice of the alleged infringement.

Significantly, a patentee that does *not* make a product or authorize another to make a product covered by its patent can recover damages for the period prior to bringing an infringement claim without regard to marking or even in the absence of notice to the accused infringer prior to filing a lawsuit.[50]

However, when the duty does arise, if the patentee fails to fulfill this duty, the patentee can be precluded from collecting damages prior to providing actual notice of infringement to an infringer.[51] Typically, actual notice is accomplished by sending a letter to an accused infringer. Alternatively, starting a lawsuit will meet this obligation.

In order for a notice letter to count as "actual notice," the patentee must specify the patent number that is alleged to be infringed, as well as the infringing product.[52]

The duty to mark and provide notice is determined on a claim-by-claim basis. Thus, if a patentee sells a product which meets some, but not all, of the claims of a particular patent, and fails to mark such a product with the patent number, then the patentee may be precluded from collecting the pre-notice damages for the claims practiced by that product, but not precluded from collecting damages for the claims that are not practiced by the sale of the product.[53]

15.5.2 Statute of Limitations

U.S. patent law places certain limits on the time in which a patentee can seek damages for patent infringements. In other words, if a patentee waits too long to bring a patent suit after an infringement occurs, it may forfeit the right to collect damages for that act of patent infringement. U.S. patent law provides a patentee up to six years from an act of patent infringement to bring a lawsuit.

This period may be extended under certain circumstances, such as when the parties enter into an agreement to extend that period, called a "tolling" agreement.

The statute of limitations will only preclude enforcement of infringements more than six years before the lawsuit began. It does not preclude a patentee from enforcing against infringements that occur

- Less than six years prior to the commencement of a lawsuit; or
- After the lawsuit commences.

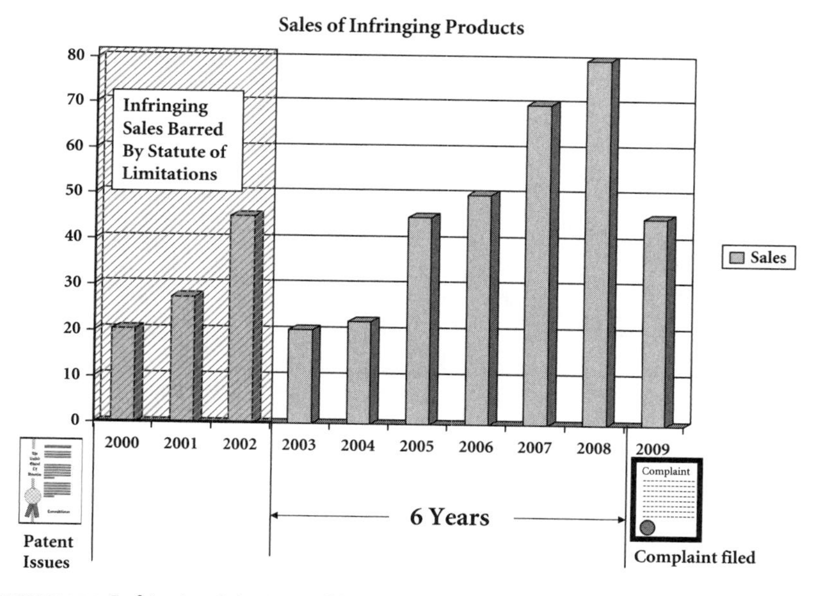

FIGURE 15.5 Infringing Sales Barred by Statute of Limitations.

Practice Note:

Generally, absent an agreement to the contrary, a patentee is precluded from obtaining damages for infringements that occurred more than six years before a complaint is filed with a U.S. district court.

15.5.3 Laches

If a patent owner takes too long to first bring a patent enforcement action, the patentee may also be precluded from seeking pre-lawsuit damages under the equitable defense of "laches."[54] This theory barring recovery is different from a statute of limitations, since it extends to all pre-lawsuit damages, not just the infringing acts which occurred more than six years prior to bringing the lawsuit.

Practice Note:
A patentee could be precluded under the doctrine of "laches" from obtaining pre-suit damages, if the patentee waits too long to bring a suit.

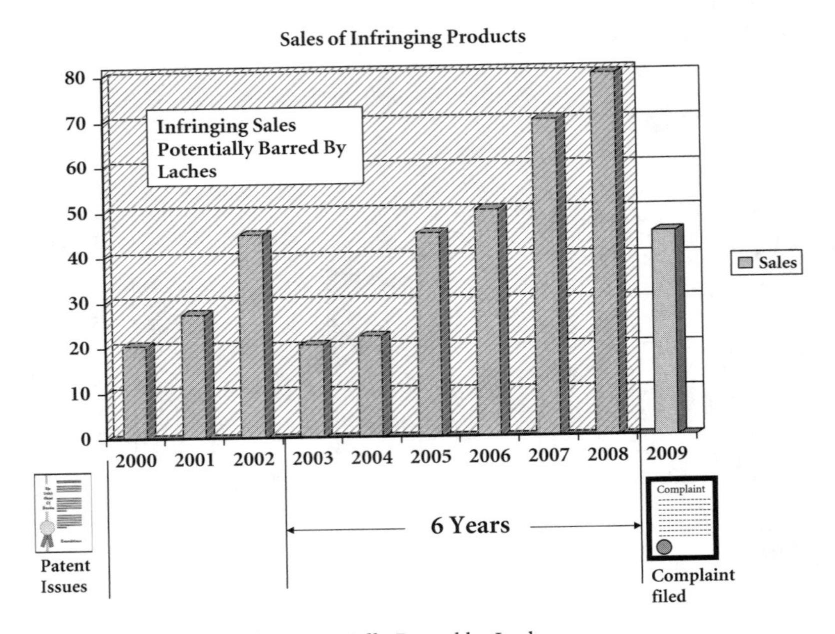

FIGURE 15.6 Infringing Sales Potentially Barred by Laches.

There are generally two elements to an equitable defense of "laches":

- An unreasonable and inexcusable delay in bringing a lawsuit; and
- A material prejudice suffered by the accused infringer that is attributable to the delay.[55]

A delay of greater than six years gives rise to a presumption of laches.[56] Delay can be measured from actual knowledge by the patentee or the alleged infringements. In some circumstances, it may be inferred from open and notorious activities of the accused infringer.[57]

This presumption of laches can be overcome. For example, a patentee may offer a justification for its delay, such as

- Involvement in other litigation;
- Negotiations with the accused;
- Poverty;
- Illness; and
- A dispute over ownership of the patent.

Similarly, a shorter delay may potentially give rise to a claim for laches, although it may be more difficult to establish.

The prejudice suffered by the accused infringer can be either evidentiary *or* economic.

Evidentiary prejudice may be found when evidence (like documents or witnesses) has been lost or becomes unavailable due to the passage of time.[58] Examples of evidentiary prejudice include, for example

- Documents destroyed in a flood;
- The death of a witness; or
- Prior art device being lost.

Economic prejudice occurs when a defendant will suffer the loss of monetary investments or incur damages which would have been prevented by an earlier suit. Courts specifically look for a change in the economic position of the defendant during the period of delay.

Since laches is an equitable doctrine, general principles of equity apply. Thus, U.S. patent law allows district courts to use their own discretion in determining whether laches has been established, and, even if established, whether the equitable remedy should be applied to preclude pre-lawsuit damages. Thus, courts may consider such factors as

- The length of the delay;
- The seriousness of the prejudice;
- The reasonableness of the excuses; and
- The defendant's conduct or culpability.[59]

15.5.4 Estoppel

An estoppel can be created by a party's detrimental reliance upon the misleading conduct of another. In the context of U.S. patent law, a patentee may be "estopped" or prevented from asserting a claim for patent infringement in certain circumstances.

This theory is different from a statute of limitations or laches because it may preclude the assertion of the patent against even post-complaint infringements.

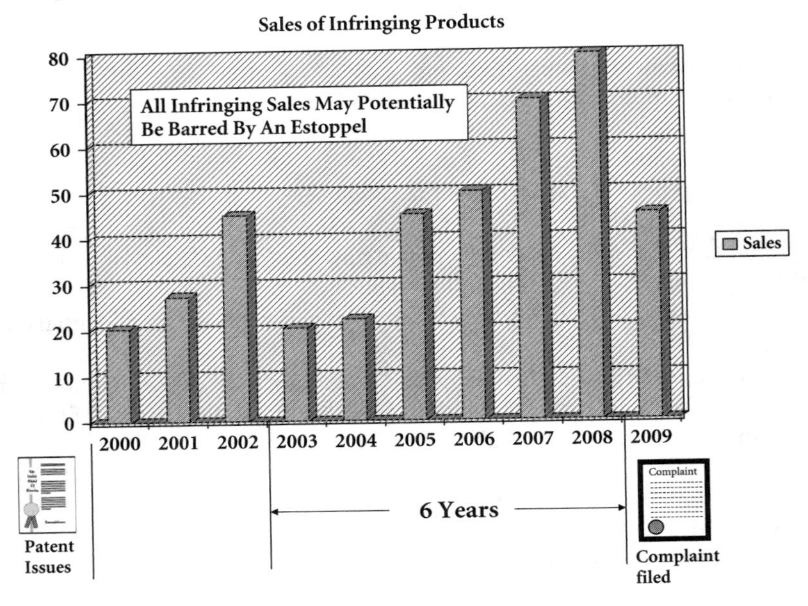

FIGURE 15.7 Sales Potentially Barred by an Estoppel.

Practice Note:

A patentee can be precluded under the doctrine of "estoppel" from obtaining any damages.

In particular, an accused infringer may establish an estoppel defense by showing the following:

- The patentee, through misleading statements or conduct, led the accused infringer to reasonably infer that the patentee did not intend to enforce the patent against the accused infringer;
- The accused infringer relied upon that conduct; and
- Due to its reliance, the accused infringer will be materially prejudiced if the patentee is allowed to proceed with its claim.[60]

Unlike laches, to assert estoppel, the defendant must know or be able to infer that the patentee has known of its activities for some time. Also unlike a laches defense, an estoppel defense can prevent a patentee from seeking damages even after a complaint is filed.

CHAPTER

16

How to Avoid Willful Patent Infringement

As discussed in Chapter 15, Section 15.4 one type of damages that can be awarded in a patent infringement action is "enhanced damages" as a result of an infringer's willful infringement of a patent claim. Such enhanced damages can include an award of three times the compensatory damages ("treble damages") and an award of attorney's fees. This type of damages can greatly increase an organization's exposure in a patent infringement suit.

While the risk of an award of enhanced damages was substantially reduced after the Federal Circuit's decision in *In re Seagate*[1] in 2007, unless an organization acts responsibly in the face of a potential patent infringement assertion, the risk remains real and potentially very costly. This chapter addresses steps the organization can take to avoid willful patent infringement.

16.1 Reviewing and Understanding the Patent and Claims

The first step to take to avoid a finding of willful infringement is not to infringe the claim in the first place.[2] Thus, the best practices would have the organization, and those charged with avoiding infringement, carefully review and understand the patent and its claims at issue. It is useful to review the patent in enough detail to understand what the subject matter relates to and whether the claims are relevant to the organization's products and services.

Practice Note:
Review and understand the patent and claim to determine if it is relevant to the organization's business.

16.2 Seeking and Obtaining Advice of Outside Patent Counsel

Once a determination has been made by the organization that a patent is relevant, best practices involve bringing in an experienced and competent patent counsel to analyze the patent in question.

Practice Note:
Seek and obtain advice of outside patent counsel on the applicability of the patent claims to the organization's business.

Such an analysis should include a review of the claims, the specification, the prosecution history, and the cited art, as well as a thorough explanation of how the potentially infringing product or service operates in relevant aspects. It is necessary for patent counsel to understand the aspects of the product or service being analyzed which might be considered the "equivalent" of the elements of the claim that might be thought to be otherwise missing. Thus, it is best to explain to patent counsel not only what the system does *not* do, but what it *does* do.

Practice Note:
Explain to counsel not only what the analyzed product or service does not do, but also what it does do.

16.3 Developing and Implementing "Design Arounds"

The goal of counsel's analysis should be to determine the exposure of the organization to the patent claims. To the extent the product or service can be modified, counsel should seek to develop with the appropriate technical staff of the organization the changes that can and should be made to minimize an adverse finding of infringement. U.S. patent law refers to such changes as "design arounds," since the goal is to design around the patent.

Practice Note:
Develop and implement design arounds which clearly avoid the patent claims.

16.4 Developing an Appropriate Record of Respect

If everything goes sour in a patent litigation and the organization is found to infringe someone else's patent, one factor the courts will look to in deciding whether to grant an award of enhanced damages is whether the organization demonstrated a level of respect for the patent, even if the organization was mistaken in its views as to the proper scope or validity of the patent. This area of U.S. patent law accepts the fact that people make mistakes. The issue is was there a level of negligent or intentional indifference to the patent rights of another such that the adjudicated infringer should be punished as a willful infringer with enhanced damages to deter future similar behavior.

One way to demonstrate to a court or jury that the organization acted in good faith is to establish an appropriate record of respect with regard to others' patents. This includes creating non-privileged documents that will demonstrate that when the organization became aware of someone else's patents, the organization tried to avoid that patent, and took appropriate steps in this effort. If the organization is put on notice from a patentee of a patent, then an appropriate written record demonstrating respect and the organization's objections to claims of infringement should be created with the patent owner. This type of correspondence is less likely to occur these days since *MedImmune*, but if it does occur, an appropriate level of respect and justification for the organization's conduct should be evidenced in such written correspondence.

Practice Note:
Develop an appropriate written record of respect for the patent claims within the organization.

In sum, when faced with knowledge of another's patent which could be relevant to its products or services, an organization should identify and analyze the patent, consult with competent outside patent counsel to confirm its views and develop an appropriate defense to any potential future assertion, implement any design arounds necessary or appropriate to reduce the risk of a finding of patent infringement, and develop an appropriate record of respect.

In the case where there is no way around the patent, the organization should seriously consider either obtaining a license to use the patent, or avoid selling the infringing product or service in the United States.

CHAPTER

17

When Can a Patent Stop a Competitor?

A patent does not grant its owner the right to practice its invention; it only grants the patent owner the right to exclude others from practicing the invention. Thus, one of the basic remedies traditionally available to a patent owner is the right to obtain an injunction (or court order) to preclude an infringer from practicing the claims of the patent.

For decades since the formation of the U.S. Court of Appeals for the Federal Circuit in the early 1980s, there was a "general rule" that courts will issue permanent injunctions against patent infringement absent extraordinary circumstances.

The fairness of this general rule was called into question in 2005–2006 when a small, non-practicing entity (NTP) was almost awarded an injunction against the maker of the BlackBerry® handheld pager (Research in Motion or RIM).[1] The prospect of an injunction against RIM was the subject of extensive negative press coverage.[2] This issue also was brought to the attention of corporate America and its leadership, which were being told that their BlackBerry® handheld pagers may cease operating and might need to be replaced.

All of this publicity no doubt had an impact on the U.S. Supreme Court when in 2006, soon after the *NTP v. RIM* case was settled for a very large sum of money, a unanimous Court, in *eBay Inc. v. MercExchange L.L.C.*, vacated and remanded a judgment of the Federal Circuit which had held that there was a "general rule" that courts will issue permanent injunctions against patent infringement absent extraordinary circumstances.[3]

The U.S. Supreme Court held that "the decision whether to grant or deny injunctive relief rests within the equitable discretion of the district courts, and that such discretion must be exercised consistent with traditional principles of equity, in patent disputes no less than in other cases governed by such standards."[4]

Thus, when the statute which granted U.S. courts authority to issue permanent injunctions in patent cases states a court "may" award an injunction, it means exactly that: "may" not "must."[5]

Under the new U.S. Supreme Court test, a plaintiff seeking permanent injunctive relief must demonstrate, and a court must apply, the following traditional four-factor framework that governs in general the award of injunctive relief:

- The plaintiff has suffered an irreparable injury;
- Remedies available at law, such as monetary damages, are inadequate to compensate for that injury;
- Considering the balance of hardships between the plaintiff and defendant, a remedy in equity is warranted; and
- The public interest would not be disserved by a permanent injunction.[6]

How each of these four factors has been applied since *eBay* is discussed in turn below.

17.1 Irreparable Harm

While U.S. patent law previously found that irreparable harm is presumed in a patent case, the U.S. Supreme Court's decision in *eBay* eliminated such a presumption. Thus, a patentee (which has the burden) must establish with evidence and not merely generalized arguments that it will suffer irreparable harm if an injunction is not granted.

In general, irreparable harm is a type of harm that cannot be compensated with just money. In determining whether there has been "irreparable harm" to the patentee, the following kinds of factors have been considered:

- Whether the parties are competitors;
- Whether licenses have been granted;
- The nature of the market for the patented items;
- Whether lost market share will be difficult to recover; and
- Demand for the patented feature.

The fact that the patentee and the infringer are competitors is an example of a case where granting an injunction may be appropriate.[7] However, this fact by itself is not dispositive as to whether an injunction will or should be granted.[8] The patentee will still be required to provide sufficient evidence that if infringing sales are allowed to continue, it will cause some permanent harm to the patentee.[9]

Often, when the patentee is merely a non-practicing entity that merely owns a patent, and does not make a competing product, injunctions have been denied.[10] The rationale for this rule was explained by Justice Kennedy of the U.S. Supreme Court in a concurring opinion in *eBay* as follows:

> An industry has developed in which firms use patents not as a basis for producing and selling goods but, instead, primarily for obtaining licensing fees. For these firms, an injunction, and the potentially serious sanctions arising from its violation, can be employed as a bargaining tool to charge exorbitant fees to companies that seek to buy licenses to practice the patent. When the patented invention is but a small component of the product the companies seek to produce and the threat of an injunction is employed simply for undue leverage in negotiations, legal damages may well be sufficient to compensate for the infringement and an injunction may not serve the public interest."[11]

However, this is not an absolute rule. Some types of non-practicing entities have been found to be entitled to an injunction.[12] For example, in some cases where a university or research laboratory is the patentee and does not itself practice the invention, courts have nonetheless granted injunctions.[13]

The fact that a patentee has licensed the patent to others may demonstrate that money damages are an adequate remedy.[14] Thus, an injunction may not be necessary to compensate the patentee. In one case, for example, the patentee's willingness to twice license its patent and forego its patent rights "is one factor to consider with respect to whether plaintiff will suffer irreparable harm" to its brand name.[15] However, the mere fact that a license has been previously granted must be taken in context and weighed with other factors.[16]

Thus, changed circumstances since a license was granted can be considered too. For example, if a license were granted to an entity which did not directly compete in the relevant market with a patentee, it might not be sufficient evidence to establish lack of irreparable harm with respect to a patentee's refusal to grant a license to a direct competitor at some later time.

The nature of the market and size of the customer base are additional factors that may be considered in determining if there has been irreparable harm. For example, where the patentee and the infringer are competitors in a two-supplier market, and the patentee has suffered a permanent loss of market share, irreparable harm has been found and an injunction has been granted.[17] Similarly, where the patentee and the infringer are direct competitors in a market with a small customer base, and the infringer sold and marketed the infringing products to the same group of customers as the patentee, irreparable harm was found and an injunction was granted.[18]

When the ongoing sale of infringing items will cause a patentee to lose market share that will be difficult if not impossible to recover, courts have found irreparable harm.[19] For example, in a case involving digital video recorders ("DVRs"), a competitor was found to infringe the patent claims. The court recognized that satellite television sales tended to have so-called "sticky" customers. In other words, once a sale was made, it was unlikely that the customer would switch television service providers. The court found that in this instance, the denial of an injunction would cause irreparable harm to the patent owner and granted the injunction.[20]

Demand for the patented features can also be a factor in at least some cases. Thus, where the demand for the patented article comes from the patented feature, irreparable harm is more likely to be found than when the patented feature is one among many features. Where the infringing goods have numerous features, both patented and unpatented, it may not be conclusively determined whether the customer demand stems from the patented features or some other factor.

In sum, cases since *eBay* have found that a plaintiff must establish irreparable harm based on a loss that cannot be compensated by money. Such irreparable harm is no longer presumed in patent cases. Mere allegations of harm are insufficient. Patentees must prove actual harm. When a patentee does not practice or license the patent, or even sell a competing product, an injunction may be difficult to justify.

17.2 Whether Remedies at Law Are Adequate

Damages have been found to be adequate when the patentee did not practice the patent, make a competing product, or would be prevented from licensing the patent as a result of the infringement.

Generally, a patentee needs to make at least a competing product to the infringing product, and needs to present evidence of how the continuing sale of the infringing product will hurt the patentee's business, *e.g.*, loss of market share, loss of future customers, etc. Mere allegations of harm are insufficient. Undemonstrated harm to a licensing program is also insufficient.

However, in *eBay*, the U.S. Supreme Court recognized that some non-practicing entities like universities and other research institutions may also be entitled to an injunction.[21]

17.3 Balance of Hardships

In addition to the harm caused by continued infringement, when balancing the relative hardships of the parties if an injunction were or were not to issue, U.S. patent law considers the relative affect on each party if an injunction were granted or denied.

For example, a court is likely to consider whether granting an injunction will put the other party out of business. Thus, where an injunction is not likely to put one of the parties out of business, courts have been more inclined to grant the injunction.[22] On the other hand, where granting an injunction is likely to put the other party out of business, court's have been more reluctant. As the Federal Circuit noted in determining whether to stay a permanent injunction pending appeal, "[a patentee] ha[s] a cognizable interest in obtaining an injunction to put an end to infringement of its patents; it did not have a cognizable interest in putting [an infringing competitor] out of business."[23]

Impact on others, such as distributors, customers, and end users is generally not considered a relevant factor for this issue.[24] Similarly, the costs to the infringer in setting up the infringing product or system should also not be considered as part of this balance.[25]

A true loss to the plaintiff will generally outweigh the damage to an infringing defendant if it is adequately established.

17.4 Public Interest

Generally, U.S. courts have not considered the public interest factor to be dispositive. Historically, the public interest factor in a typical case favors the patentee since there is a public interest in maintaining the integrity of the patent system.[26] Nonetheless, courts that have looked at this factor have taken seemingly different views on this subject.

In one case, a U.S. district court found the potential loss to the public of the Microsoft Office® and Windows® products, for even a short time, was against the public interest.[27]

By contrast, in another case, in which the manufacturer of a hybrid electric vehicle known as the Prius®, was found to infringe a patent, the district court found that even though enjoining the Prius® would increase the dependency of the United States on foreign oil (clearly a result that would be against public interest), the court found such arguments unpersuasive.[28]

Another district court took the view that the public interest in the patent system was in having technology used and improved upon, and granting an injunction in favor of a patentee that did not practice the patent would cut against such public interest.[29]

Similarly, another potential consideration that may affect the public interest is whether granting an injunction would preclude the public from accessing some irreplaceable medicine or medical procedure. However, the proofs that are necessary to establish this kind of public injury can be difficult to meet, and the ultimate determination if this proof has been met falls within the sound discretion of the trial court.[30]

In sum, these cases demonstrate that public interest is in the eye of the beholder.

CHAPTER

18

How Rights Are Transferred

A patent is a bundle of rights. These rights start off with the inventors.[1] Unless the inventor(s) transfers these rights, under U.S. patent law, the presumption is that each inventor has a whole and undivided interest in the invention.[2] This means each inventor can use and/or license rights to use the invention without accounting to the other inventors.[3]

However, as with all forms of ownership, the way in which the rights are shared and accounted for can be modified by agreement or operation of law. For example, if an inventor is hired by an organization to invent or come up with a solution to a particular problem, absent an agreement to the contrary, the normal rule of law in many jurisdictions would have the inventor's employer own the invention and subsequent patent.[4] An employment agreement may also provide for certain inventions to be owned by an employer and others retained by the employee.

An assignment is a form of agreement where all of the rights to a patent are transferred from one owner (typically referred to as an "assignor") to a new owner (typically referred to as the "assignee"). A patent owner may be an individual, a collection of individuals, an entity, a collection of entities, or a collection of one or more individuals and entities. A patent application or patent does not need to be assigned, in which case it will remain in the hands of the inventors. Alternatively, a patent application or patent may be assigned one or more times.

In order to perfect an assignment of patent rights, copies of the patent assignment should be filed (or "recorded") with the USPTO. After recording the documents with the USPTO, the documents provided will be accessible to the public when the patent application or issued patent becomes accessible to the public. Thus, when the patent application is published or the patent issued, the fact that an assignment has been filed is publicly available at one of the USPTO's Web sites (assignments.uspto.gov), and the assignment itself is available from the USPTO. The failure of an assignee to file the assignment with the USPTO risks that the assignee of record can reassign or license the patent application or patent to others as good faith purchasers for value. Such a good faith purchaser may obtain rights without the consent of the rightful patent owner.

A license is a form of agreement where less than all of the rights to a patent are transferred from the owner (typically referred to as a "licensor") to a patent user (typically referred to as a "licensee"). Licenses can come in varying forms. For example, an exclusive license may be granted, in which only one licensee is granted rights under the patent. Alternatively, a non-exclusive license may otherwise be granted in which more than one licensee may be granted rights under the patents.

License rights under a patent may be further divided up by time, field of use, and even geographically. Thus, for example, a licensee may be granted a two-year license under the patent to practice one of several particular fields of use under the patent in the states of Florida, Georgia, and South Carolina. By subdividing the rights this way, more than one exclusive license can be granted to the same patent, as long as the scope of the license (time period, field of use, and geography) are not overlapping.

In addition to granting licenses under a patent, a patent owner may forgive an infringer or licensee for past infringements by granting what is called a release. Also, a patentee may agree in the future not to assert the patent under certain conditions. The agreement not to sue on a patent is called a "non-assertion."

Epilogue

Having completed reading this Guide, it is my hope that the reader will have a better understanding of how to spot issues with respect to patent practice.

This Guide is not intended to be a "how-to" guide or a "do it yourself" guide. It is not intended to substitute for legal advice. Rather, it is intended to help non-patent practitioner users of the U.S. patent system obtain a sufficient understanding of the process, its benefits, and risks so as to be in a position to seek and obtain competent legal advice. Hopefully, this Guide has achieved that purpose.

Practice Note:
Call a patent attorney today!

Notes

Chapter 1 What Is a Patent?

1. There are other forms of intellectual property, such as trademarks, copyrights, trade secrets, etc., which are beyond the scope of this Guide.
2. 35 U.S.C. § 154(a)(2). However, this term may be extended due to delay in prosecuting a patent application attributable to the USPTO. 35 U.S.C. § 154(b)(1)(B). For certain types of inventions, such as computer-implemented and business-related inventions, this delay may be significant and could effectively lengthen the term of such a patent by years.
3. A patent only covers the territory of the country which issues it. Thus, a U.S. Patent can only be infringed in the United States. A Canadian patent can only be infringed in Canada.
4. Unlike the rest of the world, U.S. Patent Law is based on a "first-to-invent" principle. Every other country in the world, by contrast, follows a "first-to-file" principle. For a detailed discussion on the merits of each system, see Charles R.B. Macedo, *First-to-File: Is American Adoption of the International Standard in Patent Law Worth the Price?*, 18 AIPLA Q.J. 193 (1990), 1988 COLUM. BUS. L. REV. 543 (1988).
5. 35 U.S.C. § 102.
6. 35 U.S.C. § 103(a).
7. 35 U.S.C. § 101.
8. *See, e.g., Dawson Chem. Co. v. Rohm & Haas Co.*, 448 U.S. 176, 215 (1980) ("[T]he essence of a patent grant is the right to exclude others from profiting by the patented invention.").
9. *Markman v. Westview Instruments*, 517 U.S. 370, 373 (1996) (patent statute grants "inventors 'the right to exclude others from making, using, offering for sale, selling, or importing the patented invention,' in exchange for full disclosure of an invention" (citation omitted)).
10. Dayton-Wright Co., the assignee to the Wright brothers, held a number of patents in the 1920s relating to airplane design and control. *See, e.g.*, U.S. Patent Nos. 1,501,530, 1,504,663, 1,552,112, and 1,557,214.
11. Samuel Morse's invention of the telegraph was the subject of U.S. Patent 1,647, as well as extensive litigation. *See, e.g., O'Reilly v. Morse*, 56 U.S. (15 How.) 62 (1854).
12. *See, e.g.*, U.S. Patent Nos. 161,739, 174,465, and 186,787. Some of these patents were the subject of extensive patent litigation also. *See, e.g., The Telephone Cases*, 126 U.S. 1 (1888).

13. *See, e.g.*, U.S. Patent No. 227,229.
14. *See, e.g.*, U.S. Patent Nos. 4,091,426 and 4,173,319.
15. *See, e.g.*, U.S. Patent Nos. 3,906,166 and 4,881,258.
16. *See, e.g.*, U.S. Patent No. 6,377,530.
17. *See, e.g.*, U.S. Patent No. 6,452,588.
18. *See, e.g.*, U.S. Patent No. 5,745,086.
19. U.S. Patent No. 7,479,949.
20. *See, e.g.*, *Court smacks down Smucker's patent request for peanut butter and jelly*, The Washington Times, April 9, 2005; *Patently ridiculous: When peanut butter and jelly sandwiches are getting their own patent, the system intended to protect creativity is in need of a major overhaul*, St. Petersburg Times, February 24, 2003 (*available at* http://www.sptimes.com/2003/02/24/Opinion/Patently_ridiculous.shtml, last visited on July 17, 2009); Jeff Hecht, *Boy takes swing at US patents*, New Scientist, April 17, 2002 (*available at* http://www.newscientist.com/article/dn2178-boy-takes-swing-at-us-patents.html, last visited July 17, 2009); Sabra Chartrand, *Patents; In Search of the Perfect Swing, Golfers Invent More Devices Than the Players of Any Other Sport*, N.Y. Times, August 2, 1993 (*available at* http://query.nytimes.com/gst/fullpage.html?res=9F0CE7D7103CF931A3575BC0A965958260, last visited July 17, 2009).
21. U.S. Patent No. 6,368,227. On reexamination, all of the issued claims were cancelled. *See* Reexamination Certificate 6,368,227 C1.
22. U.S. Patent No. 6,004,596. On reexamination, all of the issued claims were cancelled. *See* Reexamination Certificate 6,004,596 C1.
23. *See, e.g.*, U.S. Patent No. 5,960,411; *Amazon.com v. Barnes & Noble.com*, 239 F.3d 1343 (Fed. Cir. 2001).
24. *See* U.S. Patent No. 5,806,063. *See also* USPTO Press Release #99-51, Patent and Trademark Office Orders Reexamination Of Y2K Fix Patent, Dec. 21, 1999 (*available at* http://www.uspto.gov/web/offices/com/speeches/99-51.htm).
25. For an entertaining collection of "absurd" patents on "ridiculous" devices, see Christopher Cooper, Patently Absurd: The Most Ridiculous Devices Ever Invented (Robson Books 2004).
26. *NTP, Inc. v. Research in Motion, Ltd.*, 397 F. Supp. 2d 785 (E.D. Va. 2005).
27. *See* U.S. Patent No. 6,469, entitled "A Device for Buoying Vessels Over Shoals," to Abraham Lincoln (May 22, 1849).
28. Abraham Lincoln, *Lecture on "Discoveries, Inventions and Improvements,"* delivered before the Library Association of Springfield, Illinois, Feb. 22, 1860, *reprinted in* 5 Life and Works of Abraham Lincoln, Speeches and Presidential Addresses, 1859–1865, 13 (Marion Mills Miller ed., centenary edition) (1907). President Lincoln explained in this address that the development of a patent system, along with the discovery of America and the perfection of printing, was one of the three most important developments in the world's history to facilitate all other inventions and discoveries. With respect to the patent system, he explained:

    > Next came the patent laws. These began in England in 1624, and in this country with the adoption of our Constitution. Before then any man [*might*] instantly use what another man had invented, so that the inventor had no special advantage from his invention. The patent system changed this, secured to the inventor for a limited time exclusive use of his inventions, and thereby added the fuel of interest to the fire of genius in the discovery and production of new and useful things.

29. Since its formation in the early 1980s, all appeals from decisions of U.S. district courts in patent cases are made to the Federal Circuit. (*See* Chapter 14, Section 14.1).
30. 149 F.3d 1368 (Fed. Cir. 1998).
31. In *State Street*, the Federal Circuit used the "useful, concrete and tangible result" test taken from an earlier decision, *In re Alappat*, 33 F.3d 1526 (Fed. Cir. 1994) (en banc), as the standard for determining whether the particular claim at issue was patent-eligible. (*See* Chapter 3, Section 3.4). In 2008, the Federal Circuit advised that the portion of the *Alappat* decision discussing this test should no longer be relied upon. *See In re Bilski*, 545 F.3d 943, 959–60 (Fed. Cir. 2008) (en banc), *cert granted*, 129 S. Ct. 2735 (U.S. Jun. 1, 2009). However, prior to this time, much of the discussion involving whether a particular patent claim should be considered eligible for patent protection centered on this test.
32. Prior to *State Street* and its progeny, conventional wisdom was that patents covering so-called "business methods" were not a proper subject of patent protection. In *State Street*, Judge Rich, writing for the court, shattered that conventional wisdom and called it an "ill-conceived" misconception based on a "no longer applicable" legal principle. 149 F.3d at 1375. Despite other criticisms of the *State Street* decision, methods of doing business remain patent-eligible subject matter as long as they meet other criteria, discussed in Chapter 3, Section 3.4.
33. Although the Federal Circuit in *In re Bilski*, 545 F.3d at 959, has since rejected the broad "useful, concrete and tangible result" test set forth in the *State Street* decision, patents continue to remain relevant and active in these industries.

Chapter 2 Why Seek Patent Protection?

1. This is not meant to suggest that a patent can be listed as a "tangible asset" on an organization's balance sheet. Rather, standard accounting rules apply. What a patent does is provide a tangible reality to an "intangible asset." A patent is well defined (it includes a delimitation of the organization's rights in the form of a claim), clearly identifiable (it has a specific patent number that can be referenced), and has a publicly available record that can be reviewed and analyzed by third parties, such as potential investors, to determine whether it has value. Other forms of intangible assets, like know-how and trade secrets, do not have these attributes.
2. Patents can also be used in conjunction with other forms of intellectual property (e.g., copyrights, trademarks, trade secrets, etc.) to form a comprehensive form of protection. JVC developed just such a program with its VHS licensing program, including a license to its know-how and trade secrets, popular VHS logo, and patents. Other forms of intellectual property are outside the scope of the present Guide, but nonetheless are worth considering as part of a comprehensive intellectual property business strategy. For a discussion of how various forms of intellectual property protection can be used to protect an internet website, see Charles R. Macedo, *Using Intellectual Property to Protect Your Web Site*, IP LAW 360 (May 2, 2007) (*available at* www.arelaw.com/articles/articles.html).
3. 35 U.S.C. § 292.
4. For example, false patent marking may give rise to claims for unfair competition, false advertising, and tortious interference with prospective relations among others.

5. *See, e.g., Acumed LLC v. Stryker Corp.*, 551 F.3d 1323 (Fed. Cir. 2008). *See also* Charles R. Macedo, *Permanent Injunction Affirmed in US Patent Case*, Journal of Intellectual Property Law & Practice, May 2, 2009, 4:310–312.
6. *NTP, Inc. v. Research in Motion, Ltd.*, 397 F. Supp. 2d 785 (E.D. Va. 2005).
7. *eBay Inc. v. MercExchange, L.L.C.*, 547 U.S. 388 (2006).
8. *MedImmune, Inc. v. Genentech, Inc.*, 549 U.S. 118 (2007).
9. *See also, e.g., SanDisk Corp. v. STMicroelectronics, Inc.*, 480 F.3d 1372 (Fed. Cir. 2007); *Sony Elecs. Inc. v. Guardian Media Techs., Ltd.*, 497 F.3d 1271 (Fed. Cir. 2007).
10. *See* Charles R. Macedo, Michael J. Kasdan, *Infringement Assertions In The New World Order*, IP Law 360 (Oct. 17, 2007) (*available at* www.arelaw.com/articles/articles.html).
11. *See, e.g.*, Spenser Burgess, *Unlocking the Value of Patents*, Managing Intellectual Property (Apr. 2004) ("For example, IBM started to license its unused patents in 1990, and saw its royalties jump from $30 million a year to more than $1 billion in 1999, providing over one ninth of its yearly pre-tax profits.").
12. In many patent cases, large monetary awards for patent infringement have been granted by juries and courts.
13. For example, organizations like Texas Instruments, IBM, Xerox, and Lucent, among many others, have affirmatively asserted their patent portfolios and obtained licensing revenues from competitors and others.

Chapter 3 What Is Patentable?

1. 35 U.S.C. § 102.
2. *See, e.g., RCA Corp. v. Applied Digital Data Sys.*, 730 F.2d 1440, 1444 (Fed. Cir. 1984).
3. *See id.*
4. It is a common practice in patent law to show additions to claim language by using underscores, and deletions to claim language by using brackets or strike-out.
5. *See, e.g., Schering Corp. v. Geneva Pharms.*, 339 F.3d 1373, 1377–80 (Fed. Cir. 2003).
6. *See, e.g., In re Robertson*, 169 F.3d 743, 745 (Fed. Cir. 1999).
7. 35 U.S.C. § 103(a).
8. *See, e.g., Graham v. John Deere Co.*, 383 U.S. 1 (1966) (discussing the tests to determine obviousness under 35 U.S.C. § 103).
9. *Id.* at 17.
10. While "secondary considerations" are still important in an obviousness analysis, the courts will not allow a weak case of secondary considerations to overcome a strong prima facie case of obviousness. *See, e.g., Leapfrog Enters. v. Fisher-Price, Inc.*, 485 F.3d 1157, 1162 (Fed. Cir. 2007); *see also* Charles R. Macedo, *Secondary Considerations of non-obviousness must still be considered*, Journal of Intellectual Property Law & Practice, June 2009, 4:384–385.
11. 35 U.S.C. § 282.
12. *See, e.g., In re Kahn*, 441 F.3d 977, 986 (Fed. Cir. 2006); *In re Fulton*, 391 F.3d 1195, 1200–01 (Fed. Cir. 2004).
13. *KSR Int'l Co. v. Teleflex Inc.*, 550 U.S. 398, 127 S. Ct. 1727 (2007).
14. *See* Charles R. Macedo, Jung S. Hahm, Michael J. Kasdan and Howard Wizenfeld, *KSR v. Teleflex, Redefining The Obvious*, IP Law 360 (May 3, 2007) (*available at* www.arelaw.com/articles/articles.html).

15. Prior to *KSR*, the Federal Circuit had required that in order to demonstrate that two references can be combined, there must be some teaching, suggestion, or motivation to combine prior art elements to render a claim obvious. *See, e.g., In re Kahn*, 441 F.3d 977, 986 (Fed. Cir. 2006); *In re Fulton*, 391 F.3d 1195, 1200–01 (Fed. Cir. 2004). The U.S. Supreme Court in *KSR* rejected this "rigid" test.
16. *KSR*, 127 S. Ct. at 1739–40
17. *Id.*
18. *Id.* at 1740.
19. *Id.* at 1742.
20. *Id.* at 1740–41.
21. *Sundance, Inc. v. Demonte Fabricating Ltd.*, 550 F.3d 1356, 1367 (Fed. Cir. 2008).
22. 35 U.S.C. § 101.
23. *See, e.g., Process Control Corp. v. HydReclaim Corp.*, 190 F.3d 1350, 1357 (Fed. Cir. 1999).
24. 35 U.S.C. § 101.
25. *See, e.g., Diamond v. Chakrabarty*, 447 U.S. 303, 308–9 (1980) ("Congress plainly contemplated that the patent laws would be given wide scope. . . . The Committee Reports accompanying the 1952 Act inform us that *Congress intended statutory subject matter to 'include anything under the sun that is made by man.'* S. Rep. No. 1979, 82d Cong., 2d Sess., 5 (1952); H. R. Rep. No. 1923, 82d Cong., 2d Sess., 6 (1952)." (emphasis added)); *Diamond v. Diehr*, 450 U.S. 175, 182 (1981); *State Street Bank & Trust Co. v. Signature Fin. Group, Inc.*, 149 F.3d 1368, 1373 (Fed. Cir. 1998); *AT&T Corp. v. Excel Commc'ns, Inc.*, 172 F.3d 1352, 1355 (Fed. Cir. 1999); *see also J.E.M. AG Supply v. Pioneer Hi-Bred Int'l*, 534 U.S. 124, 130 (2001) ("As this Court recognized over 20 years ago in *Chakrabarty*, 447 U.S. at 308, the language of § 101 is extremely broad.").
26. 35 U.S.C. § 101 (emphasis added).
27. *Diehr*, 450 U.S. at 185; *Chakrabarty*, 447 U.S. at 309.
28. In the majority opinion of the full court of the Federal Circuit in *In re Bilski*, 545 F.3d 943, 952 n.5 (Fed. Cir. 2008) (en banc), *cert granted*, 129 S. Ct. 2735 (U.S. Jun. 1, 2009) Chief Judge Michel coined the phrase "fundamental principles" to encompass the three judicial carve-outs from patent-eligible subject matter recognized by the U.S. Supreme Court.
29. *Funk Bros. Seed Co. v. Kalo Inoculant Co.*, 333 U.S. 127, 130 (1948); *see also Le Roy v. Tatham*, 55 U.S. (14 How.) 156, 175 (1853); *In re Bilski*, 545 F.3d at 952 (quoting *Funk Bros.*).
30. *See* Patent Reissue 1848.
31. *O'Reilly v. Morse*, 56 U.S. (15 How.) 62, 116 (1854).
32. *O'Reilly*, 56 U.S. at 117–18 ("But Professor Morse has not discovered, that the electric or galvanic current will always print at a distance, no matter what may be the form of the machinery or mechanical contrivances through which it passes. You may use electro-magnetism as a motive power, and yet not produce the described effect, that is, print at a distance intelligible marks or signs. To produce that effect, it must be combined with, and passed through, and operate upon, certain complicated and delicate machinery, adjusted and arranged upon philosophical principles, and prepared by the highest mechanical skill. *And it is the high praise of Professor Morse, that he has been able, by a new combination of known powers, of which electro-magnetism is one, to discover a method by which intelligible marks*

or signs may be printed at a distance. And for the method or process thus discovered, he is entitled to a patent. But he has not discovered that the electro-magnetic current, used as motive power, in any other method, and with any other combination, will do as well.") (emphasis added).

33. *Chakrabarty*, 447 U.S. at 309.
34. *Chakrabarty*, 447 U.S. at 309; *see also, e.g., Funk Bros.*, 333 U.S. at 131.
35. *See, e.g., Diehr*, 450 U.S. at 191–93 (finding that claim directed to a process for molding rubber products to be patent-eligible subject matter, even though the claim included an equation used a computer).
36. 35 U.S.C. § 100(b). At least one court has found this definition "unhelpful" since it is circular: it defines a "process" as including a "process." *See In re Bilski*, 545 F.3d at 951 n.3.
37. Over the years, the Federal Circuit and its predecessor courts have attempted to develop various shortcut tests to determine whether a process claim preempts a fundamental principles claim. These tests have included the so-called *Freeman-Walter-Abele* test, the "useful, concrete, and tangible result" test made famous by the *State Street* decision, and the so-called "technological arts" test. *In re Bilski* confirmed that none of these other tests should be used. 545 F.3d at 958–60. *See also* Charles R. Macedo, *Process must be tied to machine or transform matter to be patent-eligibile in the United States*, Journal of Intellectual Property Law & Practice, March 2009, 4:151–53.
38. *In re Bilski*, 545 F.3d at 961.
39. *Id.*
40. *Id.* at 958.
41. As explained in *Bilski*, the U.S. Supreme Court has "made clear that it is inappropriate to determine the patent-eligibility of a claim as a whole based on whether selected limitations constitute patent-eligible subject matter. . . . After all, even though a fundamental principle itself is not patent-eligible, processes incorporating a fundamental principle may be patent-eligible. *Thus, it is irrelevant that any individual step or limitation of such processes by itself would be unpatentable under § 101.*" *In re Bilski*, 545 F.3d at 958 (emphasis added; citation omitted).
42. *See, e.g., Corning v. Burden*, 56 U.S. (15 How.) 252, 267–68 (1853) ("One may discover a new and useful improvement in the process of tanning, dyeing, & irrespective of any particular form of machinery or mechanical device." The examples given were the "arts of tanning, dyeing, making water-proof cloth, vulcanizing India rubber, smelting ores.").
43. *In re Nuijten*, 500 F.3d 1346, 1355 (Fed. Cir. 2007) (quoting *Burr v. Duryee*, 68 U.S. (1 Wall.) 531, 570 (1863)).
44. *Id.* at 1355 (quoting *Corning*, 56 U.S. at 267).
45. *In re Alappat*, 33 F.3d 1526 (Fed. Cir. 1994) (en banc).
46. *Morley Sewing Mach. Co. v. Lancaster*, 129 U.S. 263 (1889).
47. *In re Nuijten, supra.*
48. *In re Nuijten*, 500 F.3d at 1356.
49. *Chakrabarty*, 447 U.S. at 308 (quoting *Am. Fruit Growers, Inc. v. Brogdex Co.*, 283 U.S. 1, 11 (1931)).
50. *In re Nuijten*, 500 F.3d at 1356 ("The Supreme Court has defined 'manufacture' (in its verb form) as 'the production of *articles* for use from raw or prepared materials

by giving to these materials new forms, qualities, properties, or combinations, whether by hand-labor or by machinery.' *Diamond v. Chakrabarty*, 447 U.S. 303, 308 (1980) (emphasis added) (quoting *Am. Fruit Growers, Inc. v. Brogdex Co.*, 283 U.S. 1, 11 (1931)). The term is used in the statute in its noun form, *Bayer AG v. Housey Pharms., Inc.*, 340 F.3d 1367, 373 (Fed. Cir. 2003), and therefore refers to 'articles' resulting from the process of manufacture.") (footnotes omitted).

51. *In re Nuijten*, 500 F.3d at 1357 ("[T]he Supreme Court has defined 'composition of matter' to mean 'all compositions of two or more substances and all composite articles, whether they be the results of chemical union, or of mechanical mixture, or whether they be gases, fluids, powders or solids.'" (quoting *Chakrabarty*, 447 U.S. at 308)).
52. *Chakrabarty*, 447 U.S. at 308 (quoting *Shell Dev. Co.* v. *Watson*, 149 F. Supp. 279, 280 (D.D.C. 1957) (citing 1 A. Deller, Walker on Patents § 14, p. 55 (1st ed. 1937)), *aff'd*, 252 F.2d 861 (D.C. Cir. 1958).

Chapter 5 How to Protect an Invention

1. U.S. patent law provides for procedures by which certain so-called non-statutory prior art can be "sworn" around. *E.g.*, 35 U.S.C. § 102(a) (prior art such as publications available to the public less than one year before the filing date). In other words, an applicant for a patent may submit a declaration to the Patent Office which demonstrates that it conceived of and reduced to practice the invention prior to the identified prior art. 37 C.F.R. § 1.131. This procedure can eliminate such prior art from being used against a patent application, but it requires appropriate supporting documentation.
2. 35 U.S.C. § 273(b)(1).
3. Although copyright issues are beyond the scope of this Guide, it is important to remember that a good intellectual property strategy considers all potential intellectual property rights. *See, e.g.*, Charles R. Macedo, *Using Intellectual Property to Protect Your Web Site*, IP Law 360 (May 2, 2007) (*available at* www.arelaw.com/articles/articles.html) (discussing different kinds of intellectual property rights in the context of an internet site).
4. *See, e.g.*, *Graham v. John Deere Co.*, 383 U.S. 1, 17 (1966) (Rebuttal evidence to a prima facie case of obviousness may include evidence of "secondary considerations," such as "commercial success, long felt but unsolved needs, [and] failure of others.").
5. A non-disclosure agreement is an agreement entered into between two individuals and/or organizations to retain in confidence the information exchanged as part of a larger transaction or a contemplated transaction. Non-disclosure agreements can either be "one way," i.e., serving to protect the disclosure of only one party, or "bilateral" or "two way," i.e., protecting the disclosure of both parties.
6. *See* 35 U.S.C. § 103(c) (governing the impact on patentability of joint research agreements). For a more detailed discussion on agreement-drafting guidelines under the new patent law, see Charles R. Macedo, *Drafting Joint Research Agreements Under The Create Act Of 2004*, IP Law 360 (Mar. 2, 2005) (*available at* www.arelaw.com/articles/articles.html).
7. *See* Charles R.B. Macedo, *First-to-File: Is American Adoption of the International Standard in Patent Law Worth the Price?*, 18 AIPLA Q.J. 193 (1990), 1988 Colum. Bus. L. Rev. 543 (1988).

8. *Mahurkar v. C.R. Bard, Inc.*, 79 F.3d 1572, 1578 (Fed. Cir. 1996).
9. While the law does allow for certain excuses from "diligence" (*see, e.g., Griffith v. Kanamaru*, 816 F.2d 624, 626 (Fed. Cir. 1987)), best practices still dictate that the organization and its attorneys exercise all efforts at being diligent, where practical.
10. *See, e.g., Kingsdown Med. Consultants v. Hollister, Inc.*, 863 F.2d 867, 874 (Fed. Cir. 1988).
11. Charles R. Macedo, *Effect of the Publication of Applications Under The American Inventors Protection Act of 1999*, 13–4 FED. CIR. B.J. 627 (2004).
12. *Am. Med. Sys. v. Med. Eng'g Corp.*, 6 F.3d 1523, 1537–38 (Fed. Cir. 1993).
13. *MedImmune, Inc. v. Genentech, Inc.*, 549 U.S. 118 (2007); *SanDisk Corp. v. STMicroelectronics, Inc.*, 480 F.3d 1372 (Fed. Cir. 2007); *Sony Elecs, Inc. v. Guardian Media Techs., Ltd.*, 497 F.3d 1271 (Fed. Cir. 2007).
14. *See* Charles R. Macedo and Michael J. Kasdan, *Infringement Assertions In The New World Order*, IP LAW 360 (Oct. 17, 2007) (*available at* www.arelaw.com/articles/articles.html).

Chapter 6 How to Get a Patent

1. 35 U.S.C. § 112, ¶ 4
2. *See* 37 C.F.R. § 1.56.
3. 35 U.S.C. § 154(a)(2).
4. For purposes of calculating the term of a patent, the earliest effective filing date does not include any claims for priority to non-U.S./non-PCT patent applications (e.g., a Japanese patent application priority date), or provisional patent applications. U.S. patent law allows a non-provisional patent application to claim priority to patent applications filed in other jurisdictions (*see* 35 U.S.C. § 119) and to provisional patent applications filed in the U.S. (*see* 35 U.S.C. § 111(b)), for purposes of overcoming prior art applied against claims in the patent application or patent. However, these earlier-filed applications do not count toward the term of an issued patent.
5. 35 U.S.C. § 154(d) (allowing patent term extension for USPTO-caused delay in prosecution).
6. 35 U.S.C. § 156 (allowing patent term extension to pharmaceutical inventions under certain limited conditions).
7. A list of PCT member states and non-PCT member states may be found at www.wipo.int/pct/guide/en/index.html.

Chapter 7 How to Read a Patent

1. *See* MPEP § 901.04(a).
2. Before March 2001, the United States did not publish patent applications. It would use the suffix "A" instead of "B" on these older patents to indicate it was an issued patent. For a detailed explanation of the codes used, see MPEP § 901.04(a).
3. *See* MPEP § 901.04(a).
4. *See id.*
5. *See id.*
6. Prior to March 2001, no patent applications were published except as an issued patent. Even today, not every pending patent application is published.

When seeking patent protection, one issue that should be considered at the time a patent application is being filed is whether the application needs to be and/or should be published.

7. 37 C.F.R. § 1.81(a).

Chapter 8 What Is Prior Art?

1. Different countries define prior art in different ways. The present discussion is limited to the manner in which U.S. patent law defines prior art.
2. 35 U.S.C. § 102(a).
3. 35 U.S.C. § 102(a).
4. 35 U.S.C. § 102(b).
5. 35 U.S.C. § 102(f).
6. When an invention was patented, described in a printed publication, publicly displayed or "on-sale" more than one year prior to the earliest effective U.S. filing date for a patent application, that prior art is an absolute bar to patentability. *See* 35 U.S.C. § 102(b). If these activities occurred only less than one year prior to the earliest effective U.S. filing date of the patent application, then to the extent the organization was the first to come up with the invention, it may still be entitled to a U.S. Patent. *See, e.g.*, 37 C.F.R. § 1.131.
7. Sometimes a patent may claim priority-in-part to earlier-filed patent applications because one or more continuation-in-part patent applications may have been filed. For present purposes, if there is not support for the claimed invention (e.g., disclosure of the invention) in the earlier-filed patent application, it would not be considered the "earliest effective filing" date.
8. *See* 35 U.S.C. § 102(b).
9. A full discussion of how prior art can be overcome is beyond the scope of this Guide.
10. *See* 35 U.S.C. § 102(a) and (b).
11. *See* 35 U.S.C. § 102(e)(1).
12. *See* 35 U.S.C. § 102(b).
13. *Bruckelmyer v. Ground Heaters*, 445 F.3d 1374, 1379 (Fed. Cir. 2006) (holding Figures found in a Canadian Patent Office file which were not published with application were prior art as of the date the Canadian Patent Application was laid open for public inspection).
14. *See generally* MPEP § 901.05 (discussing how the USPTO handles non-English language prior art).
15. *See, e.g., Sheller-Globe Corp. v. Milsco Mfg. Co.*, 206 U.S.P.Q. 42, 51 (E.D. Wis. 1979) (troubleshooting guide was established to be distributed to customers and acted as a printed publication), *aff'd in part, rev'd in part on other grounds*, 636 F.2d 177 (7th Cir. 1980); *Catalano v. Kawneer Co.*, 185 U.S.P.Q. 456, 459 (N.D. Ill. 1975) (holding instruction manuals distributed to customers to be prior art); *Popeil Bros. v. Schick Elec., Inc.*, 494 F.2d 162 (7th Cir. 1974) (finding distribution by Panasonic of instruction books and advertising pamphlets in Japan to distributors, retailers, ultimate purchasers, and other to be sufficient distribution to be deemed a printed publication).
16. *See, e.g., Refac Elecs. v. R.H. Macy & Co.*, 9 U.S.P.Q.2d 1497, 1504 (D.N.J. 1988) (data sheet published for distribution to potential customers was prior art),

aff'd mem., 871 F.2d 1097 (Fed. Cir. 1989); *Constant v. Advanced Micro-Devices, Inc.*, 848 F.2d 1560 (Fed. Cir. 1988); *Griswold v. Oil Capital Valve Co.*, 375 F.2d 532, 537–39 (10th Cir. 1966) (data sheet available upon request to interested parties was a printed publication).

17. *See, e.g., J.A. LaPorte, Inc. v. Norfolk Dredging Co.*, 625 F. Supp. 36 (E.D. Va. 1985), *aff'd*, 787 F.2d 1577 (Fed. Cir. 1986) (photograph is a printed publication when at least two prints were made and were distributed to at least three companies without any obligation of confidentiality).
18. *See, e.g., In re Hall*, 781 F.2d 897 (Fed. Cir. 1986).
19. *See, e.g., In re Klopfenstein*, 380 F.3d 1345, 1347 (Fed. Cir. 2004) ("The fourteen-slide presentation was printed and pasted onto poster boards. The printed slide presentation was displayed continuously for two and a half days at the AACC meeting."; held prior art that invalidated pending claim); *In re Hassler*, 347 F.2d 911 (C.C.P.A. 1965) (newspaper article was valid reference for what was disclosed therein).
20. *See, e.g., N. Telecom, Inc. v. Datapoint Corp.*, 908 F.2d 931, 936 (Fed. Cir. 1990) ("A document, to serve as a 'printed publication,' must be generally available.").
21. *See, e.g., Potter Instrument Co. v. Odec Computer Sys.*, 499 F.2d 209, 210 n.2 (1st Cir. 1974) ("limited circulation alone does not disqualify a publication from contributing to the prior art.").
22. *Compare In re Hall, supra, with In re Cronyn*, 890 F.2d 1158, 1160 (Fed. Cir. 1989).
23. *See, e.g., In re Hall, supra; In re Wyer*, 655 F.2d 221 (C.C.P.A. 1981).
24. *See, e.g., N. Telecom, supra* (because there was evidence that distribution may have been made with a restrictive notice on the documents, the court was unable to find that anyone concerned with the art could have had access to the documents).
25. *See, e.g., Jockmus v. Leviton*, 28 F.2d 812 (2d Cir. 1928) (printed catalogue, in French, sent to customers by a German manufacturer, was found to be prior art as a "printed publication").
26. *See, e.g., In re Wyer*, 655 F.2d at 227.
27. *See Mitsubishi Elec. Corp. v. Ampex Corp.*, 190 F.3d 1300, 1304 (Fed. Cir. 1999) ("demonstration at an Audio Engineering Society (AES) convention").
28. *See, e.g., Baxter Int'l, Inc. v. COBE Labs., Inc.*, 88 F.3d 1054 (Fed. Cir. 1996).
29. *See, e.g., Xerox Corp. v. 3Com Corp.*, 26 F. Supp. 2d 492 (W.D.N.Y. 1998) (demonstration via video would have been considered public use had there not been an issue of confidentiality.); *Loral Corp. v. B.F. Goodrich Co.*, 14 U.S.P.Q.2d 1081 (S.D. Ohio 1989).
30. *See, e.g., Harrington Mfg. Co. v. Powell Mfg. Co.*, 815 F.2d 1478 (Fed. Cir. 1986).
31. *See, e.g., Egbert v. Lippmann*, 104 U.S. 333 (1881); *Lockwood v. Am. Airlines*, 37 U.S.P.Q.2d 1534, 1535 (S.D. Cal. 1995), *aff'd*, 107 F.3d 1565 (Fed Cir. 1997).
32. *See, e.g., New Railhead Mfg., L.L.C. v. Vermeer Mfg. Co.*, 298 F.3d 1290, 1297 (Fed. Cir. 2002) ("The statutory phrase 'public use' does not necessarily mean open and visible in the ordinary sense; it includes any use of the claimed invention by a person other than the inventor who is under no limitation, restriction, or obligation of secrecy to the inventor.").
33. *Egbert v. Lippmann*, 104 U.S. at 336 (emphasis added).

34. *See, e.g.*, *id.* at 336.
35. 35 U.S.C. § 102(b).
36. *Pfaff v. Wells Elecs.*, 525 U.S. 55, 67–68 (1998).
37. *Rotec Indus. v. Mitsubishi Corp.*, 215 F.3d 1246 (Fed. Cir. 2000).
38. *In re Caveney*, 761 F.2d 671, 676 (Fed. Cir. 1985).
39. *See, e.g., Buildex, Inc. v. Kason Indus.*, 849 F.2d 1461, 1464 (Fed. Cir. 1988) ("the existence of a sales contract or the signing of a purchase agreement prior to [the critical] date" establishes on-sale status for purposes of section 102(b)).
40. *See, e.g., Special Devices, Inc. v. OEA, Inc.*, 270 F.3d 1353, 1355 (Fed. Cir. 2001) ("By phrasing the statutory bar in the passive voice, Congress indicated that it does not matter who places the invention 'on sale'; it only matters that someone—inventor, supplier or other third party—placed it one sale.").
41. *See, e.g., Brasseler, U.S.A. I, L.P. v. Stryker Sales Corp.*, 182 F.3d 888, 890 (Fed. Cir. 1999) (Federal Circuit declined "to establish a new exception based on the fact (alleged) that [the parties] were joint developers. . . . [W]e have never recognized a joint development exception to the on sale bar." (quotation omitted).
42. *Pfaff*, 525 U.S. at 67–68.
43. U.S. Const. art. 1, § 8, cl. 8 ("The Congress shall have Power . . . [t]o promote the Progress of . . . useful Arts, by securing for limited Times to . . . Inventors the exclusive Right to their . . . Discoveries").
44. 35 U.S.C. § 102(f).
45. *See, e.g., Ex parte Billottet*, 192 U.S.P.Q. 413, 415 (Pat. & Trademark Office, Bd. App. 1976).

Chapter 9 What to Disclose to the Patent Practitioner

1. The failure to account for this kind of change in materials resulted in at least one accused infringer being found not to infringe a patent. *See, e.g., Nystrom v. Trex Co.*, 424 F.3d 1136, 1143 (Fed. Cir. 2005) ("An examination of the term 'board' in the context of the written description and prosecution history of the '831 patent leads to the conclusion that the term 'board' must be limited to wood cut from a log."; accused products made out of "composites of wood fibers and recycled plastic" were found not to infringe).
2. 35 U.S.C. § 112, ¶ 1.
3. *See Randomex, Inc. v. Scopus Corp.*, 849 F.2d 585, 588 (Fed. Cir. 1988).
4. *Compare Engel Indus. v. Lockformer Co.*, 946 F.2d 1528, 1532 (Fed. Cir. 1991) ("The best mode inquiry is directed to what the applicant regards as the invention, which in turn is measured by the claims."), *with Cardiac Pacemakers, Inc. v. St. Jude Med., Inc.*, 381 F.3d 1371 (Fed. Cir. 2004) ("'The reason [for this limitation is] pragmatic [without it] the disclosure would be boundless, and the pitfalls endless.'" (quoting *Engel*, 946 F.2d at 1532–33)).
5. *See, e.g., In re Jolley*, 308 F.3d 1317, 1328 (Fed. Cir. 2002).
6. *See* 35 U.S.C. § 103(a).
7. 37 C.F.R. § 1.56.
8. *Digital Control Inc. v. Charles Mach. Works*, 437 F.3d 1309 (Fed. Cir. 2006).

9. *See* 35 U.S.C. § 112, ¶ 1.
10. *Ethicon, Inc. v. U.S. Surgical Corp.*, 135 F.3d 1456 (Fed. Cir. 1998).

Chapter 10 Type of Claim Coverage to Seek

1. *See DeGeorge v. Bernier*, 768 F.2d 1318, 1322 n.3 (Fed. Cir. 1985) (preamble of a claim does not limit the scope of the claim when it merely states a purpose or intended use of the invention).
2. *See, e.g., Gerber Garment Tech., Inc. v. Lectra Sys., Inc.*, 916 F.2d 683, 688 (Fed. Cir. 1990).
3. 35 U.S.C. § 112, ¶ 2.
4. *See* 35 U.S.C. § 101.
5. 35 U.S.C. § 112, ¶ 1.
6. *See, e.g., AbTox Inc. v. Exitron Corp.*, 122 F.3d 1019, 1024 (Fed. Cir. 1997) ("The written description supplies additional context for understanding whether the claim language limits the patent scope to a single unitary chamber or extends to encompass a device with multiple gas-confining chambers."), *amended on reh'g*, 131 F.3d 1009 (Fed. Cir. 1997).
7. *See, e.g., Invitrogen Corp. v. Biocrest Mfg., L.P.*, 327 F.3d 1364, 1368 (Fed. Cir. 2003); *see also* MPEP § 2111.03.
8. *See, e.g., Mars Inc. v. H.J. Heinz Co.*, 377 F.3d 1369, 1376 (Fed. Cir. 2004); *see also* MPEP § 2111.03.
9. *See, e.g.,* MPEP § 2111.03; *In re Gray*, 53 F.2d 520 (C.C.P.A. 1931); *Ex parte Davis*, 80 U.S.P.Q. 448, 450 (Bd. Pat. App. & Inter. 1948). *But see Norian Corp. v. Stryker Corp.*, 363 F.3d 1321, 1331–32 (Fed. Cir. 2004).
10. *See, e.g., PPG Indus. v. Guardian Indus.*, 156 F.3d 1351, 1354 (Fed. Cir. 1998).
11. *See* MPEP § 2111.03; *Lampi Corp. v. Am. Power Prods. Inc.*, 228 F.3d 1365, 1376 (Fed. Cir. 2000).
12. *See, e.g., WMS Gaming Inc. v. Int'l Game Tech.*,184 F.3d 1339, 1350 (Fed. Cir. 1999) ("The plain meaning of 'selecting one of said . . . numbers' is selecting a single number, not a combination of numbers."); *Bell Commc'ns Research Inc. v. Vitalink Commc'ns Corp.*, 55 F.3d 615, 622 (Fed. Cir. 1995) (construing "assigning . . . one of said trees" to be limited to assigning one and only one tree based on the language of the claim as a whole).
13. *See, e.g., Novo Nordisk A/S v. Eli Lilly & Co.*, No. 98-643 MMS, 1999 U.S. Dist LEXIS 18690, at *52 (D. Del. Nov. 18, 1999) (holding that claim limitation "comprising . . . *two* zinc ions" means *two* zinc ions and *not more than two* zinc ions).
14. *See, e.g., Elkay Mfg. Co. v. Ebco Mfg. Co.*, 192 F.3d 973, 977 (Fed. Cir. 1999) (adopting construction of term "a" to mean "one and only one" based upon the prosecution history).
15. *See, e.g., York Prods., Inc. v. Cent. Tractor Farm & Family Ctr.*, 99 F.3d 1568, 1575–76 (Fed. Cir. 1996) (relying upon definition of "plurality" as "the state of being plural" found in AM. HERITAGE DICTIONARY SECOND COLLEGE EDITION 955 (2d ed. 1982), to conclude this term requires "at least two" "in accordance with its ordinary meaning").
16. *See, e.g., Gillette Co. v. Energizer Holdings, Inc.*, 405 F.3d 1367, 1371–73 (Fed. Cir. 2005).

17. *Id.*
18. Regarding the amount of variation encompassed by the word "about," the Federal Circuit has held that "[t]he meaning of the word 'about' is dependent on the facts of a case, the nature of the invention, and the knowledge imparted by the totality of the earlier disclosure to those skilled in the art." *Eiselstein v. Frank*, 52 F.3d 1035, 1040 (Fed. Cir. 1995). Sometimes, "about" has been construed to encompass "experimental error." *See, e.g., BJ Servs. Co. v. Halliburton Energy Servs.*, 338 F.3d 1368, 1373 (Fed. Cir. 2003) (held that the term "about" was intended to encompass the range of experimental error arising in measurement).
19. *See, e.g., Anchor Wall Sys. v. Rockwood Retaining Walls, Inc.*, 340 F.3d 1298, 1311 (Fed. Cir. 2003).
20. *Liquid Dynamics Corp. v. Vaughan Co.*, 355 F.3d 1361, 1368 (Fed. Cir. 2004) ("The term 'substantial' is a meaningful modifier implying 'approximate,' rather than 'perfect.'").
21. *See, e.g., Playtex Prods. Inc v. Procter & Gamble Co.*, 400 F.3d 901 (Fed. Cir. 2005).
22. 35 U.S.C. § 101.
23. *Abbott Labs. v. Sandoz, Inc.*, 566 F.3d 1282 (Fed. Cir. 2009) (en banc).
24. 37 C.F.R. § 1.75(e); MPEP § 2129.
25. *Ex parte Jepson*, 1917 Commr. Dec. 62, 243 O.G. 525.
26. *In re Fout*, 675 F.2d 297, 301 (C.C.P.A. 1982) (holding preamble of Jepson-type claim to be admitted prior art where applicant's specification credited another as the inventor of the subject matter of the preamble).
27. *In re Ehrreich*, 590 F.2d 902, 909–10 (C.C.P.A. 1979) (holding preamble not to be admitted prior art where applicant explained that the Jepson format was used to avoid a double patenting rejection in a co-pending application and the examiner cited no prior art showing the subject matter of the preamble).

Chapter 11 How to Construe a Patent Claim

1. *Rockwell Int'l Corp. v. U.S.*, 147 F.3d 1358, 1362 (Fed. Cir. 1998).
2. *Kim v. ConAgra Foods, Inc.*, 465 F.3d 1312, 1324 (Fed. Cir. 2006).
3. *Phillips v. AWH Corp.*, 415 F.3d 1303, 1312 (Fed. Cir. 2005) (en banc) (quoting *Pure Water, Inc. v. Safari Water Filtration Sys.*, 381 F.3d 1111, 1115 (Fed. Cir. 2004)) (quotation marks omitted).
4. *Id.*
5. *Id.*
6. *Id.* at 1317 (extrinsic evidence "consists of all evidence external to the patent and prosecution history, including expert and inventor testimony, dictionaries and learned treatises." (citations and quotation marks omitted)); *see also Vitronics Corp. v. Conceptronic, Inc.*, 90 F.3d 1576, 1584–85 (Fed. Cir. 1996).
7. *See Phonometrics, Inc. v. N. Telecom Inc.*, 133 F.3d 1459, 1464 (Fed. Cir. 1998).
8. *Phillips*, 415 F.3d at 1314 ("[T]he claims themselves provide substantial guidance as to the meaning of particular claim terms.").
9. *Phillips, supra.*
10. *See Mars, Inc. v. H.J. Heinz Co.*, 377 F.3d 1369, 1374 (Fed. Cir. 2004) (emphasis added).
11. *Voda v. Cordis Corp.*, 536 F.3d 1311, 1319 (Fed. Cir. 2008).

12. *Phillips*, 415 F.3d at 1314 (the relationship of the use of a claim term to other claims, both asserted and unasserted, "can also be valuable sources of enlightenment as to the meaning of a claim term").
13. *Phillips*, 415 F.3d at 1314–15; *see also, e.g., Helmsderfer v. Bobrick Washroom Equip. Inc.*, 527 F.3d 1379, 1382 (Fed. Cir. 2008) ("Our precedent instructs that different claim terms are presumed to have different meanings.").
14. *In re Omeprazole Patent Litig.*, 536 F.3d 1361, 1379 (Fed. Cir. 2008); *see also, e.g., Phillips*, 415 F.3d at 1314.
15. *Helmsderfer*, 527 F.3d at 1382 ("As Brocar [the patentee] provides us with no evidence to rebut this presumption, we decline to construe the term 'partially hidden from view' to have the same meaning as 'generally hidden from view' or 'at least partially hidden from view.' If Brocar had intended to use these terms to describe the platform top surface, it should have.").
16. *See, e.g., Nystrom v. Trex Co.*, 424 F.3d 1136, 1143 (Fed. Cir. 2005).
17. *Markman v. Westview Instr.*, 52 F.3d 967, 979 (Fed. Cir. 1995) (en banc) (the patent specification is the portion of the patent that "contains a written description of the invention [enabling] one of ordinary skill in the art to make and use the invention"), *aff'd*, 517 U.S. 370 (1996).
18. *Markman*, 52 F.3d 967.
19. *Phillips*, 415 F.3d at 1313.
20. *Vitronics Corp.*, 90 F.3d at 1582 (resort to the specification is required "to determine whether the inventor has used any terms in a manner inconsistent with their ordinary meaning"); *Phillips*, 415 F.3d at 1316 ("the specification may reveal a special definition given to a claim term by the patentee that differs from the meaning it would otherwise possess").
21. *Phillips*, 415 F.3d at 1316 ("the specification may reveal an intentional disclaimer, or disavowal, of claim scope by the inventor").
22. *Vitronics Corp.*, 90 F.3d at 1583 (a claim construction that does not read on a preferred embodiment is "rarely, if ever" correct).
23. *See, e.g., Zelinski v. Brunswick Corp.*, 185 F.3d 1311, 1315 (Fed. Cir. 1999); *Desper Prods. v. QSound Labs*, 157 F.3d 1325, 1336 (Fed. Cir. 1998).
24. *See, e.g., Beachcombers Int'l v. Wildewood Creative Prods., Inc.*, 31 F.3d 1154, 1158 (Fed. Cir. 1994).
25. *Vitronics Corp.*, 90 F.3d at 1582.
26. *Id.*
27. *Id.*
28. *See Renishaw PLC v. Marposs Societa' per Azioni*, 158 F.3d 1243, 1248 (Fed. Cir. 1998).
29. *Nystrom*, 424 F.3d at 1143 ("An examination of the term 'board' in the context of the written description and prosecution history of the '831 patent leads to the conclusion that the term 'board' must be limited to wood cut from a log.").
30. *See, e.g., Sandisk Corp. v. Memorex Prods., Inc.*, 415 F.3d 1278, 1286 (Fed. Cir. 2005) ("Second, it is axiomatic that without more the court will not limit claim terms to a preferred embodiment described in the specification.").
31. *Vitronics Corp.*, 90 F.3d at 1583; *see also, e.g., Sandisk Corp.*, 415 F.3d at 1285.
32. *Karlin Tech., Inc. v. Surgical Dynamics, Inc.*, 177 F.3d 968, 973 (Fed. Cir. 1999) (claims of a patent may only be limited to a preferred embodiment by the express declaration of the patentee.).

33. *Digital Biometrics, Inc. v. Identix, Inc.*, 149 F.3d 1335, 1344 (Fed. Cir. 1998).
34. *See Vitronics Corp.*, 90 F.3d at 1582.
35. *Laitram Corp. v. Morehouse Indus.*, 143 F.3d 1456, 1462 (Fed. Cir. 1998).
36. *Gillespie v. Dywidag Sys. Int'l*, 501 F.3d 1285, 1288, 1290 (Fed. Cir. 2007) (emphasis added).
37. *See, e.g., Key Pharms. v. Hercon Labs. Corp.*, 161 F.3d 709, 713–16 (Fed. Cir. 1998).
38. *Modine Mfg. Co. v. U.S. Int'l Trade Comm'n*, 75 F.3d 1545, 1557 (Fed. Cir. 1996).
39. *Phillips*, 415 F.3d at 1317 (extrinsic evidence "consists of all evidence external to the patent and prosecution history, including expert and inventor testimony, dictionaries and learned treatises." (citation and quotation marks omitted)); *see also Vitronics*, 90 F.3d at 1584–85.
40. *Phillips*, 415 F.3d at 1324.
41. *See, e.g., Helmsderfer*, 527 F.3d at 1382 ("When the intrinsic evidence is silent as to the plain meaning of a term, it is entirely appropriate for the district court to look to dictionaries or other extrinsic sources for context—to aid in arriving at the plain meaning of a claim term.").
42. *SEZ AG v. Solid State Equip. Corp.*, No. 07-1969, 2008 U.S. Dist. LEXIS 48774, at *23 (E.D. Pa. June 26, 2008) (emphasis added).
43. *Laboratoires Perouse, S.A.S., v. W.L. Gore & Assocs., Inc.*, 528 F. Supp. 2d 362, 381 (S.D.N.Y. 2007) (emphasis added).
44. *Helmsderfer*, 527 F.3d at 1382–83 ("All three dictionaries cited by the district court support its construction of the term 'partially.' The first describes 'partially' as 'to some extent.' *Webster's Third New Int'l Dictionary of the English Language Unabridged* 1646, def. 1 (1993). The second defines 'partially' as '[t]o a degree; not totally.' *Am. Heritage Dictionary of the English Language* 1319 (1996). The third describes 'partially' as '[i]n partial way or degree, as opposed to totally; to some extent; in part; incompletely, restrictedly; partly.' *Oxford English Dictionary* 267, def. 2.a. (2d ed. 1989). None of these sources support Brocar's definition of partially—and the second and third sources specifically contradict Brocar's construction. There was no conflicting evidence. Based on the foregoing, the ordinary and customary meaning of the term 'partially' excludes 'totally.'" (footnote omitted)).
45. *See, e.g., Renishaw*, 158 F.3d at 1250 (construing the term "when" with reliance on the definition provided in the specification as opposed to dictionary or other common definitions because "[i]ndiscriminate reliance on definitions found in dictionaries can often produce absurd results").
46. *Phillips v. AWH Corp.*, 415 F.3d at 1321.
47. *See, e.g., Key Pharms.* 161 F.3d 716.
48. *See, e.g., Sundance, Inc. v. Demonte Fabricating Ltd.*, 550 F.3d 1356, 1363–65 n.3 (Fed. Cir. 2008) (finding that testimony of patent law expert should be stricken because he was not skilled in the art).
49. *Southwall Techs. v. Cardinal IG Co*, 54 F.3d 1570, 1578 (Fed. Cir. 1995).
50. *Engel Indus. v. Lockformer Co.*, 96 F.3d 1398, 1405 (Fed. Cir. 1996) (an inventor's "subjective intent," is considered to be "of little or no probative weight in determining the scope of the claims, except as documented in the prosecution history"); *see also O2 Micro Int'l Ltd. v. Beyond Innovation Tech. Co.*, 521 F.3d 1351, 1362 n.3 (Fed. Cir. 2008) ("First, an inventor's self-serving statements are rarely relevant to the proper construction of a claim term.").

51. *Voice Techs. Group, Inc. v. VMC Sys.*, 164 F.3d 605, 615–16 (Fed. Cir. 1999) (acknowledging that "the inventor can not by later testimony change the invention and the claims from their meaning at the time the patent was drafted and granted" but stating that the inventor may provide testimony explaining the claimed invention and its development).
52. *Bell & Howell Document Mgmt. Prods. Co. v. Altek Sys.*, 132 F.3d 701, 706 (Fed. Cir. 1997) ("The testimony of an inventor and his attorney concerning claim construction is thus entitled to little or no consideration. The testimony of an inventor is often a self-serving, after-the-fact attempt to state what should have been part of his or her patent application. . . .").
53. *See, e.g., Southwall Techs. v. Cardinal IG Co.*, 54 F.3d 1570 (Fed. Cir. 1995); *Fonar Corp. v. Johnson & Johnson*, 821 F.2d 627 (Fed. Cir. 1987) (the meaning of a term in a claim should be defined in a manner that is consistent with its appearance in other claims in the same patent).
54. *See, e.g., AbTox, Inc. v. Exitron Corp*, 131 F.3d 1009 (Fed. Cir. 1997).
55. *See, e.g., Tex. Instruments Inc. v. U.S. Int'l Trade Comm'n*, 988 F.2d 1165 (Fed. Cir. 1993) (claims cannot be construed to read an express limitation out of the claims because courts cannot broaden or narrow claims to give the patentee something different than what he has set forth).
56. *Vitronics*, 90 F.3d at 1583; *see also, e.g., Sandisk Corp. v. Memorex Prods., Inc.*, 415 F.3d 1278, 1285 (Fed. Cir. 2005) (overturning district court's claim construction which did not read on the preferred embodiment; "In sum, the trial court's speculative treatment of the preferred embodiment is unsupported by the patent specification, not grounded in the record, and contrary to the reading suggested by all parties. We conclude that SanDisk is correct in faulting the trial court's claim construction.").
57. *Karlin Tech., Inc. v. Surgical Dynamics, Inc.*, 177 F.3d 968, 973 (Fed. Cir. 1999) (Claims of a patent may only be limited to a preferred embodiment by the express declaration of the patentee.).
58. *See, e.g., Sandisk Corp.*, 415 F.3d at 1286 ("Second, it is axiomatic that without more the court will not limit claim terms to a preferred embodiment described in the specification."); *Laitram Corp. v. Cambridge Wire Cloth Co.*, 863 F.2d 855, 865 (Fed. Cir. 1988) ("References to a preferred embodiment, such as those often present in a specification, are not claim limitations.").
59. *Tandon Corp. v. U.S. Int'l Trade Comm'n*, 831 F.2d 1017, 1023 (Fed. Cir. 1987).
60. *Toro Co. v. White Consol. Indus.*, 199 F.3d 1295, 1302 (Fed. Cir. 1999) (citation omitted & emphasis added).
61. *See, e.g., In re Omeprazole Patent Litig.*, 536 F.3d 1361, 1379 (Fed. Cir. 2008) ("In any event, Apotex's construction draws no support from the specification of the '230 patent, and it would contradict claim 8's recitation of an ammonium salt as a possible alkaline salt. As ammonium salts do not fall within Apotex's construction, the claims of the '230 patent themselves do not support Apotex's proposed construction.").
62. *Amhil Enters. v. Wawa, Inc.*, 81 F.3d 1554, 1562 (Fed. Cir. 1996).
63. *See Tex. Instruments Inc. v. U.S. Int'l Trade Comm'n*, 871 F.2d 1054, 1065 (Fed. Cir. 1989).
64. *Athletic Alternatives, Inc. v. Prince Mfg.*, 73 F.3d 1573, 1581 (Fed. Cir. 1996).

65. *Halliburton Energy Servs. v. M-I LLC*, 514 F.3d 1244, 1253–54 (Fed. Cir. 2008) (rejecting broad construction of "fragile gel" offered by patentee where, under such construction, it would not be "definite" "because a person of ordinary skill in the art could not determine how quickly the gel must transition to a liquid when force is applied and how quickly it must return to a gel when the force is removed").

Chapter 12 How to Determine Infringement of a Patent Claim

1. *See, e.g.*, *Markman v. Westview Instr.*, 517 U.S. 370, 384–85 (1996); *Cybor Corp. v. FAS Techs.*, 138 F.3d 1448, 1454 (Fed. Cir. 1998) (en banc); *Gen. Mills, Inc. v. Hunt-Wesson, Inc.*, 103 F.3d 978, 981 (Fed. Cir. 1997).
2. *See, e.g.*, *Cybor*, 138 F.3d at 1454; *Gen. Mills*, 103 F.3d at 981.
3. *See, e.g.*, *Mas-Hamilton Group v. LaGard, Inc.*, 156 F.3d 1206, 1211 (Fed. Cir. 1998) ("To prove literal infringement, the patentee must show that the accused device contains every limitation in the asserted claims. If even one limitation is missing or not met as claimed, there is no literal infringement." (citations omitted)); *Sage Prods. v. Devon Indus.*, 126 F.3d 1420, 1424 (Fed. Cir. 1997); *Baxter Healthcare Corp. v. Spectramed, Inc.*, 49 F.3d 1575, 1583 (Fed. Cir. 1995).
4. *See, e.g.*, *Markman v. Westview Instr.*, 52 F.3d 967, 988 (Fed. Cir. 1995) (en banc), *aff'd*, 517 U.S. 370 (1996); *Warner-Jenkinson Co. v. Hilton Davis Chem. Co.*, 520 U.S. 17, 28–29 (1997) (adhering to rule requiring analysis on "element-by-element" basis).
5. *See, e.g.*, *Warner-Jenkinson*, 520 U.S. at 40.
6. *Voda v. Cordis Corp.*, 536 F.3d 1311, 1327 (Fed. Cir. 2008).
7. *See Festo Corp. v. Shoketsu Kinzoku Kogyo Kabushiki Co.*, 535 U.S. 722, 730–36 (2002); *Warner-Jenkinson*, 520 U.S. at 30–34.
8. *See, e.g.*, *Cybor*, 138 F.3d at 1460 (holding that application of the doctrine of prosecution history estoppel raises a question of law).
9. *See id.* at 1457; *see also Augustine Med., Inc. v. Gaymar Indus.*, 181 F.3d 1291, 1298 (Fed. Cir. 1999).
10. *Litton Sys. v. Honeywell, Inc.*, 140 F.3d 1449, 1462 (Fed. Cir. 1998) ("either amendments or arguments made by an applicant may be the basis for this conclusion."); *see also Festo Corp.*, 535 U.S. at 734–37 (holding that even amendments made to comply with Section 112 may give rise to estoppel).
11. *See, e.g.*, *Augustine Med.*, 181 F.3d at 1300–01 (reversing a jury verdict finding infringement under the doctrine of equivalents where the patentee "surrendered during prosecution the coverage it now seeks to reclaim via the doctrine of equivalents").
12. *Festo Corp.*, 535 U.S. at 734–37.
13. *Bus. Object, S.A. v. Microstrategy, Inc.*, 393 F.3d 1366, 1375 (Fed. Cir. 2005) (claims that were amended to broaden the scope of the claim were not barred from asserting infringement under the doctrine of equivalents; "Business Objects, therefore, did not narrow this limitation for purposes of patentability and is not precluded from claiming equivalents of the query engine means in the accused products."); *see also, e.g.*, *Festo Corp.*, 344 F.3d at 1366 ("If the amendment was not narrowing, then prosecution history estoppel does not apply.").

14. *Festo*, 535 U.S. at 740–41.
15. *Johnson & Johnston Assocs. v. R.E. Serv. Co.*, 285 F.3d 1046, 1054–55 (Fed. Cir. 2002); *see also Maxwell v. J. Baker, Inc.*, 86 F.3d 1098, 1106–07 (Fed. Cir. 1996). In *Johnson & Johnston*, the Federal Circuit explained:

    > [W]hen a patent drafter discloses but declines to claim subject matter . . . this action dedicates that unclaimed subject matter to the public. Application of the doctrine of equivalents to recapture subject matter deliberately left unclaimed would 'conflict with the primacy of the claims in defining the scope of the patentee's exclusive right.'
    >
    > * * *
    >
    > Moreover, a patentee cannot narrowly claim an invention to avoid prosecution scrutiny by the PTO, and then, after patent issuance, use the doctrine of equivalents to establish infringement because the specification discloses equivalents. 'Such a result would merely encourage a patent applicant to present a broad disclosure in the specification of the application and file narrow claims, avoiding examination of broader claims that the applicant could have filed consistent with the specification.'

    (citations and quotations omitted).
16. *We Care, Inc. v. Ultra-Mark Int'l Corp.*, 930 F.2d 1567, 1570–71 (Fed. Cir. 1991).
17. *Id.*
18. *See, e.g., SciMed Life Sys. v. Advanced Cardiovascular Sys.*, 242 F.3d 1337, 1347 (Fed. Cir. 2001) ("[I]f a patent states that the claimed device must be 'non-metallic,' the patentee cannot assert the patent against a metallic device on the ground that a metallic device is equivalent to a non-metallic device.").
19. *Moore U.S.A., Inc. v. Standard Register Co.*, 229 F.3d 1091, 1106 (Fed. Cir. 2000) ("[I]t would defy logic to conclude that a minority—the very antithesis of majority—could be insubstantially different from a claim limitation requiring a majority, and no reasonable juror could find otherwise.").
20. *Sage Prods.*, 126 F.3d at 1422–23.
21. *See, e.g., Muniacution, Inc. v. Thomson Corp.*, 532 F.3d 1318, 1328 n.5 (Fed. Cir. 2008) ("A conclusion of noninfringement as to the independent claims requires a conclusion of noninfringement as to the dependent claims.").
22. 35 U.S.C. § 271(a).
23. *Intel Corp. v. U.S. Int'l Trade Comm'n*, 946 F.2d 821, 832 (Fed. Cir. 1991) ("[T]here is no intent element to *direct* infringement.") (emphasis in original).
24. 35 U.S.C. § 271(c).
25. *See, e.g., Linear Tech. Corp. v. Impala Linear Corp.*, 379 F.3d 1311, 1326 (Fed. Cir. 2004).
26. *ACCO Brands, Inc. v. ABA Locks Mfg. Co.*, 501 F.3d 1307, 1313 (Fed. Cir. 2007).
27. *Dynacore Holdings Corp. v. U.S. Philips Corp.*, 363 F.3d 1263, 1274 (Fed. Cir. 2004).
28. *See, e.g., C.R. Bard, Inc., v. Advanced Cardiovascular Sys.*, 911 F.2d 670, 673 (Fed. Cir. 1990).
29. 35 U.S.C. § 271(b).
30. *See Oak Indus. v. Zenith Elecs. Corp.*, 726 F. Supp. 1525, 1541 (N.D. Ill. 1989).
31. *Manville Sales Corp. v. Paramount Sys.*, 917 F.2d 544, 553 (Fed. Cir. 1990).
32. *See, e.g., ACCO Brands*, 501 F.3d at 1313.
33. *Hewlett-Packard Co. v. Bausch & Lomb Inc.*, 909 F.2d 1464, 1469 (Fed. Cir. 1990).
34. *See, e.g., DSU Med. Corp. v. JMS Co.*, 471 F.3d 1293, 1304 (Fed. Cir. 2006) (en banc in relevant part).

35. *See, e.g., E.I. duPont Nemours & Co. v. Monsanto Co.*, 903 F. Supp. 680, 736 (D. Del. 1995) (liability for active inducement is limited to activities after date parties received notice of patent), *aff'd mem.*, 92 F.3d 1208 (Fed. Cir. 1996).
36. *Water Techs. Corp. v. Calco, Ltd.*, 850 F.2d 660, 668 (Fed. Cir. 1988).
37. *Oak Indus*, 726 F. Supp. at 1543 (citing *Water Techs.*, 850 F.2d at 668).
38. *Moleculon Research Corp. v. CBS, Inc.*, 793 F.2d 1261, 1272 (Fed. Cir. 1986).
39. *Haworth, Inc. v. Herman Miller Inc.*, 37 U.S.P.Q.2d 1080, 1088 (W.D. Mich. 1994).

Chapter 13 How to Enforce a Patent

1. *See Symbol Techs. v. Lemelson Med., Educ. & Research Found.*, 429 F.3d 1051 (Fed. Cir. 2005).
2. *MedImmune, Inc. v. Genentech, Inc.*, 549 U.S. 118 (2007).
3. *Compare Omega Eng'g, Inc. v. Raytek Corp.*, 334 F.3d 1314, 1333 (Fed. Cir. 2003) (finding that statements made during prosecution of parent application narrowed scope of claims asserted in continuation application); *Wang Labs., Inc. v. Am. Online, Inc.*, 197 F.3d 1377, 1383–84 (Fed. Cir. 1999) (considering prosecution history of parent in construing claims of child application when the subject matter was the same for both applications); *Jonsson v. Stanley Works*, 903 F.2d 812, 817–18 (Fed. Cir. 1990) (holding that when two patents issued from continuation-in-part applications derived from an original parent application, the prosecution history of the first applied with respect to the same claim limitation in the second patent), *with Adv. Cardiovascular Sys. v. Medtronic, Inc.*, 265 F.3d 1294, 1305 (Fed. Cir. 2001) (finding that statements made in prosecution histories of parent patent applications relating to different claim terms were not relevant to construing claims of a child application).
4. *See, e.g., Int'l Nutrition Co. v. Horphag Research Ltd.*, 257 F.3d 1324 (Fed. Cir. 2001) (action was stayed while assignees of co-inventors of patent disputed ownership, resulting in action by plaintiff being dismissed for lack of standing).
5. *See, e.g.*, 35 U.S.C. § 255.
6. *Chef Am., Inc. v. Lamb-Weston, Inc.*, 358 F.3d 1371, 1374 (Fed. Cir. 2004).
7. *Süd-Chemie, Inc. v. Multisorb Techs., Inc.*, 554 F.3d 1001, 1008–09 (Fed. Cir. 2009). *See also* Charles R. Macedo, *Permanent Injunction Affirmed in US Patent Case*, Journal of Intellectual Property Law & Practice, May 2, 2009, 4:310–312.
8. *BMC Res., Inc. v. Paymentech, L.P.*, 498 F.3d 1373, 1379 (Fed. Cir. 2007).
9. *Muniauction, Inc. v. Thomson Corp.*, 532 F.3d 1318, 1329 (Fed. Cir. 2008), *cert. denied*, 129 S. Ct. 1585 (2009).
10. *Muniauction, Inc. v. Thomson Corp.*, 502 F. Supp. 2d 477 (W.D. Pa. 2007) ($35 million jury verdict doubled plus interest for $76.4 million judgment; online bond-trading system), *rev'd*, 532 F.3d 1318 (Fed. Cir. 2008).
11. *Qualcomm, Inc. v. Broadcom Corp.*, No. 05-cv-1958-B, 2008 U.S. Dist. LEXIS 51748 (S.D. Cal. Jan. 7, 2008).
12. For a more detailed discussion of the *Qualcomm* decision, see Michael V. Solomita & Steven B. Gauthier, *Qualcomm v. Broadcom: Lessons In E-Discovery*, IP Law 360 (Jan. 22, 2008) (*available at* www.arelaw.com).

13. *See, e.g.*, N.D. Cal. Pat. L.R. 3-1; E.D. Tex. Pat. L.R. 3-1; N.D. Ga. Pat. L.R. 4.1(b).
14. *See, e.g.*, *Davis-Lynch, Inc. v. Weatherford Int'l, Inc.*, No. 6:07-CV-5592009, 2009 U.S. Dist. LEXIS 1644, at *6 (E.D. Tex. Jan. 12, 2009) ("The Patent Rules demonstrate high expectations as to plaintiffs' preparedness before bringing suit, requiring plaintiffs to disclose their . . . infringement contentions before discovery has even begun.").
15. *See, e.g.*, N.D. Cal. Pat. L.R. 3-3; E.D. Tex. Pat. L.R. 3-3; N.D. Ga. Pat. L.R. 4.3.
16. *See, e.g.*, N.D. Ga. Pat. L.R. 4.2.
17. *See, e.g.*, N.D. Cal. Pat. L.R. 3-2(a); E.D. Tex. Pat. L.R. 3-2(a); N.D. Ga. Pat. L.R. 4.1(c)(1).
18. *See, e.g.*, N.D. Cal. Pat. L.R. 3.2(c) (prosecution history); E.D. Tex. Pat. L.R. 3.2(c) (prosecution history); N.D. Ga. Pat. L.R. 4.1(c)(3)–(4) (prosecution history and cited references).

Chapter 14 Where to Resolve a Patent Dispute

1. 28 U.S.C. § 1338(a).
2. *In re Volkswagen of Am. Inc.*, 566 F.3d 1349 (Fed. Cir. 2009); *In re TS Tech U.S. Corp.*, 551 F.3d 1315 (Fed. Cir. 2008). *See also* Joseph Casino and David Boag, *Transferring Cases Out of Eastern Dist. Of Texas*, IP LAW 360, Oct. 15, 2008 (*available at* www.arelaw.com).
3. FED. R. APP. P. 32(a)(2).
4. *See, e.g.*, PricewaterhouseCoopers, *2008 Patent Litigation Study: Damages, awards, success rates and time-to-trial, available at* www.pwc.com; David L. Schwartz, *Practice Makes Perfect? An Empirical Study Of Claim Construction Reversal Rates In Patent Cases*, 107 MICH. L. REV. 223 (2008).
5. *See* 19 U.S.C. § 1337.
6. Examples of such procedures may include either an *ex partes* reexamination (*see* 35 U.S.C. §§ 301 *et seq.*) where, although a third party can make a submission to initiate a proceeding, only the patentee will be able to address issues raised by the USPTO, or an *inter partes* reexamination (*see* 35 U.S.C. §§ 311 *et seq.*), where both the party challenging the patentee and the patentee will be able to participate in the proceeding.
7. For example, a patentee may initiate a reissue proceeding (*see* 35 U.S.C. §§ 251 *et seq.*) to cure defects in an issued patent.
8. *See* 35 U.S.C. § 251, ¶ 1.
9. 35 U.S.C. § 251.
10. *See, e.g.*, *Hewlett-Packard Co. v. Bausch & Lomb, Inc.*, 882 F.2d 1556, 1565 (Fed. Cir. 1989).
11. 35 U.S.C. § 251, ¶ 4.
12. 35 U.S.C. § 251, ¶ 1.
13. *See, e.g.*, *Hewlett-Packard*, 882 F.2d at 1565.
14. *See, e.g.*, *In re Amos*, 953 F.2d 613, 616 (Fed. Cir. 1991).
15. The proper procedure for filing a reissue application is governed by 37 C.F.R. §§ 1.171, 1.176.
16. *See, e.g.*, *In re Morgan*, 990 F. 2d 1230, 1231–32 (Fed. Cir. 1993) (denying the request to process the reissue application because "the language of section 251 does not permit reissue of a patent which has expired.").

17. *See* 35 U.S.C. §§ 301–307.
18. *See* 35 U.S.C. §§ 311–318.
19. *See, e.g., Pod-ners, LLC v. Tutuli Produce Corp.*, CV 99-10172, 2001 U.S. Dist. LEXIS 25945, at *7 (C.D. Cal. Aug. 17, 2001); *Methode Elecs. v. Infineon Techs. Corp.*, No. C-99-21142-JW, 2000 U.S. Dist. LEXIS 20689, at *9 (N.D. Cal. Aug. 7, 2000).
20. *See* 9 U.S.C. §§ 1 *et seq.*
21. *Compare Stein Assocs., Inc. v. Heat & Control, Inc.*, 748 F.2d 653, 658 (Fed. Cir. 1984), *with Voda v. Cordis Corp.*, 476 F.3d 887 (Fed. Cir. 2007).

Chapter 15 What Is a Patent Worth?

1. Similarly, infringement of a patent after the term of a patent expires is also not actionable. *See, e.g., Elmer v. ICC Fabricating*, 67 F.3d 1571, 1580 (Fed. Cir. 1995).
2. 35 U.S.C. § 154(b).
3. 35 U.S.C. § 156.
4. *See, e.g., Nat'l Presto Indus. v. West Bend Co.*, 76 F.3d 1185, 1196 (Fed. Cir. 1996).
5. *See* Charles R. Macedo, *Effect of the Publication of Applications Under The American Inventors Protection Act of 1999*, 13–4 Fed. Cir. B. J. 627 (2004).
6. *See* 35 U.S.C. § 154(d)(3).
7. *See* 35 U.S.C. § 154(d)(2).
8. *See* 35 U.S.C. § 154(d)(1)(B).
9. *See* 35 U.S.C. § 284.
10. *See, e.g., Gen. Motors Corp. v. Devex Corp.*, 461 U.S. 648, 654–55 (1983).
11. *Rite-Hite Corp. v. Kelley Co.*, 56 F.3d 1538, 1545 (Fed. Cir. 1995).
12. *Rite-Hite*, 56 F.3d at 1545.
13. *Panduit Corp. v. Stahlin Bros. Fibre Works, Inc.*, 575 F.2d 1152 (6th Cir. 1978).
14. *Rite-Hite*, 56 F.3d at 1545 (*Panduit* test is a "useful, but non-exclusive, way for a patentee to prove entitlement to lost profits damages.").
15. *Panduit*, 575 F.2d at 1156.
16. *Stryker Corp. v. Intermedics Orthopedics*, 96 F.3d 1409, 1418 (Fed. Cir. 1996).
17. *But cf. Ryco, Inc. v. Ag-Bag Corp.*, 857 F.2d 1418, 1427 (Fed. Cir. 1988) (Court has allowed lost profits to be awarded even when the amount of profit the patentee would have made was not adequately established under the theory that the patentee "had already shown a reasonable probability that it would have made the infringing sales" made by the alleged infringer).
18. *Rite-Hite*, 56 F.3d at 1548 ("Generally, the *Panduit* test has been applied when a patentee is seeking lost profits for a device covered by the patent in suit. . . . If there are other ways to show that the infringement in fact caused the patentee's lost profits, there is no reason why another test should not be acceptable. Moreover, other fact situations may require different means of evaluation, and failure to meet the *Panduit* test does not *ipso facto* disqualify a loss from being compensable.").
19. *Id.* at 1545.
20. *Id.*
21. *Amstar Corp. v. Envirotech Corp.*, 823 F.2d 1538, 1543 (Fed. Cir. 1987) ("A patentee may recover lost profits by proving that but for the infringement, the patentee

would have made the sales the infringer made, charged higher prices, or incurred lower expenses.").

22. *Id.* at 1543.
23. *In re Mahurkar Double Lumen Hemodialysis Catheter Patent Litig.*, 831 F. Supp. 1354, 1386 (N.D. Ill. 1993).
24. *Lam, Inc. v. Johns-Manville Corp.*, 718 F.2d 1056, 1065 (Fed. Cir. 1983); *see also Micro Motion, Inc. v. Exac Corp.*, 761 F. Supp. 1420, 1430 (N.D. Cal. 1991) (awarding price erosion damages; "Lost profits as a result of price erosion are compensable damages that stand on the same ground as damages caused by lost sales. . . . In most price erosion cases, a patent owner has reduced the actual price of its patented product in response to an infringer's competition. . . . But a patent holder who proves that he would have increased his prices had the infringer not been in competition with him can also sustain a price erosion claim.").
25. *Rite-Hite*, 56 F.3d at 1549.
26. *Bose Corp. v. JBL, Inc.*, 274 F.3d 1354, 1361 (Fed. Cir. 2001) (internal quotations omitted).
27. *Bose Corp. v. JBL, Inc.*, 112 F. Supp. 2d 138, 164 (D. Mass. 2000), *aff'd*, 274 F.3d 1354 (Fed. Cir. 2001).
28. *See* 35 U.S.C. § 284.
29. *Rite-Hite*, 56 F.3d at 1545.
30. *Georgia-Pacific Corp. v. U.S. Plywood Corp.*, 318 F. Supp. 1116, 1120 (S.D.N.Y. 1970), *modified and aff'd*, 446 F.2d 295 (2d Cir. 1971).
31. 35 U.S.C. § 285.
32. 35 U.S.C. § 284.
33. *Bayer Aktiengesellschaft v. Duphar Int'l Research B.V.*, 738 F.2d 1237, 1242 (Fed. Cir. 1984) (Exceptional circumstances include, *inter alia*, "vexatious or unjustified litigation, or a frivolous suit."); *Multi-Tech, Inc. v. Components, Inc.*, 708 F. Supp. 615, 620 (D. Del. 1989) (quoting *Bayer*).
34. *Underwater Devices, Inc. v. Morrison-Knudsen Co.*, 717 F.2d 1380, 1390–91 (Fed. Cir. 1983), *overruled by In re Seagate Tech., LLC*, 497 F.3d 1360 (Fed. Cir. 2007) (en banc).
35. *Quantum Corp. v. Tandon Corp.*, 940 F.2d 642 (Fed. Cir. 1991).
36. *Knorr-Bremse Systeme Fuer Nutzfahrzeuge GmbH v. Dana Corp.*, 383 F.3d 1337, 1343–44 (Fed. Cir. 2004) (en banc).
37. *In re EchoStar Commc'ns Corp.*, 448 F.3d 1294 (Fed. Cir. 2006).
38. *In re Seagate Tech., LLC*, 497 F.3d 1360, 1371 (Fed. Cir. 2007) (en banc).
39. *Seagate*, 497 F.3d at 1371.
40. *Abbott Labs. v. Sandoz, Inc.*, 529 F. Supp. 2d 893 (N.D. Ill. 2007).
41. *Seagate*, 497 F.3d at 1371.
42. *Cohesive Techs., Inc. v. Waters Corp.*, 526 F. Supp. 2d 84 (D. Mass. 2007), *aff'd in part and rev'd in part*, 543 F.3d 1351 (Fed. Cir. 2008).
43. *Ball Aerosol & Specialty Container, Inc. v. Limited Brands, Inc.*, 553 F. Supp. 2d 939 (N.D. Ill. 2008) (refusing to reconsider prior grant of summary judgment of willful infringement), *vacated on other grounds*, 555 F.3d 984 (Fed. Cir. 2009) (vacating findings on willful infringement on grounds that patent was held on appeal to be invalid and not infringed).
44. 35 U.S.C. § 287(a).

45. 35 U.S.C. § 287(a); *see also, e.g., Maxwell v. J. Baker, Inc.*, 86 F.3d 1098 (Fed. Cir. 1996) (starting damage period from date patentee's licensee marked its product).
46. *See, e.g., Am. Med. Sys. v. Med. Eng'g Corp.*, 6 F.3d 1523, 1538 (Fed. Cir. 1993) ("The purpose behind the marking statute is to encourage the patentee to give notice to the public of the patent.").
47. *Clancy Sys. Int'l v. Symbol Techs., Inc.*, 953 F. Supp. 1170, 1173 (D. Colo. 1997); *Laitram Corp. v. Hewlett-Packard Co.*, 806 F. Supp. 1294, 1296 (E.D. La. 1992).
48. *Maxwell*, 86 F.3d at 1111; *see also Nike, Inc. v. Wal-Mart Stores, Inc.*, 138 F.3d 1437, 1446 (Fed. Cir. 1998); *Clancy Sys. Int'l*, 953 F. Supp. at 1173 ("substantially all patented articles [must] be marked to constitute constructive notice").
49. *Maxwell*, 86 F.3d 1098 (starting damage period from date patentee's licensee marked its product).
50. *Med. Graphics Corp. v. SensorMedics Corp.*, 36 U.S.P.Q.2d 1275 (D. Minn. 1995); *see also Wine Ry. Appliance Co. v. Enterprise Ry. Equip. Co.*, 297 U.S. 387 (1936) (infringer of a patent on a device that was never made or sold by the patent owner or its licensee was held liable for damages from the date of issuance of a patent, and not from the date when notice was given by filing of a counterclaim in the infringement action).
51. *Am. Med. Sys. v. Med. Eng'g Corp.*, 6 F.3d 1523, 1537–38 (Fed. Cir. 1993).
52. *Amsted Indus. v. Buckeye Steel Castings Co.*, 24 F.3d 178, 186–87 (Fed. Cir. 1994).
53. *See, e.g., Toro Co. v. McCulloch Corp.*, 898 F. Supp. 679, 684 (D. Minn. 1995) (collection of damages for "pressure ring" claims under a patent covering a vacuum/blower with "safety switch" claims and "pressure ring" claims, was not limited by sales by the patentee of products which practiced "safety switch" claims, but not "pressure ring" claims).
54. *A.C. Auckerman Co. v. R.L. Chaides Constr. Co.*, 960 F.2d 1020, 1028 (Fed. Cir. 1992) ("Laches is cognizable under 35 U.S.C. § 282 (1988) as an equitable defense to a claim for patent infringement."; "Where the defense of laches is established, the patentee's claim for damages prior to suit may be barred").
55. *Id.* at 1028, 1032. *See also, e.g., Wanlass v. Gen. Elec. Co.*, 148 F.3d 1334, 1337 (Fed. Cir. 1998).
56. *Auckerman*, 960 F.2d at 1035–37.
57. *See, e.g., Hall v. Aqua Queen Mfg.*, 93 F.3d 1548, 1553 (Fed. Cir. 1996) (holding that evidence of open and notorious activities in the industry was sufficient to conclude that the patentee had knowledge of the accused infringer's activities).
58. *Auckerman*, 960 F.2d at 1033.
59. *Id.* at 1036.
60. *Id.* at 1028.

Chapter 16 How to Avoid Willful Patent Infringement

1. *In re Seagate Tech., LLC*, 497 F.3d 1360, 1371 (Fed. Cir. 2007) (en banc).
2. *ACCO Brands, Inc. v. ABA Locks Mfr. Co.*, 501 F.3d 1307 (Fed. Cir. 2007) (reversing finding of enhanced damages for willful infringement, including attorney's fees and multiple damages since the finding of infringement was not supported by the evidence).

Chapter 17 When Can a Patent Stop a Competitor?

1. *NTP, Inc. v. Research in Motion, Ltd.*, 397 F. Supp. 2d 785 (E.D. Va. 2005).
2. *See, e.g.*, Teresa Riordan, *Patents; A Canadian company appeals in court for the right to keep selling BlackBerries in the U.S.*, N.Y. TIMES, June 7, 2004 ("Is it really possible that Bill Gates, Pamela Anderson and phalanxes of stockbrokers, layers and Congressional staff members will have to give up one of their most treasured possessions: their BlackBerries?"), *available at* http://www.nytimes.com; Mark Heinzl, *Court Deals Blow to BlackBerry Firm; Ruling Favors Rival NTP, Leaves Research In Motion with 'One Less Card' to Play*, WALL ST. J., Dec. 1, 2005.
3. *eBay Inc. v. MercExchange, L.L.C.*, 547 U.S. 388, 394 (2006). For a discussion of an early application of this case, *see* Anthony F. Lo Cicero and Charles R. Macedo, *Courts Write History on Permanent Injunctions In Patent Actions*, IP LAW 360 (Aug. 22, 2006) (*available at* www.arelaw.com/articles/articles.html). *See also* Charles R. Macedo, Michael J. Kasdan, *Infringement Assertions In The New World Order*, IP LAW 360 (Oct. 17, 2007) (*available at* www.arelaw.com/articles/articles.html).
4. *eBay*, 547 U.S. at 394.
5. 35 U.S.C. § 283.
6. *eBay*, 547 U.S. at 391.
7. Many courts since *eBay* have granted injunctions to direct competitors. *See, e.g.*, *Acumed LLC v. Stryker Corp.*, 551 F.3d 1323 (Fed. Cir. 2008) (affirming grant of injunction against competitor of orthopedic nail).
8. Many courts since *eBay* have nonetheless denied a direct competitor an injunction when other factors outweighed the fact that the parties were direct competitors. *See, e.g., MercExchange, L.L.C. v. eBay, Inc.*, 500 F. Supp. 2d 556, 590 (E.D. Va. 2007) (denying injunction where plaintiff, who repeatedly sought to license its patents, was unable to show irreparable harm), *appeal dismissed*, 273 Fed. Appx. 857 (Fed. Cir. 2008).
9. *Cf. Praxair, Inc. v. ATMI, Inc.*, 479 F. Supp. 2d 440 (D. Del. 2007) (denying injunction against direct competitor since patentee did not show market data to indicate loss of revenue or market share as a result of infringement).
10. *z4 Techs., Inc. v. Microsoft Corp.*, 434 F. Supp. 2d 437 (E.D. Tex. 2006) (denying injunction and severing z4's continuing causes of action for monetary damages due to Microsoft's continuing post-verdict infringement of z4's patents; new complaint was promptly filed on severed cause of action); *Finisar Corp. v. DirecTV Group Inc.*, No. 1:05-CV-264, 2006 U.S. Dist. LEXIS 76380 (E.D. Tex. July 7, 2006) (ordered to pay running royalty on set top boxes for remaining life of patent), *aff'd in part and rev'd in part*, 523 F.3d 1323 (Fed. Cir. 2008); *Paice LLC v. Toyota Motor Corp.*, No. 2:04-CV-211, 2006 WL 2385139 (E.D. Tex. Aug. 16, 2006) (denying injunction against Prius automobile, in favor of reasonable royalty), *aff'd in part and rev'd in part on other grounds*, 504 F.3d 1293 (Fed. Cir. 2007) (remanding to provide rationale for amount of reasonable royalty).
11. *eBay Inc.*, 547 U.S. at 396–97 (Kennedy, J., concurring) (citations omitted).
12. *See, e.g., Allan Block Corp. v. E. Dillon & Co.*, 509 F. Supp. 2d 795, 811 (D. Minn. 2007) (granting injunction to corporation involved in the development and licensing of construction technologies against licensee), *aff'd*, 287 Fed. Appx. 109 (Fed. Cir. 2008).

13. *See, e.g., Johns Hopkins Univ. v. Datascope Corp.*, 513 F. Supp. 2d 578 (D. Md. 2007) (University and licensee was competitor), *rev'd on other grounds*, 543 F.3d 1342 (Fed. Cir. 2008); *Commonwealth Scientific & Indus. Research Org. v. Buffalo Tech. Inc.*, 492 F. Supp. 2d 600 (E.D. Tex. 2007) (Australian government research lab), *aff'd in part and rev'd in part on other grounds*, 542 F.3d 1363 (Fed. Cir. 2008).
14. *MercExchange*, 500 F. Supp. 2d at 569 (lack of irreparable harm where the patentee had "continued to follow a consistent course of licensing its patents to market participants and [was] plainly willing to accept royalties for future utilization of the patent"); *But cf. Transocean Offshore Deepwater Drilling, Inc. v. GlobalSantaFe Corp.*, No. H-03-2910, 2006 U.S. Dist. LEXIS 93408, at **17–19 (S.D. Tex. Dec. 27, 2006) (noting that a permanent injunction would amount to a compulsory license which would "not contain any of the commercial business terms typically used by a patent holder to control its technology or limit encroachment on its market share").
15. *IMX, Inc. v. Lendingtree, LLC*, 469 F. Supp. 2d 203, 224–25 (D. Del. 2007).
16. *Acumed LLC*, 551 F.3d at 1328–29.
17. *Muniauction, Inc. v. Thomson Corp.*, 502 F. Supp. 2d 477, 482–83 (W.D. Pa. 2007) (injunction granted), *rev'd on other grounds*, 532 F.3d 1318 (Fed. Cir. 2008).
18. *Transocean Offshore Deepwater Drilling*, 2006 U.S. Dist. LEXIS 93408, at *13 (injunction granted).
19. *See, e.g., Black & Decker, Inc. v. Robert Bosch Tool Corp.*, No. 04C7955, 2006 U.S. Dist. LEXIS 86990, at *12 (N.D. Ill. Nov. 29, 2006); *TiVo Inc. v. EchoStar Commc'ns Corp.*, 446 F. Supp. 2d 664, 669 (E.D. Tex. 2006) (relying on "stickiness of product" to grant injunction), *aff'd in part and rev'd in part*, 516 F.3d 1290 (Fed. Cir. 2008); *Smith & Nephew, Inc. v. Synthes (U.S.A.)*, 466 F. Supp. 2d 978 (W.D. Tenn. 2006) (relying on harm to brand name), *appeal dismissed*, 269 Fed. Appx. 972 (Fed. Cir. 2008).
20. *TiVo*, 446 F. Supp. 2d at 669.
21. *eBay*, 547 U.S. at 393 ("[S]ome patent holders, such as university researchers or self-made inventors, might reasonably prefer to license their patents, rather than undertake efforts to secure the financing necessary to bring their works to market themselves. Such patent holders may be able to satisfy the traditional four-factor test, and we see no basis for categorically denying them the opportunity to do so."). *See also Johns Hopkins University*, 513 F. Supp. 2d 578 (University and Licensee was competitor); *Commonwealth Scientific & Industrial Research Organization*, 492 F. Supp. 2d 600 (Australian Government Research Lab granted injunction).
22. *See, e.g., MPT, Inc. v. Marathon Labels, Inc.*, 505 F. Supp. 2d 401, 420 (N.D. Ohio 2007) (noting that products subject to injunction were a small percentage of overall sales), *aff'd in part and rev'd in part*, 258 Fed. Appx. 318 (Fed. Cir. 2007); *800 Adept, Inc. v. Murex Secs., Ltd.*, 505 F. Supp. 2d 1327, 1338 (M.D. Fla. 2007) (noting that scope of injunction would impact a small percentage of the infringer's overall business), *rev'd on other grounds*, 539 F.3d 1354 (Fed. Cir. 2008).
23. *Verizon Servs. Corp. v. Vonage Holdings Corp.*, 503 F.3d 1295, 1311 n.12 (Fed. Cir. 2007); *see also Verizon Servs. Corp. v. Vonage Holdings Corp.*, 228 Fed. Appx. 986 (Fed. Cir. 2007) (injunction stayed pending appeal).
24. *Acumed*, 551 F.3d at 1330.
25. *Id.* at 1330; *Windsurfing Int'l, Inc. v. AMF, Inc.*, 782 F.2d 995, 1003 n.12 (Fed. Cir. 1986).

26. *MercExchange,* 500 F. Supp. 2d at 586.
27. *z4 Techs.,* 434 F. Supp. 2d 437.
28. *Paice LLC v. Toyota Motor Corp.*, No. 2:04-CV-211, of 2006 WL 2385139 (E.D. Tex. Aug. 16, 2006), *aff'd in part and rev'd in part on other grounds*, 504 F.3d 1293 (Fed. Cir. 2007).
29. *Finisar Corp.*, 2006 U.S. Dist. LEXIS 76380.
30. *Acumed*, 551 F.3d 1323 (affirming grant of a permanent injunction by district court over accused infringer's argument that the infringing product provided unique medical benefits over other available alternatives).

Chapter 18 How Rights Are Transferred

1. *Teets v. Chromalloy Gas Turbine Corp.*, 83 F.3d 403, 407 (Fed. Cir. 1996) ("an invention presumptively belongs to its creator.").
2. *Ethicon, Inc. v. U.S. Surgical Corp.*, 135 F.3d 1456, 1465 (Fed. Cir. 1998) ("Indeed, in the context of joint inventorship, each co-inventor presumptively owns a pro rata undivided interest in the entire patent, no matter what their respective contributions.").
3. *Id.* at 1468 ("'In the absence of any agreement to the contrary, each of the joint owners of a patent may make, use, offer to sell, or sell the patented invention within the United States, or import the patented invention into the United States, without the consent of and without accounting to the other owners.'" (quoting 35 U.S.C. § 262)); *Schering Corp. v. Roussel-UCLAF SA*, 104 F.3d 341, 344 (Fed. Cir. 1997) ("Each co-owner's ownership rights carry with them the right to license others, a right that also does not require the consent of any other co-owner.").
4. *Yeshiva Univ. v. Greenberg*, 681 N.Y.S.2d 71, 72 (2d Dep't 1998) ("'If an employee is hired to invent or is given the task of devoting his efforts to a particular problem, the resulting invention is the employer's, and any patent obtained by the employee must be assigned to the other . . . On the other hand, an employee whose employment is 'general' is entitled to retain any patent which he procures and need not assign it to his employer, even though his employment covers a field of labor and effort in the performance of which the employee conceived the invention for which he obtained a patent.'" (quoting *Cahill v. Regan*, 5 N.Y.2d 292, 296 (1959)), *app. dismissed*, 93 N.Y.2d 888 (1999).

Index

Note: Page references followed by "*f*" refer to figures, "*pn*" refers to Practice Notes and "*n*" refers to notes.

J

K

L

R